THE CRISIS OF
DISENGAGEMENT

THE CRISIS OF
DISENGAGEMENT

HOW APATHY, COMPLACENCY, AND SELFISHNESS ARE DESTROYING TODAY'S WORKPLACE

ANDREW J. SHERMAN

Published by Advantage, Charleston, South Carolina.
Member of Advantage Media Group.

ADVANTAGE is a registered trademark, and the Advantage colophon is a trademark of Advantage Media Group, Inc.

Printed in the United States of America.

ISBN: 978-1-59932-847-8
LCCN: 2016959524

Cover design by Katie Biondo.

This publication is designed to provide accurate and authoritative information in regard to the subject matter covered. It is sold with the understanding that the publisher is not engaged in rendering legal, accounting, or other professional services. If legal advice or other expert assistance is required, the services of a competent professional person should be sought.

Advantage Media Group is proud to be a part of the Tree Neutral® program. Tree Neutral offsets the number of trees consumed in the production and printing of this book by taking proactive steps such as planting trees in direct proportion to the number of trees used to print books. To learn more about Tree Neutral, please visit **www.treeneutral.com.**

Advantage Media Group is a publisher of business, self-improvement, and professional development books. We help entrepreneurs, business leaders, and professionals share their Stories, Passion, and Knowledge to help others Learn & Grow. Do you have a manuscript or book idea that you would like us to consider for publishing? Please visit **advantagefamily.com** or call **1.866.775.1696.**

For my fellow four-percenters who are highly engaged—we are very blessed; may our numbers continue to grow over time.
—Andrew J. Sherman

TABLE OF CONTENTS

ACKNOWLEDGMENTS

This book is the culmination of the efforts of many thought leaders who are dedicated to moving the needle and solving the crisis of disengagement. I want to first thank all of my guest contributors, Dr. Bob Rosen, Shelby Scarbrough, Alaina Love, Philip R. Styrlund, Kaihan Krippendorff, and Robert Gappa.

I also want to thank all of my partners and leaders at Seyfarth Shaw who keep us engaged and connected every day, namely Pete Miller, Paul Mattingly, Lisa Damon, Steve Meier, and Bob Bodansky. I want to acknowledge all of my clients over the past thirty-one years who have kept me challenged, energized, passionate, and who have placed their trust in my advice. I also want to thank the AMG team for all of their hard work on what is now our fourth book project together. My gratitude to good friend and long-standing client, Dave Noel, the CEO of MOI, for his research recommendations on the future of the workplace. Kudos to Georgetown Law student Sara Rafferty for all her research support—you have a very bright future ahead of you. A big "shout-out" to my assistant Evelyn Capps for her dedication and editing—thanks for putting up with me every day.

And to my family: Judy, Matthew, and Jennifer—you are my source of motivation, inspiration, and of course, eternal engagement. I am so very proud of the three of you.

INTRODUCTION

THE CRISIS OF DISENGAGEMENT

*"I am the disturbance in your sea of complacency . . .
And I will never stop shaking your waves."*

—MOHAMMED ALI

Our nation is fighting an epidemic of alarming proportions. It is *not* cancer, intolerance, racial divides, terrorism, cyberattacks, hunger, access to clean water, or the technology gap—although, unfortunately, *all* of those social epidemics remain firmly in place. Rather, it is a disease affecting the central nervous system of our economy—and it is destroying creativity, innovation, productivity, and profitability. This epidemic is a societal and workplace challenge costing hundreds of billions of dollars a year in the United States—a calamity so large that it could literally reverse the progression of our evolution if not soon corrected. It is the *crisis of disengagement.*

Dissatisfaction runs rampant in today's workplace, with many identifying inadequate challenges, pay, morale, sense of purpose, or lack of appreciation at the heart of their disdain. Many are terminally bored and apathetic, which eviscerates productivity and the ability to innovate, and in turn affects the profitability of companies and the ability to remain competitive in the world market. Social and political divisiveness and disrespect for divergent views are finding their way from society into our workplace, which is having a direct impact on disengagement, disagreements, and the divide between the haves and the have nots, the liberals and the conservatives, and those of us with difference backgrounds, raising tensions among co-workers and destroying principles of team work, culture, and productivity.

GALLUP POLL

- 31.5 percent of US the workforce defines themselves as engaged (enthusiasm is contagious).

- 51 percent of the workforce is not engaged or is disconnected (going through the motions).

- 17.5 percent of the workforce is actively disengaged (human-potential gap).

- These are all statistics that have a tremendous impact on the global economy.[1]

---

1   Amy Adkins, "Majority of U.S. Employees Not Engaged Despite Gains in 2014," *Gallup*, January 28, 2015, http://www.gallup.com/poll/181289/majority-employees-not-engaged-despite-gains-2014.aspx.

Engagement. We all crave it. We want engagement in our personal lives and in our work lives. Employers and managers want engaged workers. Business owners want engaged customers. Teachers want engaged students. Civic leaders want engaged citizens. Wall Street wants to invest in companies that can attract engaged innovators. Religious leaders want congregations who are engaged. Workers search for passion and meaning in their lives and yearn to be part of organizational cultures built on the basis of mutual trust, integrity, and respect. The irony is that in spite of such across-the-board *desire* for engagement, we are growing ever more disengaged, disconnected, distracted, and disenchanted with our work and personal lives than ever before in our history. Why is there such a gap between our desired and actual states of engagement? What can we all do to get engagement back on track in our lives and in our workplaces? How can we close this gap quickly and efficiently in order to drive up levels of workplace satisfaction, creativity, productivity, and ultimately, shareholder value?

Maybe the answer parallels the lyrics of the Rolling Stones' hit "I Can't Get No Satisfaction." Our dissatisfaction with our jobs and lives is reaching record proportions and it is both disturbing and disruptive. Many of us overtly or secretly fear being marginalized, becoming irrelevant, living a meaningless life, feeling ignored or mistreated for our efforts, or failing to leave behind a legacy, and it leads us to be void of passion, commitment, loyalty, or trust.

We would rather complain than celebrate. We would rather fight than embrace. We would rather be jealous than take pride in the accomplishments of others. Our political candidates would rather devote time and resources to attacking each other than stay focused on articulating their proposed policies or solutions. Studies have shown that users are ten times more likely to post a negative review on Yelp! or Trip Advisor than to share a positive experience. Few of us enjoy and embrace the gifts of satisfaction, passion, and happiness in the workplace.

Disengagement pervades our workforce, affecting more than the work of employees by also creating intergenerational tension. Baby boomers are unmotivated or unwilling to mentor their successors. Younger generations in the workplace feel unchallenged by the tasks they are given and unhappy with the lack of guidance they are receiving. Unhappy people eventually become unhealthy people—mentally and physically—which adds to rapidly increasing healthcare costs, which in turn leads to higher insurance premiums and smaller profits to be funneled into raises and bonuses, thereby exaggerating the problem and accelerating unhappiness overall.

Younger workers seem to be most dissatisfied, with both their pay and their workplace conditions, citing a lack of opportunity for upward mobility due to many baby boomers not being able to retire when they hoped, forcing them to fight for their jobs longer and keep client relationships close to the vest. This cultural paranoia is creating an unhealthy leadership and management deadlock. Leaders need to roll up their sleeves and get into the trenches to determine what they can do to enhance engagement with each employee, finding ways to reignite excitement and passion for the tasks employees are expected to accomplish.

If we as a nation are going to reverse this disturbing trend, we must recognize that the solution does not rest solely in increasing economic rewards. In fact, as we will discuss throughout this book, the solutions for improving current levels of engagement are more qualitative than quantitative. Yet our politicians and government leaders continue to spend too much time and hot air talking about the "1 percenters" and the gap between the "haves and the have-nots." This was especially true in the aftermath of the "Occupy Wall Street" movement and throughout the 2016 election process. If we are to remain globally competitive, the conversation must focus on new wealth creation and *not* on wealth redistribution. We need to work toward making the pie bigger, not on slicing a finite pie into smaller pieces. Rewards must be put in place for innovation and productivity. Job satisfaction is not necessarily pegged to income levels. There are millions of highly dissatisfied workers who earn well in the six figures—but there are also millions of workers in the low-to-midfive figures who approach each day with enthusiasm and passion.

On the nonfinancial side, we cannot overlook what truly drives happiness, satisfaction, pride, and engagement in the workplace. Sure, pay raises are always appreciated, but study after study underscores that most workers are equally and sometimes even more attracted to intangibles rather than cash. Key variables such as culture, teamwork, values, trust, respect, appreciation, embracing our similarities over our differences, transparency, flexible hours, creative benefits, professional development, recognition, and opportunity are cited time and time again as critical components of high levels of employee engagement and satisfaction. In the July 22, 2016, business section of *The New York Times*, economist and author Robert H. Frank wrote an article entitled "The Incalculable Value of Finding a Job You Love." In that article, Frank correctly points out that salary matters—but not as much as the satisfaction derived from developing deep experience. He advises that to be truly happy, workers need to look for career opportunities that offer professional development. Frank cites multiple studies that conclude that, in the long run, people are happier when they choose the attractiveness of workplace conditions and a strong culture over the "soul-crushing" promise of a few more dollars.[2] Companies struggling to increase their current levels of engagement and who believe that more money is the best solution can learn a lot from this article and the studies cited therein.

Disengagement has a ripple effect on all that we do, all that we produce, and all that we can become. When the lion's share of our workforce enters our doors with the goal of "just showing up" or "staying under the radar screen," spends more than half the day talking meaninglessly to friends on social-media sites, and anxiously waits for the clock to strike 5:00 p.m., we are no better as a nation than a hamster on a wheel, exerting the occasional effort, but going nowhere.

Our education and training is focused on all the wrong priorities. We teach history that is easily accessible on the Internet and math that is easily ascertainable on a calculator, while the "soft skills" which drive career success and satisfaction are ignored. As employers automate or outsource many routine tasks, the positions that often require workers to take on broader responsibilities require these softer skills such as emotional intelligence, practical experience, empathy, and critical thinking that computers can't easily simulate—and yet the teaching of these lessons are often missing from the course catalogue. Making matters even worse, it is these very skills such as empathy and emotional intelligence which have been repeatedly demonstrated to significantly increase an individual's sense of engagement, enlightenment, and sense of purpose and self-worth.

Such disconnectedness and lack of meaningful collaboration also spills over into our personal lives—affecting our families and environment. Children want trophies without winning, students

---

2   Robert H. Frank, "The Incalculable Value of Finding a Job You Love," *New York Times*, July 22, 2016, http://www.nytimes.com/2016/07/24/upshot/first-rule-of-the-job-hunt-find-something-you-love-to-do.html?_r=1.

want grades they do not deserve, entry-level employees want bonuses they have not earned, and middle-level managers want premature advancement to leadership.

Our current crisis of disengagement cannot be tolerated any longer. Our colleges are filled with distracted students, our highways are cluttered with distracted drivers, our sidewalks are filled with distracted pedestrians, our offices are packed with distracted workers, and our government offices are populated by distracted public servants. But how and when do we get serious about reversing this trend? What can business and organizational leaders do to foster and support a highly motivated, highly committed, and highly engaged workforce?

ENGAGEMENT AND DRIVING SHAREHOLDER VALUE

If you agree that your people are your most important assets, then lower levels of engagement are depressing your company's short and long-term potential. It is becoming quite common for private-equity and venture-capital firms to include key customer- and employer-engagement questions as part of their due diligence and also for commercial lenders to inquire about levels of engagement as part of their lending criteria. Buyers of companies—both financial and strategic acquirers—are putting engagement questions at the top of their due-diligence checklists. To drive long-term shareholder value, company leaders must put an engaged workforce at the top of their priority list. No investor or buyer will or should pay a premium for a workforce or a customer base that is ambivalent, disloyal, and disconnected.

This book is my heartfelt and "no-holds-barred" attempt to contribute some ideas and insights toward a meaningful solution. The observations offered do not come solely from academic research or consulting-firm reports. They also come, in part, from my own life and professional experiences.

I have been blessed to be passionate and engaged for my entire career—both when things were going well and when they were not. The road to success for me has not been well-paved and smooth; rather it has been choppy, filled with potholes, toll bridges, and traffic delays. I had a very modest upbringing and relied primarily on my own grit and determination, as well as the kindness and support of others, to accomplish everything that I have up to this point. I have taken the time to figure out what makes me happiest and have tried my best not to allow others to distract me from my life's work.

What I have learned from my forty years as an entrepreneur, lawyer, professor, author, and strategic advisor is that too many among us allow our happiness, our passion, and our enjoyment to be driven and defined by our supervisors and our team members. Misery does, in fact, love company—and it's easy to allow a frustrated and unhappy coworker to convert you into the realm of the disappointed and disengaged. We are all on our own personal journeys of fulfillment and satisfaction. We must also define our own life missions, core values, interests, and goals and then work hard to integrate ourselves into a company (and life) whose goals and culture are aligned with ours. I truly believe that there is a fantastic work setting out there for each one of us, but we cannot be lazy or complacent in achieving it.

At the Future of Work conference in Zurich in mid-May of 2016, former US Labor Secretary Robert Reich stated, "Most people in the world are doing work that they really would rather not do, but they have to do. How can we create a system where more people do what they want to do, which fulfills their dreams and sense of purpose?"

If Reich is right, and I am confident that he is, how can we expect to increase productivity, creativity, and innovation when the bulk of the global workforce is unhappy with how they spend 70–80 percent of their waking hours? How has the "social contract" between employer and employees devolved since World War II? How will it evolve in the future as advanced computers, robotics, and nanotechnology replace more and more of the menial tasks in our workdays?

Some advocate a "universal basic income" as a form of wealth redistribution, which would afford each individual a basic income and the freedom to pursue his or her true calling in life, regardless of salary and benefits that it may provide. But before we consider a complete overhaul of our economic system, can we, as employers, make a greater effort to match people's work and quest for meaning with our companies' business plans, goals, and objectives? Can we better align what we need from our workforce with what they want from us? Can we finally liberate workers from dead-end jobs which have become meaningless, irrelevant, extinct, or stale and bring an end to the eternal "paid vacations?" Can we work harder to instill more meaning into our work and our lives without overhauling our society?

OUR NATION'S DISCONNECTED STRATEGIC PRIORITIES AND WORKFORCE ATTITUDES

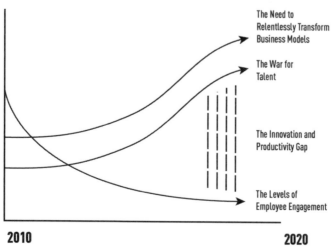

The Need to Relentlessly Transform Business Models

The War for Talent

The Innovation and Productivity Gap

The Levels of Employee Engagement

2010   2020

In addition to my own chapters, I have asked a select number of thought leaders in their respective fields to weigh in on the disengagement crisis. These guest authors reinforce the sense of urgency that we *all* must embrace in order to reverse this disturbing trend toward disengagement, apathy, and lack of passion.

Phil Styrlund reminds us that nobody is engaged when he or she feels irrelevant. Dr. Alaina Love makes the case that nobody is productive when he or she lacks passion. Dr. Bob Rosen writes that no human being will be motivated to perform without feeling appreciated and respected. Kaihan Krippendorf makes the case that no company can be driven by creativity if its employees are disconnected.

No leader can establish trust without civility and protocol is the point made by Shelby Scarbrough. And finally, Robert Gappa contends that no employee can possibly know how to advance the goals of the enterprise and create excellence in customer service without the clarity of a shared vision.

When I am asked what's wrong with our country and how it can be fixed, I often respond that as a nation we have lost our edge, our fire in the belly, our grit, our determination, and many of the other things that propelled us to world leadership. We want too much and are compelled to give too little. We want success to happen quickly. The notion of starting with nothing and building something is dependent on never forgetting that you once had nothing. It is imperative to remember where you came from—and how hard it was to accomplish your goals. Unfortunately, that determination has been replaced with a "trophy generation" mind-set in which we expect to be rewarded for only a modest effort. It has seeped like a cancer into our schools, our workplaces, our families, and even our bodies. We envy rather than celebrate the successes of those who have worked hard; we view those who have succeeded with contempt and jealousy instead of as a source of insight and instruction. We want the quick fix, the easy path. How can we be surprised that an entire generation that grew up on Facebook and video games wants to be empowered, entertained, and challenged at work? What are the consequences of forcing them into a 1950s workplace and management style? Evolution of a society includes, in fact requires, an evolution of our workplace.

It is only when we reconnect to the true joy of our accomplishments and are patient for our rewards that we can return to the path to greatness. Unrealistic expectations and impatience breed complacency and destroys creativity. We sit in our cubicles pushing paper around on a subpar basis and expect competitive salaries and generous bonuses for our actions. We fail to make the extra effort, yet we want to be rewarded like we are the star players on our team for a company that just won the championship. And on top of that, we still complain that we are not getting enough. We get what we give—but we are rarely giving enough, especially relative to our expectations.

These detours from the path to gratefulness have damaged our society from both a business and a personal perspective. There is a widening and misleading gap between the perceived "haves" and "have-nots," and a political divisiveness that has never been wider as demonstrated by the 2016 elections. Are people really that angry? Our young people in the Occupy movement were protesting and demanding jobs and student-loan relief when they should have been investing in the development of practical skills. Our aging baby boomers feel discarded and are fighting to hold onto their jobs because they are financially unprepared for retirement at a time when they should be leveraging their knowledge and experience as mentors, coaches, and catalysts for succession plans. We have wasted too many opportunities to become united in favor of becoming further divided. We focus too much of our time on the issues that divide us instead of embracing the many things we have in common. We think too much about what's tearing us apart instead of celebrating what holds us together. We invest in training people to have skills when we should be investing in lifting their spirits. We rely on metrics and data when we need to pay more attention to attitude and emotional intelligence. We need to spend more time talking face-to-face, learning about each other's needs and wants, and strengthening and fine-tuning our compassion and emotional intelligence in ways that will drive a mutuality of success.

To solve the crisis of disengagement, we must become more determined, more focused, more grateful, and more resilient.

THE BARBELLIZATION OF OUR WORKFORCE

Workplaces across America have come to look essentially like a barbell. On the left side are a handful of people who are highly engaged (HE). On the right side is an increasingly growing number of people who are actively disengaged (AD), while most in the middle make up what is called the zombie apocalypse (Z). These "zombies" are either mildly engaged or somewhat disengaged—they are just showing up for the paycheck, unless or until something better comes along. They are the true "walking dead"—capable of being reenergized but equally capable of falling into the AD category. It is important to note that engagement does not necessarily equal happiness. In fact, the irony is that the Z workers are typically the happiest among our workforce because they are often overpaid and underworked. The AD workers are cynical, frustrated, and marginalized. The HE people love what they do and where they do it, but their happiness is often *diluted* by the feeling that they work harder than everyone else for the same pay and that they are constantly picking up everyone else's slack.

We have become *too focused* on the quantitative rewards—our salaries, our bonuses, overtime—and *not focused enough* on the true joy, pride, and passion of our work. It is possible to find satisfaction inside an organization where you can be fairly rewarded for your efforts but also feel like you are a part of something bigger than yourself and do meaningful work that positively affects the lives of others. And it is possible to inspire and retain engaged employees by changing your corporate culture. Let me show you how.

Andrew J. Sherman
Washington, DC
Fall 2016

> *It is possible to find satisfaction inside an organization where you can be fairly rewarded for your efforts but also feel like you are a part of something bigger than yourself and do meaningful work that positively affects the lives of others. And it is possible to inspire and retain engaged employees by changing your corporate culture. Let me show you how.*

CHAPTER 1

UNDERSTANDING THE MAGNITUDE AND THE CAUSE OF THE CRISIS OF DISENGAGEMENT

"We can't solve problems by using the same kind of thinking we used when we created them."

—ALBERT EINSTEIN

In the summer of 2015, *The New York Times* published a controversial and critical article describing many key components of Amazon's workplace and culture. The article claimed that although Amazon's employees are well-paid and often work on ground-breaking projects, they are also pushed to the breaking point in a clear-cut, survival-of-the-fittest climate where workers tend to either quickly accept the challenge or walk out the door (if they're not shown the door first). Anecdotes of incivility, insensitivity, and callousness run throughout the story, and it triggered a larger debate for weeks about the balancing of expectations in the workplace with the defining and shaping of the workplace of the future.

This out-of-balance situation is what we term the "alignment disconnect" or the "connectivity gap."

In the year 2015, well over half of all workers in the United States claimed to be "somewhat disengaged" or even "actively disengaged."[3] I'd be willing to bet the farm that many of these workers reporting to be disengaged also felt underpaid, underappreciated, and underutilized relative to their real (or perceived) sets of skills and experiences.

THE SPILLOVER EFFECT

When a company has an alignment disconnect, there is a spillover effect on customer service, recruitment, the dilution of brand reputation, relations with vendors and suppliers, the confidence of lenders and investors, the effectiveness of leaders, managers, and employees— to the point where it will be difficult or nearly impossible to reverse the trend. When an organization has lost its "mojo," there is no dose of "cultural Viagra" that will bring it back. Examples of companies that have been affected include Kodak, Motorola, Blockbuster, Yahoo, Sony, and Sears.

Leaders of companies of all types and sizes must address this disconnect head-on at the earliest inkling of a connectivity gap. Ignoring the problem rarely, if ever, works. In today's highly connected, social-media-driven world, the general public is more likely to know

---

3   Amy Adkins, "Majority of U.S. Employees Not Engaged Despite Gains in 2014," *Gallup*, January 28, 2015, http://www.gallup.com/poll/181289/majority-employees-not-engaged-despite-gains-2014.aspx.

that your company has a problem even before you do, *unless* you are carefully monitoring posts and tweets concerning your culture. Company leaders need to get serious about engagement if they are committed to driving long-term shareholder value.

Engagement: the act of engaging; emotional involvement or commitment; the state of being in gear; a job or period of employment especially as a performer.

Multiple studies over the past seven years bolster the clear evidence that organizations with higher levels of employee engagement perform more productively and with more profitability than those with lower levels of engagement. We think of Apple, Nordstrom, Google, Starbucks, Facebook, 3M, and Netflix as being high-performing companies that have employees who genuinely seem to enjoy their work, and as a result, deliver exemplary service. However, that list is not nearly long enough if we are to remain competitive in the global marketplace.

> *Engagement: the act of engaging; emotional involvement or commitment; the state of being in gear; a job or period of employment especially as a performer.*

Gretchen Gavett of *Harvard Business Review* says: "If you're in a workplace in America right now, chances are most of the people around you are pretty checked out." Various polls and surveys confirm this thought.

Gallup, the preeminent authority on all things employee engagement, reports that only 30 percent of US workers are somewhat or highly engaged. Yes, that means 70 percent are *not* engaged. Disengagement appears to be fairly widespread: in all sizes of organizations, in all parts of the US, in all industries, and with all ages. In a word, disengagement is pervasive.

The good news is that the trend of low engagement has been somewhat stable over the last thirteen years, aside from a dip from 2008–2011, likely attributable to the recession.

But the bad news is that low employee engagement is costing US organizations dearly:

Absenteeism is 37% worse for organizations with disengaged workers compared to those with engaged workers.

Turnover is 65% worse for organizations in industries considered "low-turnover" and 25% worse in industries with traditionally higher turnover.

- Inventory shrinkage is 28% worse.

- Safety incidents are 48% higher.

- For health care, patient safety incidents are 41% higher.

- Product defects are 41% higher.

- Customer satisfaction is 10% worse.

- Productivity is 21% worse.

- Profitability is 22% worse.[4]

---

4   Brian Lassiter, "Workers Are Mad As Hell: 14 Ways to Increase Employee Engagement," Performance Excellence Network, June 25, 2013, http://www.performanceexcellencenetwork.org/pensights/workers-are-mad-as-hell-14-ways-to-increase-employee-engagement/.

Workers become disenchanted when they are in a vacuum or when they limit their relative benchmarking only to the small universe around them. If we compare our lives on a broader global scale, then higher levels of engagement and gratitude can begin to seep into our existence and our attitudes. With a flat-to-unimpressive 2–3 percent gross domestic product (GDP) growth rate, there is certainly plenty of room for improvement. Imagine the impact on our economy, our crime rate, and our standard of living if that 70 percent level of disengagement dropped by 5 percent each year!

This chapter opened with a quote by Albert Einstein. We must all commit to change the mind-set, the patience and persistence, and the attitude that can put this nation and ourselves back on track. We must embrace and appreciate what we have, not what we lack. Thomas Edison often said, "I have not failed 1,000 times. I have successfully discovered 1,000 ways to NOT make a light bulb." We need to embrace the persistence, patience, and determination that Edison adopted—instead of constantly describing ourselves as disengaged every time something does not go as expected. As individuals, we need to frame our current narrative in a way to accomplish our goals in a practical and patient manner.

THE LIMBO WORKFORCE

Many of the studies cited in this book make good-faith attempts to define our workforce as being *either* engaged or disengaged, with a few shades of gray in between. That's helpful, but it does not solve the crisis. There are a significant number of people who are neither engaged nor disengaged but rather living their lives and careers in some type of oddball zombie state. They exist, but their mission or life's purpose is unclear, both to themselves and others. They are present and accounted for, but are neither truly accretive nor dilutive to the organization. They may even be very bright people on paper, but very few of them understand how to brighten up the room with passion and energy that is truly contagious. We all know them, and many of us work for or with them.

They include:

- the "hope I don't get fired today" / "stay under the radar screen" employee;

- the "I am on cruise control so don't ask me to speed up" / "will do the minimum I need to get by" guy; and

- the "I just need to do better than anyone around me" false-benchmark guy / "blame everyone but me" guy.

In the February 12, 2016, edition of *The New York Times*, an article by Paul Sullivan was headlined "Look Closely Before Leaping From a Steady But Unfulfilling Job." The article correctly observed that many people are trapped into this limbo by their own circumstances because they do not have the viable choices. They acknowledge their unhappiness and lack of personal fulfillment but cannot sacrifice a secure, good-paying job for a chance at something different. They reach a point of resentment and numbness about their careers but do not feel empowered to pursue alternatives. It is unclear how many of us feel this way—20 percent? Thirty percent? Fifty percent? More? What *is* clear is the impact that this limbo has on our health, our productivity, and our motivation. Nobody achieved any level of true greatness or genuine satisfaction by muddling through life feeling trapped in a box.

As DeJuan Stroud was quoted in Sullivan's article, ". . .when you reach the point of 'I can't do this another day,' you choose that fear over that misery."[5]

I know that I am not alone in my concern for the breadth and depth of this phenomenon and its impact on our ability to remain productive and competitive as a nation.

THE FEW. THE PROUD. THE ENGAGED.

Even if you are reading this book as one of the "other" 30 percent who describe themselves as actively engaged in their careers—those who actually still enjoy their work, love their families, and are dedicated to their community—there is still room for improvement. You are the A and B+ players in our society, the most connected and the most productive. Do not become complacent. To advance in any situation, or on any team, the strong must get even stronger and take the time to mentor and coach the disengaged. You are the sources of inspiration for others—the touchstones. If you sway on the path, dozens or hundreds or thousands of others who follow you also sway. You are the stewards of the culture. If you shrug, we all fall.

THE CATCH-22 OF DISENGAGEMENT

At too many companies, employees express frustration and disappointment at being underappreciated, underpaid, and overworked. Employers express frustration and disappointment over the lack of loyalty, lack of innovation, and lack of productivity. They complain that today's worker is distracted and disengaged. And it is not limited to the workplace; parents and teachers complain of students and

---

5   Paul Sullivan, "Look Closely Before Leaping From a Steady but Unfulfilling Job," *The New York Times*, (February 12, 2016). http://www.nytimes.com/2016/02/13/your-money/look-closely-before-leaping-from-a-steady-but-unfulfilling-job.html.

children who are distracted and disinterested, and our young people complain that parents and teachers are burnt out.

It seems as though, over time, even as our society continues to advance technologically, and in spite of various social-media platforms to communicate in, we are losing our personal connections to each other. How can we bridge this gap and get all parties more aligned, less distracted, and ultimately more engaged in our lives, our education, and our work?

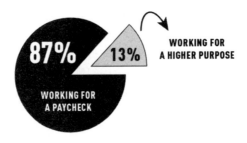

THE IMPACT OF MOBILITY

Our crisis of disengagement is being fueled in part by the impact of globalization, automation, and the overall mobility of our workforce. It is nearly impossible to have stability at the same time as excessive mobility. The so-called "gig economy," where workers drift from one temporary job to another without any loyalty or benefits, undermines all efforts to engage our workforce. Few people will be motivated to go the extra mile in their jobs if they think they will be somewhere else in the very near future. The war for talent and the intensity of mobility puts current employers in the precarious position of not being able to drive innovation and engagement, and it also fuels the paranoia of empowering your competitors when key employees are recruited. The answer to this issue does not necessarily reside in trying to reverse this trend of a gig economy—that struggle seems futile. To regain control, employers are finding creative ways to engage this workforce so that employees feel valued and *want* to be loyal to the company.

THE IMPACT OF GOING SOLO

As the demographics of our work frame shifts, so do the number of workers who choose to fight the crisis of disengagement by "going at it alone." Many people have concluded—rightly or wrongly—that the source of their disengagement is being someone's employee. According to a 2015 study by the Freelancer Union, one in three working Americans (almost fifty-four million people) defined themselves as "independent workers"—as free agents, contractors, temporary workers, full-time telecommuters, solopreneurs, home-based workers, or otherwise. Daniel Pink in *Free Agent Nation* cited a general distrust of management, a desire to set one's own schedule, and take control of one's own destiny as the drivers that will propel this number to more than sixty million by 2020. Even more interesting is that more than 80 percent of these independent workers said that they were happier and more engaged working on their own, but their happiness was driven by their autonomy and flexibility and not necessarily by their income.[6]

What can we learn about this trend and this data as leaders of companies? Is this the "new normal?" Is the solution to disengagement just to let everyone go and fend for themselves and hire them as contractors as and when needed? Will society by 2050 reject the notion of employer and employee completely, leaving us with a mar-

---

6   *MBO Partners State of Independence in America 2015,* MBO Partners, 2015, https://www.mbopartners.com/uploads/files/state-of-independence-reports/MBO-SOI-REPORT-FINAL-9-28-2015.pdf.

ketplace of knowledge workers and knowledge buyers? What will this mean for the organizational clients, office spaces, and real estate development of the future? How will it impact your recruitment and hiring plans? How will it impact your business and growth plans?

THE ALIGNMENT GAP

PRESENTEEISM: "They have quit but they are still there . . ."

In a recent Gallup survey, about 87 percent of Americans said that "they are working for a paycheck"—but 80 percent of millennials said they want to work for a so-called "higher purpose"; they want be part of something bigger than themselves and feel a connectivity to the mission and values of the organization. They are insisting on a flexible workplace and mobility to drive productivity, connectivity, and collaboration. They view the ideal company as a flat organizational chart, with a matrixed hierarchy and lots of upward-mobility opportunities. Millennials are more than 40 percent of our workforce, and that percentage is growing by the day. By 2025, they will make up 75 percent of our workforce. How can we bridge that gap? People working for only a paycheck will do the minimum they need to get by, fly below the radar screen, and rarely, if ever, go the extra effort. No company can expect to grow if the reliance on creativity and customer service is left in the hands of the engaged few.

THE CURRENT WORKFORCE

Less than one-third of American workers are engaged at their workplace.

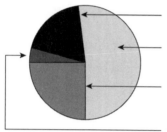

19% | Actively Disengaged
Employees are unhappy at work and not productive.

52% | Not Disengaged
Employees perform without enthusiasm or care for their work.

25% | Engaged
Employees work with passion and feel a connection to their company and their work.

4% | Deeply Engaged
Employees feel a strong bond with their work and their company and become genuine internal champions.

$500 Billion +
Is the annual cost of an unmotivated workforce.

71%

of American workers are not engaged or are actively disengaged from their work.

WHY SHOULD WE CARE ABOUT LEVELS OF ENGAGEMENT? AND WHY ARE CURRENT LEVELS OF DISENGAGEMENT TRULY A CRISIS?

Let's start with a basic observation: If you start work at age twenty-one and work continuously until sixty-five, you spend forty-four years, or 110,000 hours, either at your workplace or getting there or getting home. That number assumes a ten-hour day and a one-hour commute each way as a norm. The number also assumes a two-week vacation, an elusive concept to many of us who now work 365/7/24 with the help of technology. The bulk of our waking lives is spent at work, in transport between office and home, and in thinking about the stress of our employment while we are at home. So, why should we spend the vast majority of our adult lives unhappy and disconnected? How could we cheat ourselves of engagement in what we do to support our families and our lifestyles? Who decided that there must be firm lines of demarcation between our "work" and our "play?"

Highly engaged organizations tend to produce higher retention rates (thereby avoiding costly turnover rates and expenses and fostering candidates for succession and advertisement and monitoring); significantly improved quality of product and service lines; stronger and more durable revenues and profit margins; increased levels of innovation and creativity; health and safety rates well above industry norms; greater productivity and efficiency; stronger brands and social-media reputations; lower rates of shrinkage and absenteeism; superior training, education/advertisement, and professional development opportunities; and overall increased investment in employees.

Important Connections

Sentiment analysis aims in part to keep employees enthusiastic about their work so they're more likely to stay with the company. That engagement appears to be hard to achieve but worth the effort.

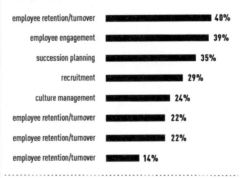

32%

Of workers in the US were engaged in their jobs in September, according to Gallup, which defines engagement as employees being involved in, enthusiastic about, and committed to their work.

Gallup says its research has found a connection between employee engagement and company performance measures including:

- customer ratings
- profitability
- productivity
- safety incidents
- theft
- absenteeism
- quality
- misappropriation of intellectual property

A survey by Globoforce and the Society for Human Resource Management found employee retention was cited most often by human-resources professionals as being among their most important challenges, with employee engagement a close second.

employee retention/turnover	40%
employee engagement	39%
succession planning	35%
recruitment	29%
culture management	24%
employee retention/turnover	22%
employee retention/turnover	22%
employee retention/turnover	14%

Source: Gallup Inc. telephone interviews with 6,926 employed adults in the US in September; margin of error +/-1.8 percentage points at the 95% confidence level (engagement figure). Gallup "State of the American Workplace" report (performance links). SHRM/Globoforce survey of 823 human-resources professionals in the US conducted Jan. 13 to Feb. 4, 2015; margin of error: +/- 3 percentage points (challenge survey).

Still not concerned? Think about how good it feels when your altruistic actions elicit satisfaction in others and what positive feelings *their* happiness and gratitude manifest in you. Sam Walton, Bill Gates, and many others often speak about the biggest satisfaction of their lives being the number of *other* millionaires that their leadership created.

Focus on *both* the selfish and selfless acts of helping people pursue their dreams in a workplace that is supportive and rewarding. How many lives can you influence? If the average family size is five and the average number of people that the average family of five directly or indirectly influences or affects is twenty-five and you have one hundred employees directly reporting to you, then the fate of 2,500 humans and their happiness rests in your hands, your decision making, your leadership, and your own levels of enjoyment. If you have one thousand, that number increases to twenty-five thousand, and so on. And this still doesn't account for customers, channel partners, vendors, and investors—or the derivative effects your influence can have on the lives of others. For that reason alone, isn't engagement among your most important priorities as a leader? Study after study illustrates that it is the *intangibles*—respect and appreciation—that keep people in their jobs and working to advance up the ladder. These are the cultures where people are genuinely willing to sacrifice to be part of something larger.

These intangibles appear nowhere on the company's financial statements and are difficult to quantify precisely. But they are important, and all of us know when we are inside a company that is driven by high levels of engagement. It's the little things—body language, eye contact, and excitement that are the clear "poker tells" indicating genuine engagement *versus* contrived engagement. It makes no difference if you are shopping at a high-end retailer or eating at a fast-food restaurant; we all have that "sixth sense" to detect levels of employee engagement and the health of the overall culture. We make our decisions about whether to return or not based on the engagement levels we observe.

THE CRISIS OF ENGAGEMENT

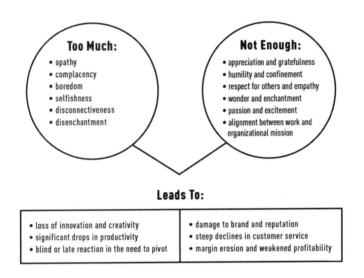

Too Much:
- apathy
- complacency
- boredom
- selfishness
- disconnectiveness
- disenchantment

Not Enough:
- appreciation and gratefulness
- humility and confinement
- respect for others and empathy
- wonder and enchantment
- passion and excitement
- alignment between work and organizational mission

Leads To:

• loss of innovation and creativity	• damage to brand and reputation
• significant drops in productivity	• steep declines in customer service
• blind or late reaction in the need to pivot	• margin erosion and weakened profitability

If I open a new Italian restaurant in a competitive hospitality marketplace, my chefs and servers will make or break the experience based on my leadership and their respective levels of engagement. If I am disconnected and care only for myself and my profit margin, then my key team members will be apathetic and unmotivated—probably already looking for their next job soon after we open. Their disengagement will spread like a disease to my customers, resulting in no repeat business and no referrals. I'll end up closed in six months.

Companies of all types are retooling their business models and reshaping their retail formats to capture the more experiential customer. The CEO of Macy's, Terry Lundgren, was recently quoted as acknowledging this about millennials: "The emerging millennial consumer has a higher set of expectations with regard to customer service, transparency, and convenience. Millennials want to be an engaged and educated part of the consuming experience."

HOW MANY "DIS-ES" CAN THE AMERICAN WORKPLACE WITHSTAND?

THREE GENERATIONS OF WORKERS—AND ALL OF THEM FRUSTRATED FOR DIFFERENT REASONS

The State of the Global Workforce (The Three Buckets of Pain)

20s/30s	Late 30s/40s	50s/60s
• in search of a higher meaning of work • desire to be involved, engaged, and challenged • struggling to keep up with rising cost of living and housing	• distracted, unfocused, out of balance • feeling the "heat" of the millennials pushing for advancement • stress of financial pressures, family pressures, social pressures, substance abuse/mid-career burnout, and rising education and housing costs	• "presenteeism" (just showing up, but won't/can't retire) • clogging the pathway to succession • resentment over inability to retire • health concerns • responsibility for aging parents • fear that their true life's work is not fulfilled

THE FUTURE OF THE WORKPLACE

Can a culture and a compensation system be friendly but also intense? Can teams be collegial and internally competitive? Can office culture be structured yet flexible? This dichotomy is now at the forefront of management debates and clearly has an impact on levels of engagement. A *New York Times* article described Amazon as a "soulless, dystopian workplace where no fun is had and no laughter is heard."[7] Workers shared stories of having suffered from

---

7   David Streitfeld and Jodi Kantor, "Jeff Bezos and Amazon Employees Join Debate Over Its Culture," *The New York Times,* August 17, 2015, http://www.nytimes.com/2015/08/18/technology/amazon-bezos-workplace-management-practices.html.

cancer, miscarriages, or other personal crises and were given no time to recover.[8]

Is this lack of empathy the "new normal" in a highly competitive economy, or is a company that tolerates such practices doomed in the highly competitive hiring market? If 60 percent of millennials leave their jobs within three years[9] and if the cost of replacement and retraining is rising, how can we incite people to stay in one place for an extended period of time? It's certainly *not* by abusing them. Yet at the same time, Amazon's ascent in a relatively short period of time to *the* dominate online retailer with a half-trillion dollar market capitalization could not happen if its workplace played ping-pong and drank craft beers all day. Where is the right balance?

We must learn to treat each other with respect, empathy, trust, and civility—but also embrace the need to recognize that our collective societal work ethic cannot be any further diluted if we expect to remain globally competitive.

---

8   Jodi Kantor and David Streitfeld, "Inside Amazon: Wrestling Big Ideas in a Bruising Workplace," *The New York Times*, August 15, 2015, http://www.nytimes.com/2015/08/16/technology/inside-amazon-wrestling-big-ideas-in-a-bruising-workplace.html.

9   "Attention, Employers: Millennials Have Made Their Demands," *The Atlantic*, http://www.theatlantic.com/sponsored/allstate/attention-employers-millennials-have-made-their-demands/219/.

THE FOUNDATION OF THE HIGHLY ENGAGED ORGANIZATION

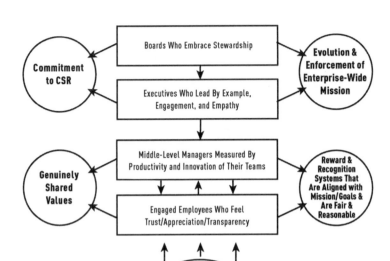

Surely we have advanced as a society where workers are no longer to be treated as "replaceable cogs in a machine," but at the same time, the pendulum may have swung too far at many companies that are unable to take action when their workers fall below acceptable levels of productivity. Leaders should focus on trust, transparency, consistency, loyalty, and supportiveness of a life outside the workplace as their top priorities.

Companies that foster and reward camaraderie among colleagues, respect at all levels, and genuine pride in all aspects of the work *will* retain employees longer and foster engagement that is more sustainable. Cultures are designed to bring out the best in a diverse group of people—and then inspire them to work with each other based on a foundation of empathy, trusted relationships, and shared values. Old-school companies that treat people as disposable are vulnerable to increasing levels of disengagement and dysfunction. Companies that serve as case studies of organizations that have mastered these cultural undertones include large retailers like Nordstrom. In the tech world, Google has surmounted corporate competitors in a short lifespan by providing employees with a slew of benefits—from gourmet meals on-site, to fitness centers and other tangible assets, to instilling more intangible cultural norms such as the sharing of quarterly reports by the CEO with all "Googlers." Employees who are engaged want to feel like they're more than just part of a team; they want to feel instrumental in the purpose of the company.

North Carolina-based packaging company, Wilton Connor Packaging LLC, also has a slew of employee services ranging from a laundry service at work for a nominal fee to coordinating and providing carpooling services, as well as offering English-language courses for a diverse workforce—all of which are a part of what the company believes is a part of "reciprocal investing" in order to ease the burden of everyday tasks for employees.

The monetary investment is slight, and the benefits of productivity have been vast. DELSTAR is an Arizona-based company that uses the same theory behind investing in employees that's illustrated by the employers mentioned above, but instead of additional perks, the company focuses on substantial training for employees. The courses go beyond technical training and teach additional job skills and life skills as well.

THE FIRST FOUR MILLENNIAL IMPACT REPORTS (2010 TO 2013) have given organizations, causes, leaders, fundraisers, and individuals around the world better insight into the next generation of volunteers, donors, and advocates. Since 2009, the Millennial Impact Project has focused on millennials' preferences when engaging with causes. By allowing millennials to describe how they wish to give to and help causes, organizations have been better able to reach them.

Throughout the first four years of the Millennial Impact Project, the following trends emerged and evolved:

- Millennials engage with causes to help other people, not institutions.

- Millennials support issues rather than organizations.

- Millennials prefer to perform smaller actions before fully committing to a cause.

- Millennials are influenced by the decisions and behaviors of their peers.

- Millennials treat all their assets (time, money, network) as having equal value.

- Millennials need to experience an organization's work without having to be on site.[10]

TIME TO HUG A MILLENNIAL?

Millennials are the generation born between 1980 and 2000. There are eighty million-plus millennials, and they will soon be the largest segment of our workforce. The perceptions of this segment of the population vary, but here are some facts based on hundreds of recent studies:

10   Derrick Feldmann, *Inspiring the Next Generation Workforce: The 2014 Millennial Impact Report*, The Case Foundation, page 4, http://casefoundation.org/wp-content/uploads/2014/11/MillenialImpactReport-2014.pdf.

PERCEPTION	REALITY
Millennials are lazy and uneducated.	Millennials are the most educated, most diverse, and most team-oriented segment of our workforce.
Millennials are money-hungry and demand empowerment.	Millennials value collaboration and personal fulfillment above almost anything else.
Millennials don't listen and don't take criticism very well.	Millennials seek mentoring, meaningful work, and professional development or they *will* be disengaged or move on.
Millennials are entitled, needy, and constantly need praise.	Millennials are hungry to learn but demand access to effective technology to drive efficiency. Technology and project management, in their view, will create more balanced lives and more time for nonwork activities.
Millennials want my job, and they are unwilling to "pay their dues."	Millennials want to learn that a career plan is in place for them, that a succession plan includes them, and that their careers will move at the same pace that the world around them moves.

How can we bridge this gap between reality and perception? How can baby-boomers and millennials peacefully coexist in the workplace and commit to more engaged working relationships to drive productivity? How can a generation focused on its advancement and a generation focused on its retirement work better *together*?

SOFTWARE, SURVEYS, AND OTHER TOOLS IN THE MODERN WORKPLACE

In the war for talent and with declining levels of engagement, many companies are turning to surveys, sentiment-analysis software, and other data-gathering tools to foster loyalty and retention and to uncover why engagement is on the decline. Our era of big data and data mining has led to many companies such as Intel, IBM, Twitter, and others using technology tools to gauge how employees feel about reward and recognition, culture, diversity efforts, prospects for advancement, and levels of engagement. Sifting through all of the data and survey results are human-resources (HR) professionals in search of the keys to the retention-and-engagement castle. The most important aspect of these tools is understanding the disconnect between what employers say and what they really mean and/or share with their friends in confidence.

Approaches vary widely, but at Intel, for example, the company surveys its 106,000 employees on an annual basis to help measure its organizational health, execution of strategy, and levels of employee engagement and satisfaction. But with more than fifty thousand hand written comments on the surveys, the sheer volume of the data currently trumps the usefulness of the knowledge to be drawn from the survey results. Some aspects of the sentiment-analysis software attempt to look at patterns to determine what can be addressed or improved and to drill deeper into what employees are *really* trying to convey beyond the mere words in their responses. Using more open-ended questions and fewer multiple-choice, survey-style question-naires forces employees to express themselves and avoids boredom in the survey process. Trust and confidentiality are key to this process—if employees feel that their responses are being shared beyond the scope of their comfort level, or even used against them, nobody will answer with candor or transparency. In other cases, monitoring social-media posts is more effective, such as IBM's Enterprise Social Pulse. In some cases, social-media posts were more reliable and more insightful than even the most advanced survey tools, which tend to miss situational analysis, humor, sarcasm, and other human emotions that may directly or indirectly influence levels of engagement.

LESSONS FROM THE CLASH

"Should I stay or should I go now? If I leave there will be trouble. And if I stay it will be double."

—The Clash

Why do people stay, and why do they leave? Are the disengaged always that way, or can a new verve and a new leader and team reignite a spark of productivity and engagement? Leaders must embrace one fact: talented and engaged people stay with one company out of mutual respect and loyalty, driven by one of the following key variables:

1. Engaged workers perceive that they are paid well relative to their efforts and market conditions.

2. Engaged workers feel appreciated and trusted.

3. Engaged workers feel that their voice is heard.

4. Engaged workers perceive concrete perks for advancement.

5. Engaged workers feel that they are involved in decision making and influencing their futures.

6. Engaged workers have access to education, learning, coaches, and mentors.

7. Engaged workers are challenged to take things to the next level by their peers and leaders.

CHAPTER 2

DISENGAGEMENT AS AN ISSUE OF LEADERSHIP AND GOVERNANCE

"Management is about persuading people to do things they do not want to do, while leadership is about inspiring people to do things they never thought they could. "

—STEVE JOBS, COFOUNDER AND VISIONARY, APPLE

"With leadership, you make a decision every day about whether you choose to follow someone. And you make it in your heart, not your head. The ability to inspire followership is so different than management, and it requires transparency, authenticity, vulnerability, and all things that are completely unnatural to you when you are trying to build and achieve and accomplish. We're all going to make mistakes. The question

is how are we going to recover when we make them, and are
we going to be respectful to others when we make them?"

—WALT BETTINGER, CEO, CHARLES SCHWAB CORPORATION

Let's be honest—leadership and governance is not as easy as it used to be. The days of the expansive, mahogany-filled corner office with fine whisky and contraband cigars—nobody looking over your shoulder or hyperquestioning your decisions—are long gone. Those days have evolved into transparent governance, multiple levels of shareholder and stakeholder activism, wage disparity protests and regulations, social-media empowerment, and overall societal democratization. Today's workplace is filled with highly matrixed and networked organizational charts with fuzzy-at-best roles and responsibilities, and with distracted baby boomers and disengaged millennials. High turnover rates and even higher employee-replacement costs, as well as an increasingly mobile workforce and rapid changes in markets and business models, are the new norm. Blurred lines between home and the workplace lead many to question whether a work-life balance is really attainable. And the microscopes that leaders live under these days are among the issues contributing to keeping leaders up at night, and to all crises being played at a very public and transparent stage.

Leaders today face the need to forge a delicate balance between confidence and vulnerability. Leaders must express hope and optimism to get acceptable levels of engagement back on track. It is nearly impossible to ask an employee to be passionate about a company whose own leaders are disconnected and apathetic. At the same time, employees expect humility and transparency. In a February 4, 2016, interview with *The New York Times* entitled "You've Got to Open Up to Move Up," Walt Bettinger, CEO of the Charles Schwab Corporation, discussed the importance of the traits of humility, candor, vulnerability, and accountability as being the most important aspects of engaged leadership. Bettinger said, "It was more important than anything to share with people the great failures in my life as opposed to the successes."[11] Sharing failures and concerns builds trust and mutual rapport.

RISING DISTRUST OF CORPORATE LEADERSHIP AND ENHANCED TRANSPARENCY EFFORTS

In 2015, our federal government promulgated a controversial new rule requiring companies to disclose the pay gap between rank-and-file employees and the chief executive. Some companies already reveal such pay-ratio information. In March, Noble Energy, Inc. disclosed that former CEO Charles Davidson made eighty-two times more than the median employee, who took home $103,500 in direct compensation in 2014. In contrast, Mr. Davidson made $8.5 million in direct compensation. The new rule requires companies to disclose median-worker pay—and compare it with the CEO's compensation. Supporters of the pay-ratio rule say the new disclosure requirement could pressure corporate boards at firms with large pay gaps to rein in CEO raises. The practice of disclosing this information could lead to greater engagement and wage parity—but it also may lead to frustration and resentment over the relationship of work to appropriate levels of reward.

---

11   Adam Bryant, "Walt Bettinger of Charles Schwab: You've Got to Open Up to Move Up," *The New York Times*, February 4, 2016, http://www.nytimes.com/2016/02/07/business/walt-bettinger-of-charles-schwab-youve-got-to-open-up-to-move-up.html.

TAKING BACK CONTROL

What's a leader to do? Throw in the towel and find a nice condo in Costa Rica? Or evolve, adapt, inspire, and embrace these challenges to make sure that culture is aligned, that resilient business models are durable and profitable, and that growth is steady and strategic? For the good of our economy and our future, I hope that it is the latter course of action.

Board members and corporate leaders are stewards over the assets of the enterprise. These assets include traditional categories such as inventory, computers, real estate, and equipment. But in today's digital economy, the three most critical assets are:

- intangible assets

- human assets

- financial assets

In my book, *Harvesting Intangible Assets*, I discussed the consequences to a company if its leaders fail to understand how to harvest its most precious strategic intangible assets. In my book, *Essays On Governance*, I discussed the financial crisis that led to the passage of the Sarbanes-Oxley Act of 2002, which created some of the laws and practices that help ensure that a board properly oversees the management of the cash flow and other financial assets of a company. Absent from these discussions, however, is the board and executive's fiduciary role to properly manage and harvest the *human* assets of the company. An underengaged workforce can never be a driver of long-term strategic shareholder value in the same way that an overweight, unmotivated jockey will never guide a racehorse to win the Triple Crown. Boards and company leaders have a responsibility to create and foster cultures of innovation, engagement, and profitability, yet they often focus on only one or two of these with any real commitment. We can study financial statements until we are blue in the face, but if we refuse to dig deeper to get to the core of the culture of the company, its systems and strategies for fostering engagement and empowerment, and its rewards mechanisms for encouraging the *right* behaviors, then I would argue that the board's role as a steward has not been satisfied.

The crisis of engagement cannot be approached casually. The aggregate costs in the United States of highly disengaged and stressed workers is well into the trillions of dollars—and has been estimated to dilute up to 15 percent of our annual GDP. Leaders *must* focus on fostering an engaged and productive workplace culture, or the consequences will be irreversible.

THE ENGAGEMENT "HOT POTATO"

Remember playing the children's game of "hot potato?" You threw the ball around a circle until the teacher blew the whistle. Whoever had the ball when the whistle was blown left the circle. The goal was to get one ball ("the potato") thrown to the next person as quickly as possible to eventually be the last person remaining. Corporate responsibility for increasing engagement seems to be the hot potato today. Boards refuse to recognize cultural challenges as being too far down the food chain in their oversight role.

Executive leaders will talk a good game about the need for stronger levels of engagement, but then push the responsibility down to the middle-level managers. Well, as it turns out, the middle-level managers are not reliable sources for fostering engagement—because they themselves are disengaged. In Gallup's recent study, only 31.5 percent of employees were self-described as "engaged," 51 percent were not engaged, and 17.5 percent were "actively disengaged."[12] Only a

---

12   Amy Adkins, "Majority of U.S. Employees Not Engaged Despite Gains in 2014," Gallup, January 28, 2015, http://www.gallup.com/poll/181289/majority-employees-

small handful described themselves as "actively engaged." Gallup goes on to share that disengaged managers cost US companies nearly $100 billion per annum through their impact on those that they manage—and that number spikes to more than $400 billion when you factor in the impact of highly disengaged managers. The "cascade effect" directly impacts employee-turnover rates (more than one out of two employees have left a job to escape a bad manager) as well as rates of productivity, focus, safety, innovation, creativity, and collaboration.[13]

So who will be accountable for improving engagement? Which organizations and companies will reward their managers for being engaged and for fostering engagement? Who can be responsible for reporting to the board on the overall levels of engagement and the strength of the culture? Every organization today must appoint, empower, and clearly define the role of the chief engagement officer (the other CEO) who can focus on the purpose and the passion of the most valuable asset of the enterprise: its people. No more passing the buck. No more head in the sand. No more hot potato!

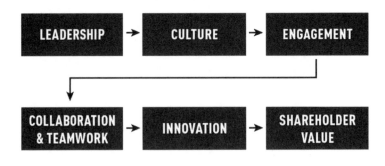

not-engaged-despite-gains-2014.aspx.

13   "State of the American Manager," Gallup, http://www.gallup.com/services/182138/state-american-manager.aspx.

Healthy leadership with a shared vision of well-communicated values is the key driver of culture. Culture fosters engagement. Engagement is at the heart of collaboration and teamwork. Cooperation and communication among teams drives innovation and combats complacency. Innovation and intrapreneurship maximize shareholder and stakeholder value. Any disconnect or break in this value chain fuels a slow erosion of the fundamental well-being of the enterprise—and that has a ripple effect on all operations of the business.

To foster greater levels of engagement, leaders must first start with a brutal reexamination of their own management styles. Multiple corporate crises have led to an environment where trust, transparency, and collaboration are expected of leaders at all levels. Humility is in; ego is out. Listening is in; dictating is out.

Empathy is in; nonchalance is out.

Empathy is in; nonchalance is out. The trend toward "servant leadership" is creating C-suite members who act with humility, listen well, admit their errors, and share the credit with others. The buck starts and stops with them. Executives such as A.G. Lafley of Proctor & Gamble and Tony Thompson of Krispy Kreme Doughnuts embody the notion of servant leadership. Lafley was featured in the October 21, 2015, edition of *The Wall Street Journal* as emphasizing that today's leaders who foster and inspire engagement and innovation must embrace humility in order to "listen well, admit errors, and be willing to share the limelight."[14]

---

14   Joann S. Lublin, "The Case for Humble Executives," *The Wall Street Journal*, October 20, 2015, http://www.wsj.com/articles/the-case-for-humble-executives-1445385076.

Leaders in 2016 need to recalibrate expectations and adjust to the new realities of the marketplace and the workspace. Employees must do the same. A new dialogue needs to be established. All companies need to take a hard look at their compensation and reward systems relative to the new realities and establish expectations accordingly. The good old days of "just showing up" and reaping rewards are long gone.

PRESENTEEISM

Leaders must directly address the crisis that Peter Farrell, a *Harvard Business Review* blogger, described recently as "presenteeism"—in other words, physically present at work but mentally absent and apathetic. We cannot expect much productivity or creativity from those who come to work and immediately want to be "anywhere but here" and just try to fly below the radar screen and hope that nobody notices. Leaders could potentially ignore this problem by choice if the percentage of workers who feel this way were a rounding error, but this is nowhere near the reality. In any company or any society where people *want* increasingly *more* but *do* increasingly *less*, there is a problem—and perhaps a disengagement crisis.

US				
Engaged		Somewhat Disengaged		Actively and Highly Disengaged
31.5 percent	→	51 percent	→	17.5 percent
GLOBAL				
Invested, Engaged, Committed to Add Value		Apathetic, Bored, Just Trying to Get by		Actively Disengaged and Toxic to Culture
10 percent	→	55 percent	→	35 percent

TRUST

At the heart of all effective leadership is *trust* and *confidence*. In general, people will respond to a leader who shares their values and is trustworthy. The apparent uptick in leaders being greedy or companies entrenched in scandals is what led to the passage of legislation like Sarbanes-Oxley. Dodd-Frank is not helping the engagement crisis, either. A June 2014 Gallup article found that while 96 percent of engaged employees purport to trust their leaders, that number drops significantly—to 46 percent—with disengaged employees, and significantly less than that with highly disengaged employees.

Where should we focus our efforts to restore trust? Well, first, make sure that your A players are content and beyond poaching or slipping into the 51-percent box. Encourage and reward them to actively get involved in mentoring, succession planning, training, and thought leadership. Support the notion that an organization can *never* have enough leaders. Motivate them, recognize them, appreciate them, advance them—or lose them, either to another company or, worse, to the pool of the B and C players who swim in the 51-percent pond. For many companies, you are almost better off losing an A player to another opportunity than you are losing him or her internally to a place of apathy and complacency. The overall economy benefits from these *A players staying A players*—whether working for you or elsewhere. The true challenge lies in converting the B and C players who live in the 51-percent box.

It is critical to accept the fact that very few, if any, of the 17.5 percent (D and F players) are salvageable. These employees may be either permanently toxic or will remain toxic unless or until they experience a "change in scenery," and this means you *must* relieve them of their responsibilities as soon as possible. Be aware that they are in active-recruitment mode and want to increase membership in their 17.5-percent club of discontentment almost as badly as you are trying to increase the pool of the currently 31.5 percent of A and B+ players. Only *you* as a leader can determine who will win this cultural "tug-of-war."

RECALIBRATING AND CORRECTING THE COURSE

How and why have we become so rudderless as leaders? Why do we lack the backbone to take decisive action and get rid of this deadwood? Is it the threat of legal action? Or is it the threat of a social-media assault? Is it the threat of workplace violence or the threat of being politically incorrect? Or is it *all* of these reasons?

Ask any serious boaters whether they can get to their destination without a rudder, and they will look at you as if you are insane. In the context of governance, a "rudder" is a steering device designed to articulate clearly set goals, a culture designed to achieve them, and a backbone to enforce performance metrics. We want leaders to pick a clear direction—even if we do not agree with it—to avoid stagnation, deadlock, and complacency. Worse yet are leaders we perceive to act like Alice in *Alice in Wonderland*—essentially apathetic—as to their destination; they burden us with even greater frustration by consuming resources and getting us nowhere.

When Congress is dysfunctional due to political divisiveness, no progress can be made, and it causes confusion and uncertainty for company leaders and their boards. This ripple effect gets in the way of a leader's ability to dictate a clear strategy. We end up with a nation run by "Alices" and an economy that remains weak or flat and a workforce that will remain disengaged and unmotivated. We cannot allow this country—or the companies we rely upon to generate tax revenues and create new jobs—to wander aimlessly from one policy to another or one strategic plan to another. Empires have fallen and companies have filed bankruptcy when leaders fall asleep at the switch and rudders are absent or dysfunctional.

THE ENGAGEMENT OF THE BOARD AND THE COMPANY'S LEADERS

Fear, ignorance, and ambivalence often act as a catalyst for complacency and employee-wide disengagement. Change is curtailed and hard questions are avoided due to concerns over how stakeholders will perceive a corporate strategy under scrutiny. The board of directors plays an important role in acting in concert with the management team to develop a clear strategy—because the board is generally more objective. An effective monitoring system can negate concerns stakeholders have of short-term failure and ensure long-term success. Benchmarks should be established to evaluate results and the strategy adjusted appropriately. The best boaters adjust their rudders as the wind direction changes and the tide turns.

One of the most essential roles of the board of directors is to weigh in annually on the company's overall goals and objectives and then hold leaders accountable for the achievement of these plans. Board meetings should be "checkpoints" to measure progress or help navigate through any forks in the road. Boards sit in the same proverbial tree as the Cheshire Cat, providing navigational tools to the executives, but they must *never* tolerate a response or report which is as rudderless as Alice's "I don't know."

Leadership is all about informed decision making based on a window of information, which is often either too early or too late. General Colin Powell had a great "40/70" rule for decision making in contemporary warfare—if he had less than 40 percent of the data he needed to make a decision, it was probably too early to decide; if he had more than 70 percent, it was probably too late. In the context of corporate governance, I would suggest modifying that to a "55/80" rule for decision making in order to protect corporate assets and drive shareholder value.

Even when a board feels that it has the right amount of information to make a decision that mitigates risks, there should always be the step of *skepticism* before the step of decisiveness, and the impact on engagement should be highly considered as a key variable. Being decisive is critical (or we wind up like Alice), but boards and leaders need a filtering process that confirms that the right quantity of information and the right level of analysis have, in fact, been gathered. The board needs a devil's advocate. In other words, when the Cheshire Cat (with its famous mischievous grin) gives its advice, someone even higher up the tree needs to confirm that the board has asked all the right questions. Asking the right questions can help boards better understand the current situation and better position themselves for evaluating future possibilities. The devil's advocate can be a particular board member, a board committee, or even an outside advisor.

The Tao of the Cheshire Cat is that if an organization does not know where it is going, then any road will take it there. Business and strategic plans are only needed after a clear destination has been selected. No shareholder wants to be part of a company that is rudderless or apathetic. The productivity of each employee team is directly aligned with the clarity of the strategic direction, which leaders should communicate on a regular basis.

> *If an organization does not know where it is going, then any road will take it there.*

NAVIGATING THROUGH DISTRACTIONS ON THE ROAD TO GOOD GOVERNANCE

Accidents are a necessary evil of both driving and life. We cannot get behind the wheel without the chance of a collision, and we cannot live our lives without the chance of making a mistake. Each year in the United States, more than forty thousand people are killed in motor-vehicle crashes, and more than three million people are injured in approximately six million accidents. Research indicates that in more than 50 percent of all crashes, driver inattention was a significant factor. Inattention isn't the right way to live our lives, govern, or lead others. The slow death of common courtesy and a diminishing commitment to our safety and the safety of others—both on our roads and in our lives—is a very disturbing trend.

How does driver distraction impact performance? Studies show that a focused driver makes approximately two hundred decisions for every mile of driving. If you take your eyes off the road for three to four seconds at fifty-five miles per hour, your vehicle travels the length of a football field. Texting while driving increases your chance of an accident by 23 percent. Pedestrians who walk into crosswalks and busy streets while texting, talking, or listening to music increase the chance of a collision.

What factors contribute to driver inattention? First, the obvious ones—alcohol or drug abuse, fatigue, reading a map or newspaper, weather and traffic conditions, putting on makeup or shaving, using smartphones, eating, drinking, smoking, changing radio stations or CDs, retrieving unsecured objects or cargo, focusing on a child or passenger in the back seat, etc. We have all seen these activities in other cars—or our own—on a daily basis. Less obvious factors include focusing on tough business or family problems while driving, stress or anxiety, running late to an appointment, engaging in an intense conversation, swerving suddenly to avoid an object in the road, or driving an unfamiliar vehicle or on an unfamiliar road.

So, what can we learn about best practices in leadership and governance by observing the distracted driver? For one thing, if directors and business leaders are distracted and not focused on the task at hand, then they are significantly more likely not only to get off course but also to hurt others along the way—especially the stakeholders who, like distracted pedestrians, rely on them to make the right decisions and stay focused behind the governance wheel. Stakeholders are handicapped because they often cannot attain the knowledge necessary to avoid the most dangerous "intersections," nor can they respond defensively when they hear allegorical "sirens" in the distance. In the boardroom, there are no sirens. The responsibility is solely the in the hands of those who lead.

It is impossible, legally or ethically, to fulfill your fiduciary duties to shareholders if you are unfocused or unprepared in board meetings. Board members who are more concerned with the menu of the postboard-meeting dinner are not likely to be effective and engaged. Those who are spending more time on their smartphones or in "sidebar" conversations than they are on board dialogue are not likely to be meaningful contributors. And board members who are too distracted by other commitments to actually read and analyze the reports sent weeks before the meeting are not likely to meet the standards of the duty of care. Distracted boards lead companies straight toward a major collision.

The ancient Syrian writer Syrus once said, "To do two things at once is to do neither." Multitasking by definition means doing more than one task at the same time. Thus, the likelihood of one or more of these tasks being poorly executed increases dramatically. Even the most-talented jugglers will drop a ball. How many times a day are you engaged in a conversation with someone while also answering an e-mail on your cell phone, only to find later that you missed something important or included something in the e-mail that you now regret?

As a whole, our society is quickly becoming unable to focus, and we're constantly encountering diversions to occupy our time and minds, making apps like "Freedom" necessary. "Freedom" sits on a computer's desktop to shut off Internet connectivity so that people can focus on work. Many people, and you may be one of them, believe multitasking actually makes them more effective. The results of a 2009 study at Stanford suggest our perceptions of multitasking are false. The brain is not wired to multitask—it processes information like a single-server processor, yet we expect it to operate as a dual-server processor. We are limited to processing one task at a time, and by overloading our brains, we are forcing them to jump back and forth between tasks. Just like a computer with too many windows open, our mind slows down and it takes more time to process each component of information. The problem is perpetuated by our inability to filter out irrelevant information while we multitask.[15]

CAN BOARDS OF DIRECTORS AVOID ACCIDENTS?

The surest way to avoid accidents is to never get behind the wheel. But organizations cannot be guided by risk elimination or nothing will be accomplished. Most progressive organizations are driven by enterprise risk management (ERM), which seeks to mitigate but not eliminate risk and where decisions are guided by principles of risk optimization. You won't travel very far, but you will be safe. If we live

---

15   Adam Gorlick, "Media multitaskers pay mental price, Stanford study shows," *Stanford News*, August 24, 2009, http://news.stanford.edu/news/2009/august24/ multitask-research-study-082409.html.

our lives in fear of a collision, we will never leave our living-room sofas. Boards and leaders today are overfocused on risk management and underfocused on opportunity recognition. Getting behind the wheel each day means that we assume the risk that we may not reach our destination without a crash or some pain along the way. Boards and company leaders accept this risk as a cost of the reward of eventually getting where they want to go. The best leaders develop stronger armor for dealing with life's adversities along the journey and know when to use the exit ramp.

FOSTERING ENGAGEMENT: ADVICE FOR THE BOARD: SEPARATING THE MESSAGE FROM THE MESSENGER

"When regard for the truth has been broken down or even slightly weakened, all things will remain doubtful."

—ST. AUGUSTINE

Since about the early 2000s, our nation's government and business leaders seem to have reinterpreted the meaning of the term "the truth" to serve their own selfish purposes. The level of deception, misrepresentation, "spinning," and omissions appears to be a daily headline to which we have become numb as we saw in the 2016 election process and in what appears to be almost daily reports of needless shootings and acts of terrorism. The lack of direction is a significant contributor to our prolonged recessionary economy. But as St. Augustine observed, we cannot have certainty without truth, and by definition, clarity requires candor and honesty.

As human beings, we tend to admire those who give us praise and have disdain for those who are critical or scornful. But we need to separate the message from the messenger. The people who offer the most value in life are the ones willing to be direct, honest, and genuine. Boards telling CEOs that they are doing a great job when they are not and managers telling their teams that they are winning when they are really losing are not governance best practices. The same thing takes place when teachers give students grades they do not deserve and when voters re-elect politicians who have not served their citizens. Often we are too fearful or too lazy to explore alternatives or be forthright.

In finance, we rely on numbers to tell a story about our viability. In marketing, we optimize accounts and campaigns based on data about consumer responses. And in operations, we increase efficiencies by evaluating internal information. Sometimes the data we rely on is positive, and sometimes it is negative. Either way, it is valuable because it accurately portrays something important about the company and allows for measures to be taken to correct mistakes and enhance successes. What would happen if the data were no longer reliable or, worse, unavailable? Would any responsible leader consider making a business decision at that point?

In online advertising, companies place a pixel on their site to determine where traffic is coming from and to track the actions of the users on their sites. They can see where the users click, how much time they spend on a page, and whether they fill out a form to receive more information. Based on this information, advertisers adjust bids for different sources of traffic until the sources are performing at an optimum level. This analysis is taking place every second and is representative of the information-rich society we live in. An advertiser would not invest in an expensive advertising campaign if it were impossible to collect data to make real-time adjustments to enhance performance. Why are companies investing capital in a workforce they are unwilling to optimize? Truths act as bids in an open marketplace of idea sharing where employees can respond to feedback in real time. We need to shift our perspective by shying away from the negative connotation of "constructive criticism" and begin to look more objectively at the truth as an additional data point that provides useful information for decision making. To harvest a more effective and efficient workforce, tell the truth and tell it often.

> *To harvest a more effective and efficient workforce, tell the truth and tell it often.*

Don't get me wrong; I am a huge fan of empathy, diplomacy, and tact. It is critical to place yourself into the shoes of the person who will be receiving the message before you deliver it and carefully craft your words before you say them. But being tactful is not the same as telling someone what he or she wants to hear just because you do not want to offend him or her.

Honesty at all levels allows for quicker, more-informed decisions. It gives everyone the license to suggest improvements. Without an open culture, employees may fear backlash or, in the worst case, termination for speaking their minds or for sharing critical information with management.

Leaders must be committed to building a culture where truth telling is a core value, both externally and internally. Managers must be rewarded for the courage of their convictions. Principles of transparency, accountability, and responsibility must be embraced, and the organizational sins of turfmanship and deception must be mitigated or eliminated. Without truth, we lack clarity. And without clarity, we cannot move toward economic recovery.

To be sure, leaders who embrace principles of fairness often win the respect and appreciation of their coworkers. Employee perceptions of fairness lead to higher retention rates and greater customer satisfaction. Employees are more committed to organizations that they perceive as fair. This is not indicative that employees expect *all* policies to be to their advantage; rather, they expect to have a good understanding of the process for establishing new policies, of the procedure for decision making, and of the communication channels and expectations when decisions are made.

"ROC" AS THE NEW "ROI"

In April of 2015, the *Harvard Business Review* reported the results of a study by KRW, a Minneapolis-based leadership consultancy. The article, "Measuring the Return on Character," found that CEOs who rated highly on four moral principles delivered better financial and nonfinancial results (including levels of engagement and trust) than those who scored lower. The four moral principles were integrity, responsibility, forgiveness, and compassion. Leaders at the top of the survey frequently engaged in behaviors that reveal strong character and which foster trust and inspire engagement, such as having the courage to stand up for what's right (even if it is painful or unpopular); genuinely expressing concern for others and for the common good; a commitment to excellence, community service, and the overall desire to leave the world in a better place than where they found it; letting go of mistakes (theirs and others); and demonstrating empathy. On the other end of the spectrum were highly distrusted CEOs who only cared for themselves and their own financial gains and led through shaming others, finger pointing, punishing well-intentioned people who made mistakes, and were caught in multiple lies and mistruths.[16]

Keeping your workers informed and offering them channels to provide input is admirable, but at the end of the day, leaders must lead and make tough decisions, whether or not they will be perceived as "fair" by those affected by them. The moral and ethical paradox of fairness is this: that which is right is not always fair, and that which is fair is not always right.

Is it better to be loved or feared? Can leaders be effective and gain *both* the respect and the attention of their employees? A recent *Harvard Business Review* study found that it is difficult to achieve both. Leadership guided by fairness often suffers from a lack of perceived power and the respect that comes along with it.[17] Say you have one hundred employees and ten need to be terminated as soon as possible for the company to move forward and remain viable to protect the best interests of the shareholders. Should you select the ten most recently hired? The ten with the lowest performance reviews? The ten who don't have families to support? The ten you like the least? The ten you perceive as least loyal to the company? In all likelihood, no matter what you decide, the consequences of your decision will be perceived as unfair by at least ten people, and perhaps many more.

The communication of the consequences of tough and unfair decisions should be guided by principles of transparency and sincerity and by treating people with dignity and respect at all times.

16 "Measuring the Return on Character," *Harvard Business Review*, April 2015, https://hbr.org/2015/04/measuring-the-return-on-character.

17 Batia M. Wiesenfeld, Naomi B. Rothman, Sara L. Wheeler-Smith, and Adam D. Galinsky, "Why Fair Bosses Fall Behind," *Harvard Business Review*, July-August 2011, https://hbr.org/2011/07/why-fair-bosses-fall-behind.

A commitment to a set of shared values, especially during times when difficult decisions will need to be made, is a key pillar of good governance.

Even if I do not agree with their views, I have always respected those who act with passion and conviction. These are people guided by deep-seated beliefs and a strong set of moral values. They understand and embrace the fact that there will be those who will perceive their decisions as unfair, no matter how much time and deliberation went into them. But governance is not a popularity contest, and executives are not cheerleaders. Governance is hard and challenging work. Nobody said it was going to be fun!

TO FOSTER ENGAGEMENT, THE "EMPEROR" NEEDS TO KNOW: DO WHAT YOU SAY, AND SAY WHAT YOU MEAN

"We want to reassure everyone that we're doing fine, but that doesn't mean we won't have to make some tough decisions."

—JEFF JOERNES, CEO, THE MANPOWER GROUP

In the famous scene in *A Few Good Men*, Jack Nicholson, playing the role of Colonel Jessep, yells back at Tom Cruise, playing the role of military attorney Kaffee, "You can't handle the truth!" How and why does it seem that Jack Nicholson's words have become a governance standard for brand leaders, CEOs, and even Congress over the past few years?

Governance and leadership require prompt, clear, candid communication with employees, shareholders, stakeholders, and citizens. The rule is pretty simple: *do what you say, and say what you mean.* There are many metaphors and sayings which reinforce this basic principle—from "walk the talk" to "where you sit depends on where you stand," even to "the truth will set you free." However, it more often appears as if our nation's leaders are playing musical chairs rather than clearly communicating their opinions. And then there are those whose opinions are so hardened in concrete that they forget that governance is also about compromise and respect for each other's positions.

Honesty and promptness are the keys to crisis management. In 1982, Johnson & Johnson set the precedent for good crisis management when its most profitable product, Tylenol, was tampered with in a store, leading to seven deaths in the Chicago area. Even though the company was not directly responsible for the isolated deaths, it recalled the product immediately from the entire US market, broadcast multiple public announcements, and made the product safer before returning it to the shelves. Above all else, Johnson & Johnson placed public health at the top of their priorities, enabling the restoration of the Tylenol brand by responding quickly, taking responsibility, and minimizing the risk to its customers. Delayed responses and incomplete information can lead to public backlashes. That was the case when Exxon failed to respond to the 1999 Alaskan oil spill in a timely manner or take responsibility for the environmental harms that resulted from the spill. In the eyes of the public, Exxon was considered deceitful and unconcerned with the environment.

We have seen the global demand for corporate transparency increase with the onset of the BP oil spill, Enron accounting fraud, and the US financial crisis. Ethical considerations, economic considerations, and innovation and learning are key forces for this shift in perspective. European retail company Marks and Spencer (M&S) is a leader in its field when it comes to sustainable business practices. It has taken stakeholder transparency and accountability to a new level with Plan A, an initiative to reduce its carbon impact and become the most sustainable retailer in the world. Rather than being a slave to the bottom line each quarter, M&S has put long-term objectives and profitability at the forefront of its business model. And all you skeptics, step aside—this is not just about doing good for the sake of doing good. As a direct result of Plan A, M&S saw an additional $70 million in profit in 2010. Stakeholders can see the successes, roadblocks, and failures along the way because M&S provides frequent updates on its website.

The rules of the game are changing as top brands become more transparent and report on socially responsible initiatives, including both how they get it right and how they get it wrong. Gap Inc.'s global compliance and integrity department shares data on its website about violations of its code of vendor conduct in the categories of management system, environment, labor, and working conditions, broken down by region. In 2010, the United States was the world's largest Global Reporting Initiative country, with 183 reporting organizations, up 30 percent from 2009.

AVOIDING "ENC SYNDROME" IN LEADERSHIP

In the children's story, *The Emperor's New Clothes*, a ruler is convinced by a shyster tailor that his suit of nonexistent clothes is the finest in the land. He then proceeds to parade down the crowded streets of his village to show them off to his community. The people are horrified by the sight of him in his natural state, but are too afraid to say anything, fearing that it will offend him. Only a small child finally speaks up to tell the emperor the truth. The story offers many insightful lessons on leadership and governance:

- **Do your due diligence on key advisors.** The tailor in this story was clearly unqualified—where was an effective vetting process?

- **Trust your instincts to overcome bad advice.** The emperor suspected that his new suit of clothing was nonexistent but followed the advice of his new tailor anyway. If something seems too good to be true, then it probably is.

- **Restrain vanity.** Even if the emperor truly believed that he had been made the finest suit of clothing, did he really need to parade around the village to show it off?

- **Build a culture where truth is validated.** The saddest part of the story is that none of the villagers would speak up. They were too concerned with telling the emperor what they thought he *wanted* to hear instead of what he *needed* to hear.

- **Let's not build a society that depends on the innocence of a child to point out our flaws.** After embarrassing himself and offending everyone around him, the emperor somewhat randomly relies on the voice of a small child to uncover the truth.

- **Be true to thyself.** Know your true strengths and weaknesses and do not try to hide them or deny that they exist.

- **Friends don't let friends walk around naked.** Build relationships based on trust and candor. True friends and objective advisors do not allow leaders to operate on the basis of vanity and ego.

The bottom line: the emperor needs to know the truth (and so do his people).

ENGAGEMENT AND EXECUTIVE LEADERSHIP

Effective leaders inspire others to act by demonstrating the path to productivity and reward. Engagement begins at the top of the organizational chart. A disengaged and disconnected CEO cannot possibly lead an organization to a path of engagement and alignment. Employees and middle-level managers look to the senior executives to set the tone and be shining examples as to what engagement looks like—both in your words and in your actions.

What are the characteristics, habits, and best practices of leaders who inspire action, foster alignment, and significantly increase levels of engagement?

For starters, they are highly credible and experienced. They are respected by their peers and their subordinates for both their accomplishments and their humility. They are authentic and transparent, confident and vulnerable, inquisitive and decisive.

To drive engagement, be the leader you yourself would want to follow. Be the leader others want to follow. Be the leader that makes them feel that the ship is moving in the right direction. Be the leader who is clear with everyone as to expectations and rewards.

What is the difference between being a good leader and

> *Good leaders can be effective in getting people to believe in them, but great leaders can get people around them to believe in themselves.*

a great leader? Good leaders can be effective in getting people to believe in them, but great leaders can get people around them to believe in themselves. A good leader can demonstrate his or her own capabilities to others, while a great leader focuses on showing others what they are capable of accomplishing. Only great leaders are capable of fostering and improving engagement at all levels of the organization.

THE PURSUIT OF HAPPINESS

Thomas Jefferson wrote that our three most basic rights as a citizen are life, liberty, and the pursuit of happiness. The first two are relatively straightforward, and the third is pretty darn subjective. Our "pursuit" of happiness is highly individualized, and people may define it very differently. The word that often gets lost in an overfocus on the happiness word is the *pursuit*. Jefferson envisioned a nation where our right to engage in a *personal quest* to find joy, passion, love, fulfillment, and the things that make us happy would be unobstructed and unlimited. Government was there to facilitate and support our journeys, not stand in the way of them.

Leaders of companies have overfocused on trying to determine whether their employees are happy and underfocused on whether their employees are engaged. Now is the time to refocus. Happiness is a byproduct of engagement. When our minds, bodies, and hearts are truly engaged in our work and in building relationships with the people around us, the more elusive feelings of happiness and satisfaction will be met. We will also naturally view our compensation for these efforts in a more holistic way—to include both the quantitative and the more intangible rewards as our motivation for high performance, personal growth, and development.

If you ask people if they are happy in the workplace, you will open up a very subjective can of worms that is difficult to manage and almost impossible to accurately measure. If, on the other hand, you ask them if they are engaged, you will still probably need to deal with responses that are challenging to analyze, *but* if you peel the onion down a few more layers, you can start to collect definable, measurable, and actionable answers to questions such as:

- Do you understand the meaning of your work and how it affects other individuals and society overall?

- Do you understand your role in our enterprise and how and why what you do furthers our mission and objectives?

- Do you feel appreciated by this organization and your peers for your efforts? Why or why not?

- Are you fulfilled by your work, and have you mapped out a path for personal and career advancement within this field? Or other fields?

- Is this company committed to serving the community in which it operates, and do you have opportunities to be part of that service?

- Do you sense a feeling of trust, respect, and *esprit de corps* among your coworkers? Why or why not? And how does this feeling manifest itself?

- Do you understand fully the purpose of your company and how each team and your individual role fit into the larger picture?

- Do you envision your current job as a career path or a stop along the way to launching your actual career?

- Is there a stove-piping system or communication gaps that are severely affecting your work environment and the greater culture of the office as a whole?

Some business leaders make the hypercritical error of assuming that the answers to all of these questions are true (thereby suffering like the emperor in the story), while others are merely in denial of the fact that their workforce is not engaged (like the line in *A Few Good Men*: "You can't handle the truth!"). Effective leaders are engaged leaders, and engaged leaders create and inspire engaged workforces.

Effective leaders are engaged leaders, and engaged leaders create and inspire engaged workforces.

Board members and company leaders need to focus with precision on our crisis of disengagement and should ask these questions:

- What are our current levels of engagement by division, by office, by team, and by individual?

- What are the direct and indirect consequences of the current engagement levels?

- What are the "ripple effects" of apathy, boredom, confusion, frustration, anxiety, stress, depression, attention-deficit disorder, lack of gratitude and appreciation, attentiveness, thoughtfulness, and civility on our customers, partners, suppliers, influencers, and others in our ecosystem over the short term, medium term, and long term?

• If current levels of engagement are not where we need them to be, then what is our game plan for improvement? What *new* rewards, incentives, training, education, organizational structures, team dynamics, leaders, motivations, and reasons need to be put in place to reverse this dangerous trend?

There are four important points here:

1. Don't make the mistake of merely throwing more money at the problem. A bigger Christmas bonus will help buy a new toy, but it won't buy genuine engagement.

2. Don't adopt the "flavor-of-the-month" business trend as the solution. You cannot change your core mission and values as often as you change your underwear and expect employees to suddenly be inspired or consistently perform when they are constantly adjusting to the business philosophy *du jour*.

3. Be who you are—but be it well and be it consistently in a fashion where your teams will either align with the mission and embrace it or self-select out of the possibility of engagement by leaving.

4. *Ask* people what tools, resources, rewards, etc. they will need to be more engaged—don't *tell* them. Nobody on the planet wants to be told that this new embroidered tote bag with the company's logo will bring us all closer together; they would much prefer to engage in a meaningful dialogue than be force-fed.

CONCLUSION

Many volumes have been written about the responsibilities of a company's board of directors and its leaders, yet "healthy governance" opens truly new ground that holds profoundly important potential and which can significantly impact employee engagement and loyalty. It is a concept suited to a time when relentlessly rapid change and compounding complexity are fast overwhelming narrow notions of what makes board members and leaders fully fit to serve and capable of driving engagement. In today's dynamic environment, capable corporate governance is every bit as much about superior leadership and people as it is about sound judgment and inviolate ethics.

Healthy boards lead to healthy leaders, which in turn will foster and maintain a healthy culture and an engaged workforce. In these turbulent times, there is no alternative to ensuring that these objectives remain a top strategic priority. Board members and company leaders who are determined to deliver superior, sustained value creation to shareholders will embrace the holistic concept of healthy leadership and act decisively to build a team committed to healthy governance. A sharing culture is a critical component of the evolving equation for taking the company to the next level.

CHAPTER 3

REFLECTIONS ON DRIVING A CULTURE OF ENGAGEMENT: ROOTS OF HEALTHY LEADERSHIP

BY GUEST ESSAYIST BOB ROSEN

The marketplace is changing, workers are changing, and the nature of business itself is changing. One in four workers today has been with his or her employer for less than a year. Ten years before this writing, there was no Facebook. Ten years before that, we didn't have the Web. Now, Google's executive chairman, Eric Schmidt, predicts the entire planet will be online by 2020. Apple offers this head-turning statistic: products less than four years old generate roughly 60 percent of their revenue. No segment of business is immune from the forces of rapid change and insecurity.[18]

Many leaders are not adapting well to this brave new world. Some accept outmoded ways of thinking because if it worked in the past, shouldn't it keep working? Some react by oversimplifying their worldview. Others lose their ability to prioritize. The result is an ever-widening gap between the leaders we have and the kind we need.

Effective leadership requires a deep, holistic approach to personal and organizational excellence. The bottom line is that leadership is personal, and who we are is a function of how we're grounded and how well engaged we may be in the larger vision of the organization. Becoming "grounded" is how we build organizations that not only stay afloat in stormy weather but outperform increasingly intense competition. The roots of being grounded are in physical health, emotional health, intellectual health, social health, vocational health, and spiritual health. Here are short descriptions of how they underpin the healthy-leader model:

THE SIX ROOTS OF HEALTHY AND GENUINELY ENGAGED LEADERSHIP

Physical health matters because unhealthy executives produce unhealthy companies, and unhealthy companies have unhealthy employees, and the levels of apathy, frustration, disconnectedness, and disengagement begin to spread like wildfire. Unhealthy workers are costly workers, whether they occupy the corner office or stand on a factory assembly line in Asia.

Your body can do remarkable things: It can repair itself, as when bones knit together after a break. It can tell you when it is com-

---

18 Bob Rosen, *Grounded: How Leaders Stay Rooted in an Uncertain World* (San Francisco: Jossey-Bass, 2014).

promised, as happens with infection. It can lift moods through the production of endorphins.

Energy management is a twofold challenge. Whereas body-mind awareness looks largely inward, energy management asks you to consider your physical and mental reserves and use your interactions with your environment to create positive energy. You harness personal energy while simultaneously generating organizational energy.

Are your attitudes and habits geared to physical health? Ask yourself:

- Do I make sure I have time to exercise regardless of where I am or what is going on?

- Does my schedule include regular breaks for rest and relaxation?

- What gets in my way?

- Do I set a good example for my team and my organization?

- Can I find ways to contend with the stresses of running my organization that are both personally and physically reinvigorating?

Emotional health is critical because we've all been in meetings with executives who make everything about them. Self-centeredness, bluster, arrogance, ego—these are all signs of emotional immaturity. In any people, these traits are annoying. In leaders, they can be disastrous.

Emotionally healthy leaders have a nimbleness that's evident in their reactions, thinking, and behavior. Leaders light on their emotional feet are not derailed by unpredictability. When things go wrong, they manage their emotions, monitor how colleagues are faring, and try hard to make decisions that benefit the organization in the long term. And they cultivate this practice—knowing that emotional health is a process, not a "solid state" of being.

The bedrock of emotional health is self-awareness. These questions may help you assess where you are in self-awareness terms:

- Do you talk openly about your emotions? How often?

- Do you have a trusted confidante who offers supportive feedback, both in your personal and work life?

- Are you the kind of person who can't stand sudden changes in routine?

- When you experience a strong emotional reaction to something, do you have a method to help you stop and evaluate alternative responses?

Emotionally healthy leaders strive to stay mentally in the present and are not sidetracked by what's happened in the past or their worries about the future. They focus on listening and understanding what truly motivates others. This present-centeredness keeps them from going down strategic dead ends.

Emotionally healthy leaders express hope and optimism, and their energy is contagious, which helps put acceptable levels of engagement back on track. Be honest about yourself and what matters, and let coworkers know that humanity is as important as productivity.

Intellectual health matters because many leaders are linear thinkers. But today's world is not linear; it's web-like. Interconnected variables are arranged in multifaceted mosaics. You need an adaptive mind-set, wherein your thinking is both flexible and systemic. An adaptive mind is also self-transforming. It possesses a clear point of view, but it's also open to the unexpected, able to handle uncertainty and complexity.

One of the reasons leaders have difficulty managing through complexity is that their view of the surroundings is too narrow and too shallow. By expanding your mental range, you can solve more complex problems. You embrace complexity but are never paralyzed by it.

The main ingredient of intellectual health is what we call deep curiosity. Without engagement and passion, there can be no curiosity.

Some people are natural intellectual explorers. Others need to develop the habits that lead to an adaptive mind-set. Here are questions for your journey toward more adaptive thinking:

- Try to remember the last problem you faced. How far did you go to seek out its root causes? To get diverse perspectives? Recognize patterns?

- How often do you research a topic you don't know much about?

- When was the last time you admitted that you didn't have an answer to something? What did you do about not knowing?

- When you do not understand a concept a colleague has proposed, do you ask questions until you do? Do you ask in the moment or later?

- What was your last big new idea? How did you promote that idea?

What inhibits intellectual health? Fear kills curiosity and significantly dilutes engagement by curtailing a willingness to leave one's comfort zone. Disapproval discourages curiosity and fosters disengagement—as happens when we hear things like "That's beyond your level," or "We've always done it the other way."

Finally, lack of support inhibits curiosity. Bosses can explicitly or tacitly discourage people who try something new, often by planting the suggestion that exploring beyond "how we do things around here," regardless of outcome, will compromise their job security.

Social health is important because whether you are calling a customer, running a meeting, presenting to your board, or having a performance discussion, the impact on yourself and others is a deeply personal one. The leader who is not fully connected to his team cultivates distrust, discord, and disengagement. The result is a host of ailments, from disengagement and cynicism to lapses in integrity to stagnant earnings.

Social health starts with personal authenticity. Being your real self is reflected in having the courage to expose yourself psychologically.

If you're unsure of your social health or disease, ask yourself:

- *Can I honestly say I'm comfortable in my own skin?*

- *Do I have a "work personality" and another one for family and friends?*

- *Do I keep my promises, even the small ones, or do I let some commitments slide?*

- *Do I guard against the "big-boss disease," i.e., the tendency to isolate myself and cut myself off from potential criticism?*

- *Do I shoot the messenger when I get bad news?*

- *Do I share my intentions only on a "need-to-know" basis?*

- *Do I give people chances to take the initiative, or do I prefer to keep a tight hand on the reins?*

- *Do I like showing off my power, influence, money, or status?*

- *Can I make fun of myself and admit mistakes so others can see me as a complete person? Or do I strive to appear faultless?*

Some socially healthy leaders testify that being forced to go public with their most personal selves has made them better at business. They understand that what we stand for as individuals is incredibly important in how we function in groups. We are born to bond into mutually rewarding relationships. When we don't, we suffer physically and psychologically—and we create unhealthy and thus ineffective organizations.

Vocational health has three elements. First, leaders who are grounded in this way have a sense of meaningful calling. They're doing work that matters to them deep down. Second, they enjoy and pursue personal mastery. Their daily efforts merge talent and passion, and they demonstrate to others how to become better at what they're good at. And, third, they possess a strong drive to succeed. They know that easy achievements are not half as satisfying as those that demand persistence and hard work.

Stepping back and giving vocational health more attention is critically important. One study of one thousand people by York University School of Human Resource Management found a strong correlation between meaningful work and job satisfaction. Employees with meaningful work (meaning they felt it was both self-actualizing and had a positive social impact) experience less burnout.

The pursuit of vocational health puts many on a journey of discovery. What they discover has as profound an impact on others as it does on them. Unsure where you fall along this path? See how long it takes you to answer these questions:

- What would you do with a million dollars?

- What is your biggest professional regret, and why?

- If you had a year to live, how, where, and with whom would you spend it?

- What do you like most about yourself?

- When you have a completely free day, what do you most enjoy doing?

- How would you describe your ideal job?

Finding the right balance between self-improvement and helping others is the secret. For many of us, that takes spiritual health—the last of the six healthy roots that keep us grounded.

Spiritual health can be an amorphous concept. Some say spirituality is a belief in a higher purpose, belief in a personal God, or having a profound sense of inner peace. Others feel that it is having a moral core, or experiencing the fullness of life in a universe larger than us. Spirituality is all of these and more. It's about connection at the macro level and a set of truly shared core values which foster engagement.

A business devoid of spiritual health promotes parochial and narrow financial interests above humanity and social responsibility. In the process, trust deteriorates, and the environment is neglected or destroyed.

Research into the power of consumer-product brands has identified a link between a brand's power to convey a company's higher purpose and that company's financial performance and levels of true and meaningful engagement. What makes a brand especially compelling to consumers is how it evokes spiritual values like

- experiencing joy (through feelings of happiness and wonder);

- helping people relate to one another;

- giving people a sense of warmth and vitality; and

- challenging the status quo in ways that improve daily life for many people.

Values-based brands grew much faster over a ten-year period. They outperformed a larger group of companies by 400 percent. Businesses who embrace corporate social responsibility (CSR) are aware that commercial success cannot be considered separately from a broader context of respect for community, people, and planet. The concept is best expressed as a formula: social responsibility = higher purpose + global connectedness + generosity of spirit.

> *Social responsibility = higher purpose + global connectedness + generosity of spirit.*

What differentiates leaders grounded in spiritual roots? It can mean holding firm to values in times of doubt and economic uncertainty. They imbue their organizations with a spirit of authentic meaning (and foster a climate that supports vocational health as well).

Companies that commit to social responsibility understand that by doing for others, they do for themselves. They also see immediate payoffs in employee engagement and performance well before the stronger financial results described above. Look around your organization for where you can apply your healthy leadership. With a firm grasp of who you are, enlist others in the quest for higher performance.

ENGAGED GOVERNANCE: HOW TO BUILD HEALTHY, HIGHLY EFFECTIVE BOARDS

In a world changing faster than at any time in history, the "context" in which boards and leaders must govern is outpacing their capacity to feel secure and confident, making some boards reluctant to lead in an era when board leadership is vital. There is a compelling need for boards to refresh themselves. My belief is that by cultivating a new mind-set grounded in the concept of "healthy governance," boards can become more resilient and adaptive in the face of rapid change and growing complexity.

BE A HEALTHY BOARD MEMBER

There are six keys to healthy governance that board leaders can apply to build board effectiveness and engagement. The most effective board members show up as complete human beings, tapping into their intrinsic positive instincts and working as "healthy leaders."

1. **Physical health**: Sustain the energy and stamina needed to tackle tough challenges; stay fully engaged; achieve big goals.

2. **Emotional health**: Adapt and respond wisely to the unexpected; practically embrace an uncertain future; lead others through change; recover from setbacks.

3. **Intellectual health**: Think critically and creatively to solve complex problems in exciting new ways; make well-informed choices; take decisive actions.

4. **Social health**: Bring your full self to the board; value diversity; build productive relationships and teams; inspire collaboration, trust, and respect.

5. **Vocational health**: Sustain peak performance; find fulfillment in the role; shape an environment that fosters success; strive to stay ahead of global threats and opportunities.

6. **Spiritual health**: See the world through the lens of higher purpose and interconnectedness; have a humble appreciation for life's lessons; lend perspective to change and uncertainty; embrace diversity and global perspective.

The healthy board member bravely faces questions others might fear: *How do I show up? Am I fully engaged? Can I keep my ego and my self-interest out of the way of creating long-term sustained company value? What legacy do I want to create as a unique, lasting contributor to this board and the company? Have I cultivated all the strengths required to be a good, and hopefully great, board member?*

High ethics as well as respect and trust of other board members and executive management are, as always, essential. Industry knowledge, technological insight, functional experience, and relevant geographical and cultural expertise are also vital. Yet even for board members who possess all those strengths and more, learning remains a must, as does conscientious cultivation of the six dimensions of healthy leadership.

BUILD AN ENGAGED BOARD

Typically, a board is a gathering of strong individuals who work together only intermittently. As such, mature team behavior is critical. The board's challenge to work as a team may be compounded by the need for diversity. Greater diversity allows for a wider range of perspectives and real value creation, but it tests each member to maintain empathetic connection and extend the trust that brings team stability and continuity.

Clear lines of honest and transparent communication are essential to engaging and aligning healthy companies. In much the same way, mutually respectful, professional interactions are hallmarks of a healthy board. The best boards understand the complexity of human communication. Members carefully weigh not only what they wish to say but also how it will be received. The team values self-awareness and forges trusting relationships with open communications.

A healthy board is open and inclusive in discussing how it should operate. Guiding principles are clear, and goodwill is assumed. Every member is deeply involved personally yet remains sufficiently "detached" to do what is best for the company and its shareholders.

HEALTHY VS. UNHEALTHY BOARDS	
HEALTHY, EFFECTIVE BOARD	**UNHEALTHY, INEFFECTIVE BOARD**
REALISTIC • readily tackles tough questions • probes for valuable information • prioritizes strategy options	REACTIVE • avoids controversy • parses information • recycles ideas, offers "kitchen-cabinet" advice
COLLABORATIVE • brings full humanity to interactions • navigates balance of parts to drive decisions • solicits honest feedback	DIVISIVE • ego driven • exhibits poor focus/agenda management • puts personal agendas first
CONSTRUCTIVE • creates strategic value (without creating the strategy) • tolerates productive failure • is proactive and adaptive	CONFRONTATIONAL • struggles to think/act strategically • prone to indecision and inaction • listens passively

CONFIDENT AND HUMBLE	CONSERVATIVE AND CYNICAL
• continually revisits "what business are we in and where should we be" • confirms sizable bets without betting the company • embraces social responsibility	• rubber-stamps executive decisions • rigid mind-set • lacks higher purpose
OPEN-MINDED	NARROW-MINDED
• draws value from board's diversity of experience and roles • effectively balances short-term and long-term imperatives • confronts "hijacks" and blind spots	• lacks open, curious adaptive mind-set • reacts primarily to current noise • fails to use anxiety positively

MAKE BOLD CONTRIBUTIONS

Healthy boards govern for today *and* tomorrow. Ongoing pressure for quarterly results and dealing with crises as they arise certainly require the board's immediate attention. Yet a healthy board maintains a long-term view, articulating with the CEO a bold vision for the company and working as one toward vision fulfillment. In this way, the board steadily guides the company even as the business continually adjusts to changes in the market and adapts in strategic response to new competition.

The best boards are a truly strategic resource to management, helping the company's executives choose the right people, craft an effective organization, sustain superior business processes, and take decisive steps, as needed, to safeguard the company in changing circumstances. In a global economy, understanding constantly changing customer needs in different geographies is also vitally important, and direct interaction with key customers is generally advisable.

Short- and long-term business strategies are shaped and managed by the executive team, but they are well *understood* and closely *monitored* by a healthy board.

ADOPT A HOLISTIC NOMINATING APPROACH

Nominating committees have traditionally focused on what potential board members *do* and *have done*, taking inventory of nominees' achievements and experiences, while also giving consideration to candidates' value-adding expertise, competencies, and skills. Our view is that as the global context demands increasingly bold contributions from the board, nominating criteria must become more holistic. That is, when weighing what an individual might add to your board, consider the full human being—not just what he or she does but also who he or she is. Systematically assess each candidate across the six keys of health we cited above: Physical, Intellectual, Emotional, Social, Vocational, and Spiritual.

Adopting a holistic mind-set allows current board members to look more comprehensively at who they are and more accurately identify whom to add to the board to successfully navigate the twists and turns of the marketplace, awaken hope, and create fresh possibility for the company.

Bob Rosen—trusted global CEO advisor, organizational psychologist, and best-selling author—has long been on a mission to transform the world of business, one leader at a time.

He founded Healthy Companies International more than twenty years ago with the singular goal of helping top executives achieve their leadership potential and build healthy, high-performing, and sustainable companies. Shortly before launching the company, he was awarded a multi-year grant from the MacArthur Foundation for an in-depth study of leadership. Since then, Bob has personally interviewed more than four hundred CEOs—in fifty countries—in organizations as diverse as Ford, Motorola, Johnson & Johnson, Singapore Airlines, Brinks, Northrop Grumman, Toyota, Lego, Booz Allen Hamilton, Citigroup, PepsiCo, ING, and PricewaterhouseCoopers. He has become an advisor to many of these companies.

Bob has distilled his most critical findings into The Grounded™ Leader Model, which shows leaders at every level how to further develop six specific dimensions of themselves for greater impact. The Grounded™ Leader Model is also the basis for his firm's ongoing work. Clients include Global 2000 corporations, government and non-governmental organizations, and selected associations around the world.

Bob is a frequent media commentator who has been quoted in the *New York Times, Wall Street Journal, Fortune, Bloomberg Businessweek, Financial Times, Time, Chief Executive Magazine*, and more. Bob is a best-selling author of works including *The Healthy Company, Leading People, Just Enough Anxiety, Global Literacies, The Catalyst,* and his latest *New York Times* best seller, *Grounded*. He is also in demand as a global keynote speaker with a special focus on personal leadership.

Bob graduated from the University of Virginia. He subsequently earned a PhD in clinical psychology at the University of Pittsburgh. Bob teaches in executive education programs around the world and has been a longtime faculty member in psychiatry and behavioral sciences at George Washington University's School of Medicine.[19]

---

19   "Meet Bob Rosen," http://bobrosen.com/biography/.

CHAPTER 4

DISENGAGEMENT AT THE PEER AND TEAM LEVELS

"Teamwork is the ability to work together toward a common vision. The ability to direct individual accomplishments toward organizational objectives. It is the fuel that allows common people to attain uncommon results."

—ANDREW CARNEGIE

With an incredibly integrated society, the ability to effectively work on a team—especially a large team—is important to businesses and organizations of all sizes. From specialized internal-practice groups to cross-sector collaborations, teamwork and peer-to-peer interactions are not just frequent—they are inevitable.

Our ability to feel a sense of teamwork and trust of our various teammates drives engagement and ultimately our company's success.

The impact on engagement is significant—while we all work for organizations, most of our work is spent day-to-day working on a set of smaller work teams on various projects.

As the complexity of technology continues to increase and the amount of information available advances, many individual workers are honing their skills into narrower specializations. Simultaneously, there is only a finite amount of knowledge that one person can reasonably know, so to ameliorate what has been coined as this "personbyte" deficiency, organizations are increasing the size of their teams (teamwork gives us added personbyte). This term, created by Massachusetts Institute of Technology physicist Cesar Hidalgo, is utilized in his argument to emphasize that this tacit knowledge in teams is a critical component to the modern economy. The individual has been a celebrated figure in Western society for centuries, but with the increase in technology and narrowing of specialties, we may be at the point in time where teamwork is celebrated, and the work done in a collaborative effort is the new normal. (And this is why you must rethink how you build relationships.)

Although there is clearly strength in teams, vulnerabilities manifest in weak links that can be detrimental to the overall success of an organization. Tim Harford highlights the importance of extracting weak links and illustrates how harmful they potentially can be by giving several poignant examples: the simple seal that destroyed the Challenger space shuttle when it failed to serve its purpose, resulting in the deaths of seven astronauts; string quartets ruined by one offbeat player; gourmet meals thrown off by one ingredient. As economies become increasingly more dependent, so, too, do collaborations of individuals, and teamwork becomes increasingly more integral.

GROUP EFFECTIVENESS

MIT Professor Alex Pentland is one of the researchers who has provided the greatest insight into this question. His Human Dynamics Laboratory invented the sociometric badge, an unobtrusive device that people in a group wear on their clothing. It typically measures the tone of voice a person uses, how often they gesture, and how much they talk, listen, and interrupt one another. It does not record what people say; in explaining team performance, the words themselves turn out to be practically irrelevant.

While researching groups, Pentland and his lab found that the members of the very best teams interact in three distinctive ways. First, they generate a large number of ideas in short contributions to conversations; no one went on at great length. Second, they engage in what Pentland calls "dense interactions," with group members constantly alternating between advancing their own ideas and responding to the contributions of others with "good," "right," "what?" and other very concise comments. Third, everyone contributes ideas and reactions, taking turns more or less equally, ensuring a wide diversity of ideas.

The most important factor in group effectiveness turned out not to be what everybody thinks but rather the social sensitivity of the team members. That's what encourages those patterns of "idea flow," to use Pentland's term. Those three elements of interaction were about as important as all other factors—individual intelligence, technical skills, and members' personalities, combined.

IT MATTERS TO MATTER

This is not a new way of thinking. In 1981, University of Maryland Professor Morris Rosenberg first conceptualized the concept of mattering to others as an integral component of an individual's feelings of self-worth and self-esteem. The feeling of being needed, being relevant, being of significance to others, put meaning into our lives and into our work. Levels of engagement and appreciation in the workplace often tie-back to the core roots as to how people perceive themselves relative to the needs and wants of the organization or institution—does this company care about my thoughts, ideas and feelings? Does what I do here truly matter to my co-workers, my supervisors, our customers and constituents? How do I affect the well-being of our stakeholders? We all want to be relevant, we all want to make a difference, we all want to leave a legacy, and we all want to know that our limited time on this planet truly mattered. This is how we define meaning in our work and the key to re-engaging our satisfaction.

Rosenberg's research highlights five aspects of mattering:

- attention; the feeling that one is noticed

- importance; a belief that one is cared about

- ego-extension; the feeling someone else will be proud of what one does or will sympathize with failures

- dependence; a feeling of being needed

- appreciation; the feeling that one's efforts are appreciated by others

It's really a theory of feeling like you belong, like you have friends, you are important, and simply, that you matter. It should be no surprise that these can be hard to come by for many college students and for anyone that is taking on a new endeavor in life, especially for us new professionals. If you don't get those five aspects, you can feel marginalized, depressed, and likely to give up on your environment and all forms of meaningful engagement.

Mattering is the ability to go home at the end of the day and share a great day that you accomplished with your family. Mattering is the ability to look at yourself in the mirror and feel a sense of pride and accomplishment, coupled with a commitment to humility and continuous self-improvement. Matter is when your colleagues at work truly miss you on your day off. Mattering is a feeling of being significant—and in my view, very few significant people are also dissatisfied or disengaged. Mattering is being a true difference-maker in the lives of others and to find your appreciation in the art of sharing, the art of growing and the joy of its consequences, rather than solely being focused on the reward of the payback.

SOURCES OF WORKPLACE AND TEAMWORK DISENGAGEMENT

Sit down for a face-to-face with any of your disengaged employees and you are likely to hear one or more the following observations, if there is a foundation of candor and transparency:

- "This company doesn't really care about me, so why should I care about it? Why should I go the extra mile?

- "Our CEO talks a good game about teamwork and collaboration, but at the end of the day, everyone is out for themselves."

- "This company is a dinosaur. Our products and services are badly out of date—everyone knows it, and nobody seems to be doing anything about it. I wouldn't be surprised if we were out of business in three years. I am just biding my time here until the Titanic hits the iceberg."

- "It's all about the nepotism and the cronyism here. If you are not 'in the club,' you are on the outside looking in. My career's going nowhere fast here."

- "I have met or exceeded all of the goals this company has set for me and had favorable performance reviews—yet I have not had a raise in more than five years. Our CEO just bought a new mansion and took his family on an around-the-world vacation. What's wrong with this picture?"

- "When I first joined this company, there was a buzz of excitement and enthusiasm down every hallway. But since then, we have had three different CEOs, and nobody seems to know anymore where we are heading and our true reason for existence. The apathy around here has truly become contagious. Many of us feel like zombies—dead and directionless, yet we still show up every day to collect a paycheck."

- "Every time I get comfortable in a role, somebody either moves me to a different division or redefines my position description. I can't seem to get any momentum or rhythm—it's like *Groundhog Day*, and often I feel like I am a hamster just running on the wheel."

- "I am lacking some of the technical skills I need to advance in this position, so I have hit a capability and advancement glass ceiling. I can't afford to get these skills on my own, and our company's training and education budget seems to be shrinking by the day. I would be willing to invest in myself if this place would invest in me."

- "Nobody seems to care about this company anymore. We are losing customers and market share by the month. Wall Street has given up on us—our stock price is down another 20 percent this year, and my option strike price is now well above what I can buy the shares for online. If our shareholders have given up on us, why should I still believe in this company?"

The Bucketization of Disengagement

Underappreciation (Real/Perceived)	Culture	Leadership Vulnerability
Under-rewarded (Real/Perceived)	Lack of Competitive Vision	Strategic Goals and Compensation Rewards Disconnects
Training and Education Vacuums	Evolving Workforce and Work Relationships	Shrinking Pool of "A" Players

- "We used to be a well-run family-owned business. The founder and his son who took over the business knew all of our names. We had company picnics at their homes and had really enjoyable holiday parties. But ever since this company bought us, things have not been the same, and they seem to be getting worse. All we ever hear about now is metrics, key performance indicators, and our profitability. I mean I know that finances are important, but what happened to caring about the people who create the performance that drives the numbers? Don't we matter anymore? They are probably just gearing up to sell us again in a few years, and who knows if I'll even have a job here after that. So I just keep a low profile and hope nobody notices that I am even here."

- "This is the third time this year that we have had massive job cuts. Who knows when or if I am next? The consultants call it downsizing or rightsizing, but I call it wrong. We cut all of the fat out of this company two years ago, but now we seem to be cutting into the muscle and the bone. Most of my coworkers have left, and some of them are freelance consultants to the company, making more money and having more flexibility than they did when they worked here. Maybe I should just leave now and get a head start on my path to entrepreneurship?"

- "I seem to be the only one around here that still cares about my job. I work three times harder than any of my peers, yet we all make about the same money. They are on the phone all day, talking and texting with their friends and family or on the web for nonwork-related reasons, and I am picking up the slack. Nobody seems to do anything about it or even seems to care, so why should I? My parents always told me to work hard, stay focused, and appreciate my job, but now I seem to be in the minority here at the company."

- "Nobody listens to me or seems to care about my opinion here. I have submitted some really good ideas in the employee-suggestion box, spoken to several of my supervisors about my ideas and observations—but nothing seems to get done. Are my ideas that bad, or is it that nobody *wants* to listen? Or is everyone really that arrogant to think they are smarter than me or don't *need* to listen?"

- "I feel directionless and rudderless here. I am really not sure what I am supposed to be doing all day or if what I do when I do it is a good job or a bad job—or whether it is really helping the company advance the ball downfield. I played a lot of sports when I was a kid and am used to either winning or losing, but here I feel in limbo—like we are always at practice but never on the game-day field. I have no idea whether *we* are winning or if *I* am winning—or what a win even looks like. We need some clearer and better coaching."

- "A few years ago we were sold to a big conglomerate headquartered in X country. Our culture has changed to adapt to the norms of X's systems and rewards, but I don't really understand it, and few of us really understand what's expected of us. There still seem to be a lot of disconnects between how we do things and how they do them at headquarters. I am not sure there was a very effective integration plan in place, or if there was, it seems like it was abandoned in midstream. Now a lot of us just kind of make it up as we go along and hope for the best."

- "When this company recruited me, they talked a lot about valuing and rewarding my innovation and creativity. I found that really attractive and left a company where I was pretty happy and appreciated by the powers that be. But since I have been here, all I seem to experience when I prepare or try to develop new ideas, processes, products, or services is red tape, politics, turfmanship, and budget constraints. If everything I try to do here hits a brick wall, then eventually I am just going to stop trying . . . or just take my ideas and talent elsewhere. I feel like I've been 'bait and switched,' and I'm wondering why they even wanted me here in the first place."

- "I have been 'passed over' three times for promotion opportunities here. The last person they brought in for that new district-manager position is half my age with a third of my experience. Nobody can seem to clearly tell me why I am not being considered for that promotion, and I am starting to question my own skills, abilities, and sense of self-worth. My wife has become increasingly more critical of my lack of advancement, often in front of friends and family. Many days I just feel like I am sinking into a deep hole. Everyone is talking about career paths and career mapping, but I just feel lost. I am forty-two and still have at least twenty years of work ahead of me. I need to get out of this rut, but don't know what to do next."

- "I really don't like it here, and many days, I truly hate it. I resent my job and can't stand my boss or her boss or his boss above him. My coworkers are jerks and my work is boring. But I am trapped. My retirement savings took a big hit in the last market correction and feels more like a 101(K) than a 401(K). And with the twins in eleventh grade and both looking at small liberal-arts colleges, I am probably looking at $400k over the next four years that I don't have, and there are no scholarships in sight. I'll just stick it out here as long as I can or until something better comes along."

- "I am just burnt-out. I can't remember the last time I felt challenged or passionate about my work. I don't love it and I don't hate it—it just is what it is. I'm good at it now after twenty years but feel empty and unfulfilled. The other day, I wasted five hours online just looking for a new yoga class and reading the reviews and social-media pools about the local yoga instructors. It was the most excitement I have had in months. Pretty sad, right? But what am I supposed to do to get reenergized about my work? I spend most of my time focused on everything I plan to do when I get outta here. My life outside of work has become much more interesting than the work itself. I never thought I would ever become a 'nine-to-fiver,' but now I am looking at my watch every ten minutes after lunch. It's sad but true."

- "I used to belong to a 'wine-of-the-month club.' Every month we would try new wines and buy more of what we liked and often give away as gifts what we didn't enjoy. Our CEO seems to be subscribing to the 'management-philosophy-of-the-month club.' Every month he reads a new book, attends some new seminar, or hires some new consultant—and suddenly we all have to adapt and adjust. I can't keep track if we are riding on a bus, managing by objective, keeping a scorecard, or calling plays in our daily huddle. I wish he would just pick something and stick with it long enough to see if it actually works. His constant change in direction is turning all of us into members of the 'whine-of-the-month club.'"

- "When I first joined this company, we really stood for something. All of us had a very clear idea of our mission, our vision, our values, and how they shaped and influenced our culture and how we were rewarded. I strongly embraced those values and, back then, I could not wait to get up in the morning and go to work. I mean, who wouldn't be excited to change the world! But as we have grown, those values have been diluted or even abandoned in part, and as the company loses its way, motivation is waning. I keep waiting for the reset button to be pushed so we can all be reenergized, but our leaders seem to be content with the way things are now and are ignoring the 'please reboot' warning, even though it is flashing on their screen every hour."

- "I still love it here, but I appear to be in the minority of the minority. I try to maintain a positive attitude and influence others accordingly, but nobody seems to care or want to listen. I never thought that I would be the maverick or the outlier by being appreciative of my job and the opportunities here, but that's how it seems now, and I feel powerless to change it."

- "I really don't like it here and feel that I have been underappreciated and treated poorly. I should probably leave, but I think I'll exact my revenge by staying and not only doing a poor job for as long as I can but also devoting my day to telling as many of my coworkers or anyone else who will listen on my social-media accounts just how bad it is here. Oh, I just thought of another nasty tweet I can write . . . gotta go now."

- "All of the 'cool kids' work in the ABC division here. Our CEO is always talking about the great performance of that division and how it will be the key to our company's performance, growth, and global competitive edge. I have tried several times to transfer to that division, but so far without success. I guess that I am not one of the cool kids. Many of us in the other divisions feel unloved, like abandoned stepchildren. It's tough to stay motivated and engaged when your parent company loves one child a lot more than the others."

One of the many ironies of our disengagement and dysfunctionality in the workplace is how we choose to spend our evenings. We complain all day about how much we hate our jobs, yet we come home at night and watch television shows like *Happyish, The Office, Getting On, Horrible Bosses, Parks and Recreation, 30 Rock, Workaholics,* and many other shows which reinforce bad behaviors and disengagement at work. What message about our work lives and careers does this send to our children? How can we find joy and entertainment at night watching our own lives during the day?

TEAMWORK/HONEST ASSESSMENT

Is your team weighing you down, doing nothing, or making you stronger?

Your productivity is a reflection of the weighted average of the five people with whom you interact the most with each day. Teamwork and collaboration are key components to the success of any company. Your views on teamwork may be influenced in part by whether you see the world and its scope of opportunity as either finite or infinite. Although the foundation to a healthy and successful environment for teamwork calls for respect, dependability, and accountability, this is only part of the equation. Individuals comprising the team must recognize their specific roles and how their roles are a function of the overall goal of the business.[20] This generates a more collaborative culture, where the "team can focus on executing

---

20   Adam Bryant, "Management Be Nimble," *The New York Times,* Jan. 5, 2014, page BU1.

the strategy instead of worrying whether colleagues will do what [they are] supposed to do."[21] And just as a united team can drive the company to attain organizational goals, a fractured culture or even one toxic employee can be detrimental to the overall productivity of the organization. Although individual employees require varying degrees of management, the onus is on managers to constructively confront organizational challenges head-on.

There are a slew of resources available for managers to constructively confront troublesome employees in a value-adding manner to get to the crux of an issue plaguing your company. These include: having the tough conversations employees hate and managers fear; trusting that the employee also wants harmony within the organization; giving critical feedback without bruising egos; and not taking aggressive employee reactions personally.[22]

WORKPLACE RUDENESS IS AS CONTAGIOUS AS A COLD

Rudeness in the workplace can spread as easily as a common cold.

Researchers from the University of Florida have found that incivility in the workplace—from snippy remarks to eye rolling—is contagious and has big consequences for employees and their work.

The researchers conducted three experiments among university students, placing them in simulated workplace situations, such as witnessing a worker gruffly chastise a colleague for being late. ("How can you be this late;

---

21   Ibid.

22   "Managing the Most Difficult People at Work: 15 Cornerstones for Handling Constructive Confrontations," C4CM, https://c4cm.com/product/managing-difficult-people-work-15-cornerstones-handling-constructive-confrontations/.

what is wrong with you?" one rude experimenter said.) The researchers found that not only can coarse behavior spread easily throughout an organization but also that the contagion seems to happen involuntarily. This according to Trevor Foulk, the lead author of the paper and a doctoral candidate at the University of Florida.

"If someone is rude to me, it is likely that in my next interaction, I will be rude to whomever I am talking to," he says. "You respond to their rudeness with your own rudeness."

The research suggests that witnessing or enduring rudeness causes our minds to subsequently interpret even ambiguous or benign actions as uncivil and leads us to respond with equal effrontery.

"It is an automatic cognitive process and occurs deep in our brains," says Mr. Foulk.

The effect may be worse in workplaces where the bulk of communication occurs electronically, a realm in which it is easy to misinterpret messages as more abrupt or unfriendly than intended.[23]

If you ask any CEO of a typical high-performing and successful company what his greatest asset consists of, the answer will almost always be "our people." Ask that same CEO what his greatest challenge consists of and the answer will almost always also be "our people." Why?

Why are the *recruitment, motivation,* and *rewarding* of the growing company's most critical asset so difficult to manage? Why is

---

23   Rachel Silverman, "At Work," *Wall Street Journal*, August 11, 2015, http://www.wsj.com/articles/at-work-1439335893.

the process of motivating your workers, keeping them focused on a shared vision, and instilling a culture of innovation and performance such a daunting task?

Well, as to the timelessness of the difficulty of effectively managing human capital, consider the following quote:

> *"People can be stubborn and troublesome. Your job as a leader is to help them overcome their shortcomings."*

Would it surprise you to learn that these were allegedly the words of God in the Old Testament upon handing the Ten Commandments to Moses? Clearly this has been a challenge for some time. Jack Welch's success at General Electric is well summarized with the following quote:

> *"My main job was developing talent. I was a gardener providing water and other nourishment to our top 750 people. Of course, I had to pull some weeds, too."*[24]

Is the process of building and managing engaged teams as simple as first recognizing that we are human and that all of us have our share of talents and flaws? And that a good leader's job is to nourish that talent and manage those flaws? Is building a performance-driven culture as simple as some basic lessons that we all learned as children, such as "treat people the way you want to be treated," "share toys in the sandbox," and "you get what you give?" Certainly it is more complex than that. Or is it?

In a recent *Fortune* magazine article, which focused on how the most admired companies find the best talent, the Top Ten

---

24   Shane Cultra, "10 of My Favorite Business Quotes: 'The Business of Business is Business,'" March 10, 2011, http://domainshane. com/10-of-my-favorite-business-quotes-the-business-of-business-is-business/.

Companies list included firms as diverse as Proctor & Gamble, BP, General Electric, UPS, Google, Nordstrom, Starbucks, PepsiCo, and Anheuser-Busch. So what did an oil company, a clothing retailer, and a coffee-shop empire all have in common?

1. **Communication**: They communicate early and often, up and down the ranks. Top management is accessible, and employees are engaged in the company's vision, understand its goals, and work toward achieving them.

2. **Excellence and Versatility**: These companies expect excellence from employees at every level and empower them with the tools, resources, and training that they need to achieve excellence. People are challenged regularly and rotate into different positions to avoid complacency and turfmanship.

3. **Opportunity for Advancement**: These companies provide career tracks and opportunities *at all levels* for promotions and advancement. At UPS, more than 90 percent of the senior management started on the loading dock, often on the night shift, and came up through the ranks.

4. **Loyalty**: In classic "you-get-what-you-give" fashion, all of these companies have a low turnover rate. (Proctor & Gamble's annual turnover rate is below 2 percent.) And when people *do* leave, they are treated like alumni, not as traitors.

MOTIVATION TIPS FOR KEEPING YOUR TEAMS ENGAGED

In order to motivate and increase the engagement levels of your teams, it is concurrently essential for you to enhance your own engagement with others. It is important for managers to look inward just as critically as outward when trying to raise the level of engagement in their businesses. Four core areas of engagement to focus on as individual leaders include: physical engagement, intellectual engagement, emotional engagement, and spiritual engagement.[25] If organizational managers and leaders make a paradigm shift within themselves and start viewing the concept of workplace engagement as a choice instead of something out of their control, the overall structure can be taken to a higher level.

Fostering an atmosphere of workplace civility goes beyond good manners toward one another; it generates a respectful environment that leads to increased cooperation and collaboration within and across departments.[26] If managers tolerate harmful behaviors by employees—from the troublesome, whiney, or toxically negative employees—they not only do a disservice to themselves but to the broader organization. By identifying problem people, managers can extract the negative influence these employees may have on the organization, which can manifest in reduced productivity, damaged office morale, or high office-turnover rates.[27]

25   Alec Horniman, "Four ways to enhance your engagement with others," *The Washington Post*, January 25, 2015, https://www.washingtonpost.com/business/capitalbusiness/four-ways-to-enhance-your-engagement-with-others/2015/01/23/676ceade-a0ef-11e4-9f89-561284a573f8_story.html.
26   "The Growing Problem of Workplace Incivility: How to Reduce Rudeness, Encourage Courtesy & Create a more Professional Atmosphere," Business Management Daily, http://www.businessmanagementdaily.com/glp/47976/index.html?campaigncode=WLB647.
27   "Keep Negativity from Infecting Your Workplace: Dealing with Troublemakers, Whiners, Pessimists and other Difficult Employees," Business Management Daily, http://www.businessmanagementdaily.com/glp/44738/index.html.

ELEVEN KEY STRATEGIES AND BEST PRACTICES FOR BUILDING EFFECTIVE AND ENGAGED TEAMS

1. **Employees like to feel that they are working with others, not for others.** They do not enjoy being micromanaged, and they welcome the flexibility and autonomy to make decisions for themselves. Encourage your people to be proactive, not just reactive when it comes to problem solving. Reward them when their efforts yield results.

2. **Win the respect of your team.** Most workers get caught up in the vision of the founder and the romantic heat of a company on a rapid ascent. But that passion can be fleeting if the leaders do not continue to share and communicate their vision.

3. **Don't use threats, guilt, or yelling to motivate your team.** Fear will yield short-term results, but is not likely to be an effective long-term motivator.

4. **Do not be afraid of some degree of employee turnover,** provided that your turnover rates stay below industry standards. Aiming for a zero turnover rate may lead to mediocrity by keeping people in positions for which they are unqualified. A certain degree of turnover helps bring a new perspective and fresh ideas.

5. **Take the time and effort to ask what benefits the employees want and need to get the highest motivational results.** Offer options that reflect the diversity in your workforce and avoid a "one-size-fits-all" approach. Carefully monitor what benefits your competitors are offering to ensure that your programs keep pace. Remember to focus

on more than just cash; often it is the intangible factors that make the real difference.

6. **Technology is great, but don't forget the value of human interaction.** Many emerging-growth company leaders are so dependent on e-mail, voicemail, cell phones, and tablets that they do not spend enough face-time with their team. To really listen to feedback, new ideas, and performance goals, you need to meet with your staff in person. The unspoken and visible social signals that are absent from digital communication can predict the performance of a group. Examining a variety of elements, such as who is talking, how long they are talking for, the amount of interruptions that occur, the level of gesturing—down to the way people face each other—are relevant indicators in determining the success of the group as a whole.[28]

7. **The way to hold on to quality people is not just to pay them well but also to treat them well.** A positive and challenging workplace where everyone is treated with respect can be very hard to leave, even for the promise of more money.

8. **Do what you say, and say what you mean.** Maintain open communication channels with your staff, and keep the promises you make to them.

9. **Big bonuses and stock options are important, but they are not the only thing.** A pat on the back, a big smile, a

---

28   Geoff Colvin, "What Really Makes Teams Work," LinkedIn, August 8, 2015, https://www.linkedin.com/pulse/what-really-makes-teams-work-geoff-colvin.

congratulatory company-wide e-mail, or a small gift can go a long way in motivating and rewarding employees.

10. **Be quick to celebrate and share achievements publicly, but give criticism privately.** In a recent study, only ten percent (10 percent) of the CEOs of growing companies felt as if they celebrate the company's overall success (or a team's success) often enough, yet a much higher percentage admitted to the mishandling of a disciplinary situation. Shouldn't those priorities be reversed?

11. **Finally, don't fool yourself into thinking that you have what it takes to motivate people.** Don't fall into the trap played by Steve Carell in the hilarious role as the boss in the sitcom *The Office,* where he perceives himself as the fearless leader of the paper supplier in Scranton. Your role as the leader of an emerging-growth company is to create a culture that inspires and empowers people to motivate themselves and that properly rewards self-motivation.

COMPENSATING YOUR EMPLOYEES FOR WIN-WIN RESULTS

In your desire to build your business and maintain a strong and committed workforce, you must strike a balance between your personal success goals and those of your employees. You must avoid the appearance of achieving wealth at the expense of the rank and file. At one extreme, a motivation-and-compensation plan that is structured with the objective of making the owners and investors in the company wealthy, while neglecting the needs of mid and lower-level workers, will not win you favors with the majority of your staff. At the opposite extreme, if, like so many dot-coms have done, you lavish your staff with perks, such as free meals and liberal leave policies, topped off with six-figure salaries and stock options, you will quickly find yourself out of business. Although the latter arrangement may help you retain employees and attract an abundance of applicants, no company can sustain itself with that type of cost structure.

MOTIVATING YOUR WORKFORCE: IT TAKES MORE THAN MONEY	
Keeping your team motivated takes more than money; it means finding the right mix of the following components:	
• culture of respect	• career-advancement opportunities
• strong leadership	• base compensation
• constant innovation	• bonuses and benefits
• empowering management styles	• opportunities for ownership
• training	

MOTIVATION AND COMPENSATION SYSTEMS

A critical set of assets for a rapidly growing company are its human resources, which must be properly motivated and compensated if they are expected to stay around for the long term and to stay focused on meeting the company's growth objectives. In an economy with very low unemployment rates and a shortage of well-trained technical and professional workers, it becomes hypercritical that the emerging-growth company take the appropriate steps to ensure that employees at all levels are motivated to come to work each day, be highly productive, and feel rewarded for their efforts with a competitive compensation package that includes a bundle of benefits and perks.

The leadership of the company must strike a balance between the two extremes. They need to talk to their employees to determine what benefits are feasible and affordable and analyze the compensation and benefits being offered by their competitors. Motivating people is far from an exact science. There is no secret formula. Rather, it is an art form, which can be as varied as the number of employees working at the company.

CREATING A CULTURE THAT FOSTERS MOTIVATED TEAMS

Regardless of each employee's specific performance motivators, there are certain steps that the leadership team of an emerging-growth company can take to boost morale, which in turn will serve as a motivator for *all* employees.

These steps start with building a corporate culture

- that demands personnel at all levels be treated with respect and dignity;

- that is relatively free from egotistical behavior, nepotism, and politics;

- that encourages open communication among all employees;

- that is committed to teamwork and values working together toward organizational goals—not striving to achieve selfish personal objectives;

- where every employee feels valued;

- where employees feel secure in their positions and their opportunities for advancement;

- where teamwork as well as individual performance is rewarded;

- in which roles and performance targets are clearly articulated to each employee;

- where each employee understands how his or her role fits into meeting the overall objectives of the organization; and

- where the employees trust the ability of the company's leadership to make the right decisions.

THE POWER OF PERSPECTIVE AND ENGAGEMENT

Leaders must be committed to breaking down the organizational and communication silos and barriers that stand in the way of each employee understanding how he or she is contributing to the larger mission of the enterprise. Each person can either be treated as another cog in the wheel or as part of something much larger, much more significant and bigger than him or herself. When people embrace the larger mission, they gain perspective, and when they gain perspective, they are engaged.

As the old story goes, a man passes by three construction workers and asks them what they are doing. The first says, "Buddy, I am laying down bricks and building a wall, isn't that pretty obvious?" The second responds, "I am making $16.50 an hour, with benefits." The third responds, with a proud smile, "I am building a school to help kids with learning disabilities overcome their challenges."

That old story tracks well with the Gallup studies and related data, which indicate that most of us are working mechanically without any connection to the larger purpose, others are waiting for a paycheck, and very few of us are aligned with a larger, greater purpose.

ARE YOU REINFORCING THE RIGHT BEHAVIORS TO FOSTER GROWTH?

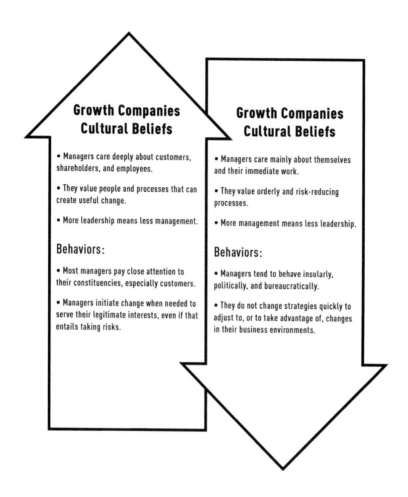

Growth Companies Cultural Beliefs

• Managers care deeply about customers, shareholders, and employees.

• They value people and processes that can create useful change.

• More leadership means less management.

Behaviors:

• Most managers pay close attention to their constituencies, especially customers.

• Managers initiate change when needed to serve their legitimate interests, even if that entails taking risks.

Growth Companies Cultural Beliefs

• Managers care mainly about themselves and their immediate work.

• They value orderly and risk-reducing processes.

• More management means less leadership.

Behaviors:

• Managers tend to behave insularly, politically, and bureaucratically.

• They do not change strategies quickly to adjust to, or to take advantage of, changes in their business environments.

Source: Healthy Companies International

DEVELOPING EFFECTIVE TEAMS

Once recruitment, motivation, and reward systems are in place, you must also ensure that the superstars you have hired and trained also function well as a team. Our "playing-well-with-others" rule must be articulated if the company is going to meet its growth objectives. Recruiting all-stars and letting them take the floor without a unified agenda will not win championships. Undermining leads to underperformance.

Even the original Dream Team, the US Olympic basketball team in 1992, made up of all-stars Jordan, Johnson, Baskley, Ewing, and Bird, was led by cocaptains Magic Johnson and Larry Bird, who earned their fame, on and off the basketball court, by being genuine team leaders. Yet, the 2006 US team in the World Basketball Classic could not pull it together to beat Mexico, South Korea, or Canada despite an all-star and Hall of Fame line-up.

Effective teams must be built on trust and respect and have a unified vision. The team must have a collective sense of purpose. Every team member must clearly understand his or her role and feel as though he or she contributed in some meaningful way to the success of the team. The challenge is that trust building takes time and patience, and in today's fast-moving marketplace, growth companies need to find ways to expedite this process.

Team building needs to follow the Dan Brooks model. The US Olympic hockey team in 1980 made world history by beating the Soviet Union in Lake Placid by focusing on personal chemistry and character. In building the team, Coach Brooks was criticized by the committee and even his assistant coaches for overlooking some of the big names in building his roster. His response was, "I'm not lookin' for the best players, I'm lookin' for the right players."

WHEN TEAM MEMBERS GO ASTRAY

Some people seem to thrive on the discouragement of others. In their worlds, the unhappier others are around them, the happier and more competent they will appear to their boss. These people have clearly never played at team sports. Winning is not about being the best among nonperformers; winning is about being among the performers, surrounded by a talented team that complements each other's skill sets.

When team members who are usually engaged and productive fall into a rut, it is incumbent on the team to get them reenergized, not circle around them like vultures. Employees who suddenly turn unproductive and uncooperative can be turned around, but if the situation is ignored, it will become contagious. Misery loves company.

Get to the heart of the problem early on in the process. Listen carefully with empathy and compassion to separate the work related from the personal and the fixable from the unfixable. Reinforce what drew the employee to the company in the first place. Try to reignite that spark. Establish challenging goals and clearly define tasks, especially if the employee has lost touch with the essence of his or her position on the team. Offer up coaching to get him or her back on track. Be frank and transparent with feedback, but also offer earned doses of encouragement and praise.

THE CRISIS OF DISENGAGEMENT

How can we better define passion in the workplace? Is it just a "you-know-it-when-you-see-it" type of phenomenon, or can it be more objectively defined? Consider this definition of passion in a work setting, offered by Jim Whitehurst, president of Red Hat, a software company and industry leader:

> For me, a passionate employee is someone who pays attention to the whats and the hows of the company's strategies and tactics, someone who is involved and curious and who constantly questions what the company is doing and their own role in making it successful. And they do that not because someone ordered them to, but because they want to. That's the kind of intrinsic reward today's workers seek out, not the lavish perks or financial bonuses that we mistakenly assumed motivated workers of the past. For example, at Red Hat, where I serve as president and CEO, we have at least three associates who are so passionate about our company's role changing the world through open source technology that they have gotten a tattoo of "Shadowman" icon wearing a red fedora in our company logo. How many companies can say the same? That's a level of permanence and sense of mission that no economist could ever have predicted with a chart.

To foster this passion, Whitehurst offers the following guidance:

> Let people show their emotions. We often use the term "emotional" like it's a bad word, especially when it comes to the workplace. But inspiration, enthusiasm,

motivation, and excitement are emotions too. If you ask your people to check their emotions (both the good and the bad) at the door, you can't tap into their passion.

Hire passionate people. One way to get passionate people into your organization is to rely on the people who already work there to refer people they want to work with. Create a flexible incentive program that rewards people for bringing in candidates who are a perfect fit for your culture.

Fan and fuel the flames. Find ways to share and celebrate the passion of your team. Augment your company newsletter by shooting videos of your people in action or find opportunities to throw culture-inspired parties to celebrate your joint accomplishments.

Don't sedate your rock stars. Give your people the autonomy to do the work that interests them. Then watch what happens when they put their energy and talent into whatever role they operate in.[29]

SUCCESSFUL BUSINESS GROWTH-FOCUSED TEAMS POSSESS TEN CHARACTERISTICS

1. Balance of complementary talents, styles (*dreamer, schemer, reamer*), and ability to wear multiple hats (general utility infielders)

2. Truly shared vision and core values with a genuine sense of loyalty to the team

---

29   Jim Whitehurst, "How to Build a Passionate Company," *Harvard Business Review,* February 15, 2016, https://hbr.org/2016/02/how-to-build-a-passionate-company.

3. Communication channels that foster open dialogue, room for disagreement, and methods for resolving conflicts (without fear of repercussion or a culture of revenge for speaking one's mind)

4. Accountability and willingness to share in the fruits of success and be responsible for errors in judgment

5. Collaborative and empowered process for establishing (and modifying) goals and objectives

6. Egos parked at door

7. A track record of success (longer together is better) that builds "tacit" knowledge and confidence in each other (as long as it does not lead to complacency or a lack of long-term creativity)

8. Integrity, trust, fairness, and respect *by* and *among* team members

9. Strong, cooperative work ethic (no imbalances in commitment that lead to jealousy, infighting, and dysfunctional compensation systems)

10. Compensation and reward system that balances the need to reward the team for teamwork without defeating the need/benefit of recognizing individual accomplishment

(Note: The relationship between the "star" of the team and the other players will ultimately define the team's *overall* and *sustainable* success.)

BUILDING DIVERSE TEAMS

Diversity is not about black, white, or grey. Engaged and truly diverse teams must embrace and include all types of people, personalities, and cultural backgrounds.

- religion

- age

- gender

- sexual preference

- cultural background

- physical and mental abilities

- regional heritage

- personality type

Physical characteristics and appearance (weight and height), socioeconomic background, personality types, and management styles are all attributes that contribute to a diversity mix that can be harnessed as fuel for business growth. Diversity objectives must be linked to the company's strategic business plan and woven into the fiber of the company's operations. Diversity will fail as a strategic initiative if it is allowed to be merely a stand-alone program or division within the human resources.

Building a culture that both fosters and yields motivated workers must also be custom tailored around the styles of leadership, which will vary from company to company. The more charismatic leader may rely on company chants, songs, and regularly scheduled motivational meetings that look more like a Tony Robbins seminar than an employee meeting as the basis for keeping employee motivation and loyalty at a high level. The more financially focused leader may rely on periodic bonuses and other financial incentives to ensure employee happiness. And the more "management-by-objectives" style leader may adopt techniques such as "open-book management," with rewards tied to the company's overall performance as a motivational technique. The motivational framework ultimately selected should be consistent with and reflective of the company leadership's overall style, or it will be ineffective. The focus on diversity should not solely be on the workforce—it must also be implemented at the board and leadership levels.

Diversity Initiatives Must Penetrate Many Areas, Not Just Our Workforce

DIVERSITY IN THE BOARDROOM

Diversity is not only the right thing to do; it is the smart thing to do, especially when serving a diverse set of customers and markets. A diverse work team leads to better decision making, better results, and a greater level of innovation and creativity. But when it comes to diversity in our nation's boardrooms, *we still have a lot of work to do.*

Women and minorities remain grossly underrepresented in US corporate boardrooms, crimping companies' potential to lead in the global economy, a report by the Alliance for Board Diversity (ABD) recently showed. White men held 73 percent of board seats at Fortune 100 companies in 2010, up from 71 percent in 2004, according to the ABD, which advocates the inclusion of women and minorities on corporate boards. White women accounted for 15 percent in 2010, compared with 14 percent in 2004, while minorities made up 13 percent, down from 15 percent.

Citigroup Inc., IBM Corp., and Procter & Gamble Co. were among only fifteen companies in the Fortune 500 whose boards as of 2015 had representation from each of the US Census Bureau's major groups: men, women, Whites, African-Americans, Asian-Americans, Pacific Islanders and Hispanics. Companies cannot truly drive shareholder value until boards are reflective of the markets they serve or hope to serve, with leaders from different backgrounds, ethnicities, and genders.

New government regulations passed in 2011 in Norway, Spain, France, the Netherlands, Iceland, Italy, and Belgium, designating a required number of women in the boardroom, which resulted in dramatic increases in the number of board seats held by women in Europe. Worldwide, the United States lags behind the pack—it has only increased the number of women on boards by 3.3 percent since 2004, surpassing only Japan with a 1.1 percent increase.[30]

In the United States, we are inching toward a realm where diversity considerations are top priority in board composition. In 2009, the Securities and Exchange Commission (SEC) adopted "The

30   Bryce Cover, "Companies In This Country Now Have to Have At Least 30 Percent Women on Their Boards," March 9, 2015, https://thinkprogress.org/companies-in-this-country-now-have-to-have-at-least-30-percent-women-on-their-boards-1e5e8bdfc024#.81ufgbct9.

Governance Disclosure Rule," which requires companies to disclose how diversity influenced their consideration of candidates for director positions. This rule was adopted because commenters believed disclosure of diversity considerations would help inform investors on the corporate culture and governance practices—and it resulted in a demonstrated correlation between diversity and improved corporate-financial performance. The SEC did not define what diversity meant for the purposes of this rule, leaving companies to decide the appropriate definition.

Recent Gallup research has also delved into the connection between gender diversity and engagement and the impact these two subjects have on the overall financial success of businesses. Unsurprisingly, the results illuminated the positive effect gender diversity has on company performance, as well as the importance of engaged individuals within a company.[31] Specifically, within gender-diverse companies, the study found these companies help not only attract, but retain talented women.

A lack of gender diversity has subjected companies like Facebook to public criticism for having no women on its board. While preparing for the biggest initial public offering (IPO) to date, stakeholders questioned the ethical implications of the oversight, leaving potential investors wondering if Facebook was leaving money on the table, so much so that Anne Sheehan—the corporate governance director for the second-largest pension fund in the United States, the California State Teacher's Retirement System—sent a letter to Mark Zuckerberg, urging him to increase the size and diversity of the board prior to its IPO. According to an Ernst and Young report,

---

31   Sangeeta Bharadwaj Badal, "The Business Benefits of Gender Diversity," *Gallup Business Journal*, January 20, 2014, http://www.gallup.com/businessjournal/166220/business-benefits-gender-diversity.aspx.

even less-qualified gender-diverse groups outperform more-qualified homogenous groups. This underscores the impact of gender-diverse boards and their positive effect on shareholder value.[32]

WHAT IS GENUINE DIVERSITY?

Diversity is not about quotas, affirmative action, or doing the "politically correct" thing; diversity means not settling for "tolerance." Diversity is a commitment to embracing all viewpoints and perspectives at the board level for the selfish purpose of driving shareholder value. The business case for diversity reminds us that diversity of thought at the board level helps to ensure productivity, creativity, and better understanding of *all* markets the company serves. Diversity objectives cannot merely be gender or racially driven; they must include diversity of religious beliefs, backgrounds, training, global experience, political, and philosophical perspectives. Diversity drives debate, and debate drives effective decision making, which in turn will drive shareholder value. It is the convergence of different perspectives that leads to effective leadership and decision making.

EXAMPLES OF EXECUTIVE PERKS AND EMPLOYEE BENEFITS AN EMERGING-GROWTH COMPANY MIGHT OFFER

- life and disability insurance plans
- comprehensive health-care insurance plans
- dental/eye-care/pharmaceutical reimbursement plans
- drug and alcohol-abuse counseling programs
- on-site child-care facilities or child-care assistance subsidies
- casual-dress policies

---

32 "Board Brief: Why Gender Diversity Matters," Texas Wall Street Women, http://www.txwsw.com/pdf/board_brief.pdf.

- early eligibility for benefits

- SERPs (supplemental executive retirement plans)

- stock-option plans

- laptops/cell phones/tablets provided at little to no cost

- pension and profit-sharing plans

- waiver or dilution of noncompete clauses

- aggressive 401(K) And 403(B) retirement plans (including rollover features with employer contributions and matches)

- executive/employee dining rooms with free/subsidized meals

- executive mentoring of lower-level managers

- low/no-interest consumer loan programs

- flexible work arrangements/job-sharing programs

- free transportation home when working late nights

- charitable contribution funds and directed-giving programs

- golden parachutes (e.g., change-in-control agreements that provide for big severance packages if the company is involved in a merger or acqui-sition—including "gross-up" payments to cover tax liability)

- prepaid legal-services plans

- aggressive vacation policies (including a vacation stipend)

- training costs and educational reimbursements (may be tied to grades)

- seniority/tenure-rollover from previous job

- loans or partial payments on housing costs

- signing bonuses

- reimbursement of moving or relocation expenses

- car allowances

- stipends toward residential-living costs

- transportation and commuting subsidies

- employee-innovation renewal programs

- reserved parking spots or parking subsidies

- outplacement services

- flexible work hours

- elder-care assistance programs

- telecommuting options (allowing work from home)

- on-site facilities for doctor appointments

- aggressive family- and health-leave policies

- college-tuition subsidy program (for employees or their families)
- financial-planning, estate-planning, and retirement-planning Seminars
- group home and automobile insurance programs
- executive and management Training retreats
- access to the corporate jet, vehicles, or apartments
- stress, time-management and wellness seminars
- first-class air-travel upgrades

- inexpensive take-home meals
- on-site health and fitness facilities (or arrangements for discounts with a nearby facility)
- adoption-assistance programs
- on-site executive concierge, massage, custom tailors, dry cleaning, shoe shines, or spa/salon services
- tickets to local sporting events and theatre
- half-day Fridays (summers only)
- employee appreciation days, picnics, and ice-cream socials
- "Be the CEO for a Day" / "Spend a Day with the CEO" programs

CHAPTER 5

REFLECTIONS ON CIVILITY, PROTOCOL, AND MANNERS IN THE WORKPLACE

BY GUEST ESSAYIST SHELBY SCARBROUGH

Civility is an essential component in any engagement effort. Why? Because being *nice* matters. The fundamentals of trust, respect, honor, loyalty, humility, courtesy, and kindness are the pillars that build the bridges to connect us with one another and break down the walls that come between us.

The very issues that cause our disengagement are *precisely why* we must emphasize civility in a *systematic, systemic, and mindful way,* top-down and inside out.

Is disengagement the result of incivility, or is the other way around? Regardless, civility and engagement are two sides of the same coin. Civility provides a platform for behavioral cues and communication tools for humans to achieve their goals.

All forms of engagement are not necessarily positive or easy, but it is through civility, a tool unique to humanity, that we can navigate controversy and conflict to remain connected and "at the table."

Engaging in mere manners does not mean we are truly civil. But a commitment to basic social graces is interrelated, and it's a good place to start. The traditions of manners in the civilized world are rich and well established. But, in this day and age of super shorthand, we sometimes want to dismiss manners as out-of-date, stuffy, and old-fashioned. Our society wants quick-and-easy, fast-and-delicious, laborless outcomes without consequence.

What do we sacrifice when we forgo the protocols of the past? It is civility that suffers—our humanity. It is not just *nice* that is neglected. It is the core of our evolutionary journey, the progression of mankind from simple hunter-gatherers to humans who can work together for the betterment of mankind.

But civility is more than manners. And civility without trust and respect is simply superficial and disingenuous. Civility is a protocol for understanding. It's a pathway for discussion in communication.

Civility starts with being self-aware, being a good listener, and being willing to help even if it's not your job. Some people are not natural givers. Believe it or not, I believe you can fake civility and be effective. And at times, perhaps faking it is the best way forward because if you are good at it, then at least you will move off of square one in a conversation and, who knows, you may even learn something.

But what actions will actually change behaviors? Following is a list of simple, proactive activities that can be implemented in the workplace today to immediately increase the level of civility without much emotional or financial cost.

- **Utilize the One-Word Open/Close.**

Each meeting participant declares one word at the start of the meeting that describes how he or she *feels*. Feelings have typically not had much permission to exist in the workplace. This small effort brings the room together as one immediately and helps focus the room on the agenda as a unified group. At the same time, each person feels heard and validated right from the start. In turn, the end of the meeting is closed with a one-word close by each participant.

- **Cut the Cross Talk and Circular References.**

How many times do people cut one another off in meetings? It's so easy to do and so much harder to listen all the way through until someone is done speaking. Our natural inclination is to second guess what the person is trying to say or spend the time thinking of what we are going to respond with instead of listening, really listening, to the other person. Cut the cross talk and watch the level of civility rise exponentially.

On the same lines, meetings, along with attitudes and attention spans, take a nosedive when something that has been said already is repeated over and over by others in the meeting. While it's tempting to want to hear our own voices, if we can be more aware of either concurring with another's point—or offering a constructive alternative to what was said rather than repeating—meetings move along without going in a circular motion.

- **Speak from Experience.**

Think about it; memorable, credible stories usually come from personal experience. They are engaging for sure, and they diminish the realm of opinion and keep discussions fact or experientially based. This enhances the opportunity for civil engagement. Start a sentence with "In my experience" rather than, "I think."

- **Give Credit Where Credit Is Due.**

In my experience, (see what I did there?) taking credit for the ideas of others is one sure-fire way to erode trust and respect. It is the height of incivility. President Reagan had a plaque on his Oval Office desk with an old saying that went: "There is no limit to what a man can do or where he can go if he doesn't mind who gets the credit."

- **Re-"Constitute."**

In some work environments or groups, it may make some sense to go so far as to draw up a form of group-conduct agreement for meetings. For example, the Entrepreneurs' Organization forums draw up "constitutions" that provide for the conduct they agree to uphold for the benefit of the whole. That includes such things as leaving technology at the door for the duration of the meeting and paying a self-imposed fine into a kitty for the group's use if late for a meeting. These are aspects of a civil approach to interpersonal accountability. The key is to agree on things up front and together.

- **Stop the Sales Pitch.**

Very importantly, members do not solicit one another. In an organization of entrepreneurs, this is especially useful so as to provide a safe environment for members to talk about their challenges and hopes without fear of being sold or solicited for business. How might this manifest in a traditional workplace? Selling or soliciting someone is inherently about achieving *your* needs, rather than what is best for the other person.

If our communications were restated as open-ended questions or giving statements that are about helping another person achieve his or her goal rather than from a more self-centered perspective of trying to get something, then the discussion would have the opportunity to flourish into a civilized and fruitful conversation.

Imagine the difference in response when instead of whipping off an impatient, curt e-mail to a coworker or direct report about a looming deadline or expectation, you walked into his or her office and said "I am just checking in. I know you are busy and wanted to see if you needed any assistance to reach x goal." In short, demanding something of an employee promotes less authentic engagement and connectedness than working with him or her on a mutually beneficial goal.

- **Use the Round-Robin Approach to Gather Feedback.**

One technique that adds a simple, civil sense to meetings is to make sure each person in the room is asked if he or she has something to contribute. Before moving on to the next topic, make sure *each person* is specifically asked if he or she has something to add—not just a general "Anyone have a comment?" but "Joe, anything to add? Sue, Jim, Ethel, Horace . . ." In these moments, people are usually appreciative of the opportunity, but they use pretty good judgment when considering making any comment. Particularly, if they employ the "circular-reference rule," then there is trust and a strong sense of involvement even if they choose not to say a word. Even in silence, they were heard.

- **Practice Gratitude.**

In the mindfulness or self-help section of a bookstore, much can be found these days on the practice of gratitude. It could not be more appropriate in every aspect of our lives. Engaging in expressions of gratitude can hardly ever be wrong. Set the tone by finding moments, both regular and unexpected, to put gratitude front and center. Encourage the change or behavior we wish to see. Honor humility, reward respect, and create awareness of courtesy and kindness.

- **Find and Share Joy.**

Joy is contagious in a good way. I find that giving joy is uplifting and provides a valuable opportunity for greater emotional connection. It can be in the simple act of holding the door for the person behind you or dropping off that cup of coffee on a coworker's desk, just the way he or she likes it.

- **Practice "Face-to-Face" in a Faceless World.**

We know that in our techno-centric modern workplace, we are disengaged in large part due to the walls that connectivity builds between us. As the human factor, we need to get up, get out of our offices, walk down the hall, look over the cubicles, and hang out at the water cooler a little more. And *smile* more.

Study after study shows that when we smile, we feel better, and we make others feel better.

- **Cultivate the Creative-Design Process.**

The creative-design process (CDP) is a way to engage employees and other stakeholders in a solutions-oriented exercise, and it attempts to chaperone participants down a creative path so as to let the creative juices flow in an orderly and sequenced format so that each step can be documented and progressive to a positive outcome. Executed well, the energy, collaboration, and engagement among small groups can be electric and civil.

This CDP is a contemporary way to engage teams in solving whatever challenges an organization faces. The steps listed below can be modified or adapted to the situation at hand. CDP could be the basis for a meeting agenda or a discussion framework.

Each step employs interactive tools such as journey maps, mind mapping, sketching, and storyboards to engage teams in identifying salient points.

The solutions are clear and simple. Build trust, respect with humility, and rational thinking. Acknowledge feelings, but avoid making decisions based on emotional conditions.

When we put a human face on incivility, we are less likely to poke, prod, or lapse into unproductive territory. Only once we have built solid relationships and well-developed communication channels built on trust and respect can we speak in shorthand or send one-lined e-mails for the sake of efficiency.

Our humanity will always keep us challenged to sort our emotions from reason and keep making an effort to continue on our civilized journey to civility. The more bridges we build together and the fewer walls we build, the greater the opportunity for engagement.

Treating people with dignity and respect can never be wrong. Civility is engaging, and engaging in civility leads to a better bottom line.

Shelby Scarbrough combines an entrepreneurial background with the pride and responsibility of public service to bring new perspectives to each endeavor. Her skills and experience blend protocol with practicality for business and government executives alike.

She demonstrates a diverse background with experience in small business, entrepreneurism, government affairs, international relations, public relations, marketing, fundraising, and philanthropy, and she takes ownership of whatever she tackles.

As global board president for the Entrepreneurs' Organization (EO) (www.eonetwork.org), an international association of more than ten thousand highly motivated entrepreneurs worldwide in forty countries, she spent three years traveling the globe speaking to international businesses on behalf of the organization. As a chief "EO Ambassador," she initiated legacy programs in global sponsorships and external awareness, and she raised the global stature of the organization with a yearlong, global twentieth-anniversary celebration.

Shelby is a public speaker, covering topics ranging from customer service to civility. In August 2015, she was chosen as graduation speaker and reunion chairman for her Harvard Business School graduation class in the Owner-President Managed program.

An avid angel investor, Shelby cofounded Courage Entrepreneurs, an angel fund in association with The Rice University Business Plan Competition and serves as an advisor for business development, strategic relationships, and planning for a number of startup companies.

Throughout her career, Ms. Scarbrough worked with such notable figures as: His Holiness Pope John Paul II, Presidents Reagan, Bush, Ford, Carter, and Nixon, President Walesa of Poland, Her Majesty Queen Elizabeth, and members of the Royal Family, Prime Minister Margaret Thatcher, and President Nelson Mandela. She planned events and meetings in locations ranging from the Vatican to Buckingham Palace to the Kremlin and the White House.

Her career began in the White House office of presidential advance, and as a protocol officer at the US Department of State. Upon the death of President Reagan, she was asked to serve as the deputy lead in Washington, DC, for his state funeral.

In 1990, Shelby founded Practical Protocol (www.practicalprotocol.com), an international special-events management and business-protocol training organization specializing in custom-designed logistic plans that address the unique needs of high-profile clients.

She is a published contributing author for *The Power of Civility*—a book that explores the various ways civility is part of our world and how civility still remains a worthy goal of society.

A champion of customer service and small-business ownership, starting in 1993, Ms. Scarbrough was a Burger King franchisee with ten restaurants in northern Virginia, which she recently sold. She graduated from the University of California at Los Angeles with a BA in English.[33]

---

33   Shelby Scarbrough, "Meet Shelby Scarbrough," 2016, http://www.shelbyscarbrough.com/meet-shelby/.

CHAPTER 6

DISENGAGEMENT AT THE COMMUNITY LEVEL

"The greatest use of a life is to spend it on something that will outlast it."

—WILLIAM JAMES

"If we could read the secret history of our enemies, we should find in each man's life sorrow and suffering enough to disarm all hostility."

—HENRY WADSWORTH LONGFELLOW

Look around you. Everywhere disengagement is tearing at the fiber of our neighborhoods. Two years before this writing, my wife and I as empty nesters moved full time into the city. In the three blocks that I walk to the gym every morning, I see littering and abandoned trash left by the residents and visitors to our neighborhood, who clearly are disengaged and disinterested in having a clean and rodent-free community. In those same three blocks I am nearly hit several times crossing the street by distracted drivers staring down at their smartphones. And in those three blocks that I walk each morning, nobody says hello to one another or even acknowledges one another's existence.

Why does it take a crisis or a natural disaster or an act of needless violence or an act of terrorism before we feel part of a community, dedicated to something much larger than ourselves? Why must we rely on the horrifying consequences of a school shooting or a terrorist attack or a hurricane before we show empathy and caring toward one another? How has apathy overtaken the sense of belonging that made our cities and our states so great for so long? When did it become okay to be so disengaged toward one another and toward those whose job it is to protect us?

GETTING WHAT YOU GIVE

Call it what goes around, comes around—or the laws of karma—but everyone seems to know that we can only expect out of life and each other what we are willing to invest. Yet this fundamental principle seems to have been forgotten, ignored, or discarded at both the company level and the employee level. What has happened to the core value of empathy? To our sense of emotional intelligence? To our basic ability to walk in another's shoes before arriving at conclusions, judgments, or prejudices? Why can we not all embrace the African principle of "Ubuntu," the notion that none of us can be complete as an individual without each other? That our meaning in life is defined by embracing those around us? A commitment to engaging our community will naturally lead to a stronger sense of purpose and engagement at an individual level.

Adam Grant has not forgotten. As the youngest tenured professor at The Wharton School of the University of Pennsylvania, he is the author of *Give and Take,* and the basic premise of the book is that *giving* may be the secret of getting ahead—as a company and as a person. He is often at the helm of advising companies as to how to get the most out of their employees and how to help employees get the most out of their jobs. Grant points out in *Give and Take* that both

> *A commitment to engaging our community will naturally lead to a stronger sense of purpose and engagement at an individual level.*

employees and leaders who have a rose-colored view as to what they can expect from their jobs or each other will quickly grow dissatisfied and move on, on a perpetual basis, until they either adjust their outlook or until their careers come to a miserable conclusion. Grant regularly studies "workplace dynamics" and is a strong believer in the core principle that *helpfulness* lies at the core of an organization's growth and productivity. In Grant's model for building a healthy culture and society, givers give without expectation of immediate reward, they are never too busy to help someone else, they share credit for success without thinking twice, and they mentor others generously. He contrasts "givers" with "matchers" (who always expect something in return for whatever they give) and "takers" (who seek to always come out ahead in every exchange and will do almost anything to protect their turf).[34]

---

34   Adam Grant, *Give and Take* (New York: Viking, 2013).

Grant's work resonates on many levels. First, he makes a strong case for the true benefits of the nonfinancial rewards that our work is capable of giving to us. Second, his findings support my position that appreciation lies at the heart of a fulfilling career—and you will rarely be appreciated if you are only concerned for yourself. Third, he offers a wide variety of case studies to support his premise that the desire to help others must be genuine to be meaningful—and if the help truly influences and affects another in a positive way, then it is that much more likely to be returned as a personal and organizational dividend. In the workplace today, there needs to be a paradigm shift from the view of employees that jobs are a *right* because that misses the reality that jobs are a *privilege* deserving of appreciation and gratefulness.

More companies are integrating work tasks and projects with community initiatives to drive engagement. People are more engaged when they feel they are part of something bigger than themselves and when they can see that their work has meaning and impact.

THE BIG PICTURE

Giving not only positively impacts companies but also can rein-vigorate and rebuild communities that have become disengaged over time. Although the events of 9/11 were brutally tragic, the one positive aspect of the aftermath has been the rise of the "post-9/11 generation"—a reinvigorated civil society, consisting of an amalga-mation of grade school-, high school-, and college-aged individuals in some of their most formative years who have the terrorist attacks firmly imprinted in their minds. The result of this rejuvenation has been an uptick in political interest and activism. This is illustrated through data collected in 2010, which showed that "from 1967 to 2000, the share of college freshman who said they had 'discussed politics' in the previous twelve months dropped from 27–16 percent;

since 2001, it has more than doubled and is now at an all-time high of 36 percent."[35] The paradigm shift coincides precisely with September 11. Putnam and Sanders attribute this to a social awakening that the fate of individuals within our complex society today is highly interdependent.[36] These authors further assert that civic restoration is contingent on greater engagement.[37]

So what was the impetus for individuals to volunteer in droves to the victims of 9/11 and lend support to New York City? Kraig Beyerlein and David Sikkink argue that those supplying relief for the victims of 9/11 were overwhelmed with sorrow and solidarity for the recipients of this attack. Some of the elements the authors suggest were the level of personal identification with the victims (through actually knowing someone), personal feelings of responsibility, and the involvement in a social event such as community candlelight vigils.[38] These community gatherings "reframed" the tragic event and reinforced its significance in a communal setting.[39] While some have argued anger was part of the civil-engagement efforts in the aftermath of 9/11, these authors suggest the emotional culprit was actually sorrow and identification with the victims. Specifically, the authors point to involvement in religious congregations as resulting in increased attendance at vigils, as well as facilitating mobilization of volunteers.[40]

---

35   Thomas H. Sander and Robert D. Putnam, "Still Bowling Alone? The Post 9-11 Split," *Journal of Democracy* 21, no. 1 (January 2010): 11.

36   Thomas H. Sander and Robert D. Putnam, "Still Bowling Alone? The Post 9-11 Split," *Journal of Democracy* 21, no. 1 (January 2010): 12.

37   Ibid.

38   Kraig Beyerlein and David Sikkink, "Sorrow and Solidarity: Why Americans Volunteered for 9/11 Relief Efforts," *Social Problems* 55, no. 2 (May 2008): 190. doi: 10.1525/sp.2008.55.2.190.

39   Ibid.

40   Ibid.,195

Although many studies have been conducted by social scientists on a multitude of man-made and natural disasters that have struck the country, none seem to compare to the attacks of 9/11.[41] One study suggests this was due to the immense level of a "lost sense of personal safety and security" following 9/11.[42] Most importantly, the study highlights the importance of Americans rallying around each other due to a form of patriotism mixed with the complex concept of social trust.[43] This seems to be a common thread of increasing civic engagement; it is built upon social trust and perhaps that is what is lacking in the jobs of individuals working in the US—a lack of the basic foundation of trust required to form healthy and collaborative relationships in the office.

ENGAGEMENT AFTER NATURAL DISASTERS

Ten years post Hurricane Katrina, the city of New Orleans had become "a hub for startups, a seedbed of social innovation, a model of school reform and a magnet for educated young people."[44] Tulane University President-Emeritus Scott Cowen recently reflected that the secret of New Orleans becoming a "comeback community" was that the city rebuilt itself primarily by itself and that this is key to a close-knit community—specifically giving the individual residents a voice in the rebuilding process.[45] Both the attacks of September 11 and Hurricane Katrina espouse similarities that scholars are beginning

---

41 "How Americans Responded: A Study of Public Reactions to 9/11/01," Institute for Social Research, The University of Michigan, 1.

42 Ibid., 2

43 Ibid., 3

44 Scott Cowen, "The New Orleans Model for Revival after Hurricane Katrina," The Advocate, June 23, 2015, http://www.theadvocate.com/baton_rouge/opinion/our_views/article_1ccbcf3c-caa1-5271-970b-42a99eae136c.html.

45 Ibid.

to focus on as important examples of entrepreneurial spirit that have led to a revitalization through rebuilding communities.[46]

Analysis has centered on these two historic events as examples of state and local governments that, when faced with adversity, created policies that left the communities more resilient and more engaged than ever before. One could argue that this type of free-market approach is what generated community involvement to etch out their own path of what they wanted their new community to look like. Even the Federal Emergency Management Agency (FEMA) recognizes that community engagement is crucial after a disaster, specifically articulating that successful civic engagement affords "*all* residents in a disaster-impacted community a way to interact and provide their input on future development . . . legitimiz[ing] the planning process, empower[ing] residents and giv[ing] the community *ownership* of the process."[47] This led to nonprofits and businesses in the communities partnering to diversify the economy to make the city more resilient.

The collaboration within the community is what allowed the city to create a strong foundation to rebuild upon. Both sectors have emphasized the necessity of both the private industry and public entities to rigorously communicate and coordinate to create a more stable economic climate.[48]

---

46   Kevin F. Gotham and Miriam Greenberg, "From 9/11 to 8/29: Post-Disaster Recovery and Rebuilding in New York and New Orleans," *Social Press*, 87, no. 2 (December 2008): 1039

47   "Lessons in Community Recovery: Seven Years of Emergency Support Function #14 Long Term Community Recovery from 2004-2011," FEMA, December 2, 2011, 1.

48   Scott Shalett, "New Orleans, Reinvented," *Politico Magazine*, April 16, 2015, http://www.politico.com/magazine/sponsor-content/2015/04/new-orleans-reinvented#.V-qxX_krJD8.

FINANCIAL DISENGAGEMENT AND INNOVATION

Hurricane Katrina brought to surface the shaky local economy in New Orleans, just as the recession of 2008 brought the economy of Detroit to a halt, leading it to be dubbed "the poster child of the Great Recession."[49] Some have even gone so far as to call what Detroit has experienced a "social Katrina."[50] The city's population declined 25 percent between 2006–2016—the city also faced extreme poverty levels, some of the highest unemployment rates in the country, and as a result had thousands of abandoned or empty buildings. What was previously a leading, booming economy in the US had now gone through a transformative period of dissolution.

But the city is resilient, and most recently, residents have attributed the "strong sense of community" as "h[olding] them together through the bad times."[51] The community itself became reengaged and recharged with a mission to turn the city around. "Visionaries and ordinary citizens . . . decided to quit waiting for someone to fix [the city]" and began investing in the community again.[52] For example, a local nonprofit, Southwest Solutions, tried to rebuild the distressed communities across the city by using a "holistic, integrated approach" to the crisis at hand, specifically focusing on both the wellness of the physical places in the city and the wellness of the people to cultivate a strong system of community support.[53] This

---

49 Bill Morris, "Detroit 2025: After the Recession, a City Reimagined," *Popular Mechanics,* September 27, 2012, http://www.popularmechanics.com/technology/infrastructure/a8137/detroit-2025-after-the-recession-a-city-reimagined-13108807/.

50 John Van Camp, "How do you rebuild a city?" *Politico Magazine,* September 10, 2014, http://www.politico.com/magazine/sponsor-content/2014/09/how-do-you-rebuild-a-city/#.V-r8M_ArLIU.

51 Ibid.

52 Bill Morris, "Detroit 2025: After the Recession, a City Reimagined," *Popular Mechanics,* September 27, 2012.

53 John Van Camp, "How do you rebuild a city?" *Politico Magazine.*

included a wide range of focus areas, from education and professional training to health-care services and community housing. However, the most important ingredient to the work of Southwest Solutions was "bringing the residents right alongside [us]," and the pivotal shift from rebuilding to creating opportunities that incentivized residents to stay and reinvest in their local communities.

Southwest Solutions was not alone in the fight to bring back the innovative character of the city. Young people also moved back to the city that was once their home and saw a clean slate to reenvision what the city could be. "The allure of the city on the mend has inspired a return by young people who grew up here, whose families still live nearby and who feel a sense of loyalty to the place."[54] It was the interconnection of these external forces that breathed new life into the sense of community gripping the city. So what is it about the city that pulled the community together and engendered a hotbed of ideas for young innovators to return back home? One underlying theme is simple: the opportunities. The opportunity to "affect the outcome"—which was an alluring factor in the decision for some to pack up their bags from Silicon Valley and head home.[55]

The city's depression also lured major investors, such as Dan Gilbert, founder and chairman of Quicken Loans, to invest and develop the community, starting with the center of the city and building out. The holistic approach adopted by Gilbert and other innovators did not just involve renting an empty building downtown but also making a "mark on the entire area."[56] This is something that

54   Liz Gannes, "Tech-Savvy 'Boomerangs' Come Back Home to Rebuild Detroit," Recode, February 11, 2015, http://www.recode.net/2015/2/11/11558854/tech-savvy-boomerangs-coming-back-home-to-rebuild-detroit.
55   Chuck Salter, "How A Young Community of Entrepreneurs Is Rebuilding Detroit," Fast Company, May 2013, https://www.fastcompany.com/3007840/creative-conversations/how-young-community-entrepreneurs-rebuilding-detroit.
56   Ibid.

could be expanded on in the internal workplace—ownership and opportunity.

THE CONTEMPORARY IRONIC DILEMMA: FINDING MEANING IN YOUR WORK AFTER YOUR CAREER

An article on retiring, published in 2016 in the *New York Times,* really struck me. I came across it in the personal business section—only the article was not the typical "how to retire early" or "saving smart for your retirement." Instead, the article spotlighted several retirees who returned to the communities they grew up in and the community-building work they started *after* retiring from jobs as accountants, producers, and lawyers.[57] It was ironic to me that the snippets of these personal-interest pieces focused on finding meaning in your work *after* your career. But I think it is possible to find this type of altruistic meaning in your work concurrently *with* your career. It is up to employers and employees to figure out what truly engages the workplace.

Is it that traditional capitalism and our notion of corporate governance centered on businesses maximizing short-term shareholder value is responsible for the worsening of the social and environmental challenges we face? Many believe so. As demonstrated through the efforts of the multifaceted Occupy Movement, many perceive that companies (and their investors) are prospering at the expense of the environment and the communities in which they operate. The latest results from the Chicago Booth/Kellogg School Financial Trust Index survey confirm the erosion of trust between Americans and their financial system. In the spring of 2011, only 13 percent

---

57   John F. Wasik, "Retirees find Meaning Serving the Needs of Their Communities," *The New York Times*, February 14, 2015, http://www.nytimes.com/2015/02/14/your-money/retirees-find-meaning-as-volunteers-meeting-community-needs.html?_r=0.

of the survey respondents indicated that they trusted big corporations. Only 12 percent trusted the stock market, and only 32 percent trusted banks.

Are businesses and the quest for profitability inherently bad for society and the environment? Or can sound governance practices help business leaders drive economic growth without increasing the social and environmental challenges we face?

Traditional business leaders have been leveraging governance and management principles to maximize short-term shareholder value. In the process of doing so, they have been contributing to the social and environmental challenges we face. However, a growing proportion of innovative business leaders in sustainable businesses and social enterprises have successfully been leveraging sound governance principles to maximize long-term stakeholder value. These leaders have been diligently working over the past twenty-five years. As a result, consumers and investors have increasingly been demanding more transparency as well as environmental- and social-performance metrics from the traditional firms they buy from or invest in.

CSR INITIATIVES: A GOOD START, BUT OFTEN NOT GOOD ENOUGH

Over the past few years, we have seen a tremendous increase in corporate social responsibility (CSR) and corporate citizenship initiatives from traditional businesses of all industries and all sizes. At most big companies that operate globally though, social and environmental responsibility remains most often a strategy used to mitigate brand-equity risks. It is true that these CSR initiatives can lead to a tremendous positive impact when measured on an absolute scale. However, in most cases, they remain limited efforts as compared to the size of the overall negative impact generated by these same companies. Most global companies now issue an annual corporate responsibility report. Indeed, the 2008 KPMG International Survey of Corporate Responsibility Reporting showed that while only about 35 percent of companies listed in the Global Fortune 250 issued a CSR report in 1999, 80 percent of such companies issued an annual CSR report by 2008.

However, a major challenge remains to integrate each company's social and environmental performance into its annual core business report. A number of new standards enable companies to do so. For instance, the Global Reporting Initiative (GRI) has been gaining momentum as a way to report social, environmental, and financial value creation for any business in any industry. While the adoption of GRI reporting has been increasing in Europe and the Asia Pacific region, its adoption among companies headquartered in the US has been tepid at best. Consulting firms such as KPMG or Deloitte now offer specialized advisory services and training programs to assist companies that seek to integrate their environmental- and social-performance metrics into their annual core business reports.

DEFINING CSR

CSR can be defined in many ways:

- It can be a form of citizenship or conscience that shapes how a corporation will interact with its community and its constituents (top-down vs. bottom-up).

- CSR can be voluntary and self-regulating or be "cajoled" by competitive peer pressure, government interaction and influence, fines and penalties, or due to a crisis or scandal.

- CSR seeks to serve all stakeholders in the ecosystem(s) in which the company operates.

- It is a form of marketing and branding versus a reflection of our moral and ethical responsibilities to our community.

THESE INITIATIVES CAN MANIFEST THEMSELVES IN A WIDE VARIETY OF PROGRAMS AND INITIATIVES:

- cash support of various community initiatives and/or charities (philanthropy)

- do no (or minimal) harm mind-set and values

- in-kind donations

- standalone general and/or specific-purpose foundations

- corporate legal department pro-bono work

- direct support and/or staffing of educational centers and initiatives

- ethics training programs and adoption or enforcement of a clearly defined code of conduct

- workforce health and wellness (including families) programs

- resource management, efficiency, and recycling programs

- safe and responsible working conditions and respect for L&E laws

- enforcement of CSR with supply chain, channel partners, and strategic alliance partners

- "triple" bottom line (profit/people/planet)

SUSTAINABLE BUSINESSES: THE GAME CHANGERS

In contrast with the more typical and often compartmentalized CSR initiatives championed by global corporations as discussed above, *sustainable businesses* take it to the next level and integrate social, environmental, and economic value creation into their organization. Examples of successful sustainable businesses have been documented in a number of industries. For example, in the retail industry, Whole Foods and Trader Joe's have emerged as leaders in maximizing profitability while focusing on socially and environmentally responsible product lines. In the food industry, pioneers such as Organic Valley, Newman's Own, or Stonyfield Farm have shown that high profitability can be achieved by sustainable governance practices that help local famers and ensure long-term environmental sustainability. In the clothing industry, models such as REI, Patagonia, and Eileen Fisher have demonstrated that sustainable sourcing practices and governance principles focused on long-term value creation for all stakeholders can lead to healthy profits, higher consumer loyalty, and lower employee-turnover costs.

SOCIAL ENTERPRISES—THE CROSS-SECTOR PIONEERS

Whereas sustainable entrepreneurs and leaders create businesses that have economic, social, and environmental value creation integrated into their governance structure, social entrepreneurs use market-driven approaches to eradicate a social or environmental challenge. One of the best-known social-enterprise models is *microfinance*. By lending money to the poorest of the poor, microfinance institutions (e.g., Grameen Bank, SKS Microfinance, Project Enterprise) have developed profitable entities while enabling their clients to lift themselves out of poverty.

However, social enterprises operate in all industries. For instance, Harbor City Services in Baltimore, MD, is a nonprofit that offers warehousing, shredding, and moving services to customers while creating vocational opportunities, treatments, and support for workers who are recovering from mental illness and substance abuse.

Another example is Berrett-Koehler, a publishing company that produces books that create a better world. The books they publish introduce new thinking that challenges the status quo and fosters positive change at the individual, organizational, and societal level. An example in the apparel and shoe industry is TOMS Shoes, which started out centered around the mission of providing each child with a good-fitting pair of shoes. To achieve its mission, TOMS developed a "One For One" model. For each pair of shoes sold, TOMS gives a pair of shoes to a needy child. In the hypothetical scenario that *all* kids eventually have a good-fitting pair of shoes, TOMS Shoes will need to reinvent its mission (and business model). They are mitigating this unlikely risk to their business survival by broadening their product line to eyewear.

COCA-COLA: A CASE IN POINT

Corporate social responsibility (CSR) has become an integral way for companies to engage stakeholders and build or maintain trust in the company—a case in point is Coca-Cola.

At Coca-Cola, the notion of *shared value* (a CSR value proposition developed by Michael Porter) takes on a specific resonance. Coca-Cola is, of course, one of the most famous and iconic of global brands. At the same time, through local bottlers, Coca-Cola is involved in communities around the world. In the issue of future or current access to potable water, sustainability takes on a double meaning—environmental responsibility as well as a sustainable source for the main ingredient of the company's product. Coca-Cola has taken its global involvement with water seriously for some time, working with nongovernmental organizations to find solutions and making commitments to replenish water the company uses. It also protects sources of water, using treatment plants to ensure the water the company uses is treated to a high standard before being returned to communities.

Employees as well as leaders of Coca-Cola relate that CSR has become a substantive part of the company's way of thinking about its business, not a separate activity. It is a way to engage consumers and other stakeholders, a way to build shared value and even for employees to act as advocates. Boards should note that CSR can often only be sustainable when it is directly related to a company's core business. Through the lens of business strategy, management practices—such as communicating with stakeholders, ethical behavior, and building brands standing for organizational values—can also be seen as central to the long-term sustainability of the exterior business.

Since about the early 1990s, seed and growth capital to social entrepreneurs (along with advisory services) have been provided by social incubators such as Echoing Green, Ashoka, Endeavor, or the Draper Richards Kaplan Foundation. Furthermore, impact investors such as Investor's Circle, Calvert Foundation, RSF Social Finance, and Opportunity Finance Network have allowed social entrepreneurs to scale and drive social change across different ecosystems. Not all businesses are social enterprises. Indeed, many are hybrid organizations that can be formed as businesses or as nonprofits. Many social enterprises combine revenue-generation schemes with grants or program-related investments (PRIs) to achieve their social mission.

US-based social entrepreneurs have been burdened in their mission by the lack of legislation enabling them to operate as business/nonprofit hybrids. To respond to this need, pioneer social entrepreneurs have advocated for the creation of a new legal form of business entity in the US. The low-profit limited liability company (L3C) is meant to act as the needed entity that can receive for-profit and nonprofit investments to achieve its social mission. The L3C legislation has also proven useful to simplify compliance requirements related to the Internal Revenue Service's rules related to PRIs in social businesses. As of January 2012, L3C legislation had been passed in eight states (Illinois, Louisiana, Maine, Michigan, North Carolina, Utah, Vermont, and Wyoming), as well as in the federal jurisdictions of the Crow Nation. Furthermore, as of this writing, L3C legislation is being discussed and might be introduced in at least ten other states. According to InterSector Partners' latest survey, there were more than 540 L3Cs operating in the US as of January 2012.

SIGNIFICANT TAKEAWAYS IN FOSTERING COMMUNITY DEVELOPMENT AND COMPANY ENGAGEMENT

Opportunity. The major theme that binds communities together after a man-made or natural disaster, making communities resilient, is the individuals who frame the problem as an *opportunity* and seize it. It is the visionaries who step up and harness the problems that have surfaced in the wake of tragedy or disaster, and through community engagement, make changes for the better. The other similarity between the two instances discussed earlier, New Orleans and Detroit, is that they both needed to become more economically flexible. New Orleans worked on innovative ways to diversify their economy from the hospitality and oil industry to tech. Innovators flocked to Detroit to rebuild the economy back into the mecca of innovation it once was. What they have in common is the opportunity that was presented through these pivotal events. In the workplace, this could be established through a major shift in policy, mission, or focus.

Collaboration. Another key element to the successful recovery of these "comeback communities" has been the level of collaboration. The high degree of working together to reinvigorate these disparate communities into focused entities involved communication *within* the community. The ability for politicians, the private and public sectors, nonprofits, and individuals to work together to reshape their communities has been incredible. This translates to the workplace as well—communication is key. When people know what is going on and the hiding and secrecy of information is minimalized, people feel more invested—they feel like they are a part of something and not just another cog in the wheel.

Ownership. Ownership goes in tandem with collaboration. Detroit is the prime example of this. Where there is opportunity and collaboration to work to better the community, there is fertile ground for ownership of the ideas as well. People—and employees more specifically—do not just want to seize opportunity or work with others to attain a goal; they want to feel as though there is a sense of ownership in their contribution. Investors flocked to Detroit, and just as the individuals in the community wanted to take a part in deciding what the city would be rebuilt like moving forward, employees want to feel a sense of ownership in their work and that their contribution is adding value in a way they deem palpable.

CHAPTER 7

REFLECTIONS ON HOW PASSION AND PURPOSE DRIVE ENGAGEMENT

BY GUEST ESSAYIST DR. ALAINA LOVE

"Learn to love the job you've got. Take the job, learn to live in the moment and love it, master it and doors will open for you if you're good at what you do."

—BEN CHESNUT, CEO, MAIL CHIMP

The crisis in employee engagement in the United States is staggering. Studies indicate that half of today's workers are unhappy in their jobs, creating a prime breeding ground for disengagement. But why is this happening, especially in a country that is currently enjoying a significant improvement in jobs growth? What is it that leaders are missing that would help close the human-potential gap and drive sustained engagement? I can tell you that it goes a lot deeper than unlimited vacation days and annual picnics.

My company, Purpose Linked Consulting, has studied employees at all organizational levels and spent time diving into the engagement drivers that motivate a company's best and brightest. What we've learned boils down to four simple and unalterable realities:

1. Beyond a certain baseline level of pay and perks, giving employees more money will not guarantee their engagement or loyalty.

2. Both millennials and baby boomers alike are searching for more fulfillment from their jobs.

3. Leaders have both the responsibility and the capacity to shape a work culture that fosters engagement.

4. Choosing to ignore these facts assures two outcomes for your organization: its human-potential gap will only widen—and its productivity will ultimately suffer.

During the early years of the industrial revolution, this mind-set may have been sufficient, but the work environment and employee expectations have changed significantly over time. Behavioral economists have since discovered the concept of "market-driven norms," and it's impacting the way your employees think about their compensation and the way their pay impacts their level of engagement.

Behavioral economics indicate that the psychology of pay is based on each person's perception of his or her worth in the marketplace. Social-norm behavior comes into play when we ask someone to volunteer his or her skills or services. It's similar to what happens if a friend asks you to help move a piece of furniture on a Saturday, or if you see a woman with a baby trying to change a flat tire on the side of a busy highway. You are likely to stop and try to help. So is it possible to tap into this kind of behavior among your employees for the benefit your organization? The short answer is, "yes." Our research shows that employees at both ends of the generational spectrum are looking for more from their work than pay.

By studying more than six thousand leaders and employees at all age levels, we've learned the following:

1. There is a direct connection between being motivated at work and feeling a sense of personal fulfillment from the work in which you are engaged.

2. Fulfillment escalates when there is an opportunity to translate your purpose in life to tangible work contributions.

3. Allowing individual purpose and passion to have a rightful voice in the dialogue of the organization may have far-reaching consequences because individuals increasingly believe that a focus on purpose and passion is essential for making a positive impact on today's social, political, and economic challenges.

> (Note: These findings are not limited by employee age.
> They are true for baby boomers and millennials alike.)

In other words, the ultimate form of compensation derived from social-norm behaviors is "fulfillment" rather than money.

What our research indicates is that individuals at all levels are seeking the freedom to bring the whole of who they are to the work environment, and they are aware that by doing so they will be better contributors to the organization and society. This suggests that purpose and passion are *internal constructs* that can significantly influence the *external environment* that shapes your workplace's culture and engagement. In a nutshell, *passion fuels engagement.* And, in a world of hard numbers and stretch goals, the connection between engagement and productivity is undeniable. The evidence overwhelmingly points to the fact that tapping into employee passions provides your organization with a substantial competitive edge because doing so ignites the human spirit.

Identifying your passions and those of your employees is easier than you might imagine and is one of the key drivers of genuine engagement. But first, passion must be defined and translated into something concrete and measurable. Our research has shown that passion can be codified into ten distinct "archetypes" or patterns. The context of passion archetypes is rooted in a conceptual framework based on the notion that an individual's purpose functions as the primary catalyst for igniting his or her passions. Your passions, then, are the *outward manifestation* of the deeper inner purpose that drives you. They influence your overall approach to work and life.

Passion Archetypes can now be identified and measured using an online tool called The Passion Profiler™. Each of the ten archetypes is present in all of us, to greater or lesser degrees. The key is in understanding the top three passion archetypes operating in each of your employees and tapping into the "language" of those passions in how you lead and manage them. We call those three passions your "Passion Archetype Cluster." In brief, the ten Passion Archetypes are:

1. **The Creator:** The archetype of art, beauty, and aesthetics, the Creator focuses on translating mental concepts into forms or representations that can be shared with others. The goal of the Creator's work is to touch others emotionally.

2. **The Conceiver:** Conceivers are passionate strategists who avidly dissect plans, concepts, or information to develop a more extensive comprehension of their underlying complexities. Individuals with this archetype are powerful "idea junkies" who thrive in the exploration of multifaceted concepts and assimilate them so rapidly that others struggle to keep up.

3. **The Discoverer:** An archetype that thrives in exploration, Discoverers are the truth-seekers of the organization. They relentlessly focus on a hypothesis and will work tirelessly to determine its accuracy.

4. **The Processor:** Processors are the practically minded sustainers of structure, function, and tradition in the organization. They are highly analytic and enjoy sifting through data to determine what it reveals. They are gifted at utilizing information and data to identify unseen landmines that the organization might encounter in the future.

5. **The Teacher:** These are the knowledge exchangers and mentors of the organization who enjoy taking others under their wing. For the Teacher, the focus is on both sharing information and learning from the insights of others who assimilate that information.

6. **The Connector:** Avid relationship nurturers and negotiators, Connectors are the bridge builders of the organization. They are gifted networkers, good listeners, and adept communicators who are passionate about interfacing with others to seek common ground from which to work.

7. **The Healer:** As the clinicians of the organization, Healers are the first to notice pain or dysfunction on a team or within the organization at large and take personal responsibility for eradicating it. Healers work selflessly to assist others with navigating through painful or difficult situations.

8. **The Altruist:** As the moral compass of the organization, the Altruist will challenge the team to achieve goals while contributing to society as a whole. The Altruist is an archetype of social conscience.

9. **The Transformer:** "If it ain't broke, fix it" might be the mantra of this archetype. Transformers gravitate toward change and chaos and thrive in finding the new order that will emerge.

10. **The Builder:** Builders are the architects of the organization who boldly take on seemingly insurmountable challenges. They enjoy designing the blueprint for the organization and making it a reality. Builders are masters at constructing new businesses or organizations in previously uncharted territories.

Understanding the passions inherent in each employee's personality is essential for assuring his or her sustained engagement in the work of the organization. Beyond understanding those passions, your most critical role as a leader is in creating the culture and structuring the opportunities in which those passions can be utilized. This requires that you look beyond the current set of skills that each of your employees demonstrates and examine the passions he or she possesses as well.

As a leader, it's not sufficient to merely understand the passions that drive you or your staff. You must also develop "organizational passion mastery." Implementing the following enhancements could make a big difference in the success of your organization:

- Make a practice of understanding the passions of all new hires to your organization or team, just as well as you understand their skills and education.

- When you select teams, look for a diversity of passions as well as skills so that creative ideas are generated from individuals with broad perspectives.

- When engaging in developmental planning for your employees, it's important to understand their passions. Why develop an employee for a role that doesn't excite him or her?

- Succession planning is among the most essential responsibilities for any leader. Beyond examining the readiness of succession candidates for higher positions, it's important that you also identify the passion characteristics of the roles for which you're considering them.

- Finally, when developing action plans for executing strategies, identify more than the skills and tactical steps required to accomplish the goal. Examine the passions that might be critical contributors to success, and be sure to have individuals with those passions working with you.

Developing personal-passion mastery requires a commitment to deeply understanding yourself and your impact on others. When you understand your own passion archetypes, you're in a much better position to identify behaviors aligned with your passion strengths and self-correct behaviors associated with your passion vulnerabilities. Develop a frequent practice of reflective contemplation. Reflection (rather than constant action) prompts you to examine your values, convictions, biases and weaknesses, and the connection between your passions and your professional and personal life. It's the kind of reflection that allows you to understand the role that you play in relationships with others, especially work colleagues and staff. It's the crucial work of a great leader. It's how you prepare yourself to create a culture that increases employee retention.

Mastering your passions and committing to helping others find an outlet for theirs *inside* the organization is probably the most important work you'll ever do and will put you on the steady and durable path to engagement in your work and your home lives.

Alaina Love, creator of Passionality® and president and cofounder of Purpose Linked Consulting, is a nationally recognized expert in leadership and individual purpose and passion. She is coauthor of the best-selling McGraw-Hill book, *The Purpose Linked Organization: How Passionate Leaders Inspire Winning Teams and Great Results*. Alaina and her husband, business partner, and coauthor, Marc Cugnon, have spent the last eighteen years focusing their research and programs on employee, leadership, and individual purpose and passion. Their work has shown that personal fulfillment and inspirational leadership are the keys to engagement and outstanding business results, as well as leading a thriving personal life. Alaina is currently working on a new book entitled *Passionality*, which focuses on the art and science of bringing purpose and passion into our daily lives and offers readers practical tools and techniques for doing so.[58]

---

58   Alaina Love, "Alaina Love Biography," http://www.mypassionality.com/meet-alaina-love/.

CHAPTER 8

DISENGAGEMENT AT THE INDIVIDUAL LEVEL

"If I am not for myself, then who shall be for me?
If I am only for myself, then who am I?"

—RABBI HILLEL

"He who is not busy being born is busy dying."

—BOB DYLAN, "IT'S ALRIGHT, MA (I'M ONLY BLEEDING)"

Ask average American citizens about their jobs and you will see their body language change dramatically. Shoulders shrug, faces scrunch up, eyes roll back, bodies hunch over, and arms cross. Most people I know will use words like stress, tired, burn out, frustration, underpaid, and underappreciated in describing their jobs. In multiple recent Gallup surveys, fewer than 5 percent of Americans described themselves as highly engaged and truly happy and passionate in the workplace. Ask average students about school (at any level of education) and you will also see their body language change and hear words like "It's okay," and if you dig deeper you will hear words like distracted and disconnected. More than 40 percent of our student population describe themselves as chronically disengaged in the classroom. The future looks truly bleak if the two places where we need to be the most engaged—the classroom and in the workplace— are actually the places where we are the unhappiest.

The extent of our disengagement at the individual level is not limited to our roles as workers or students. We are often disengaged as citizens, as neighbors, as family members, and as friends. We are increasingly disengaged from each other and often even from ourselves. We travel aimlessly through the maze of life, stopping from time to time to enjoy a few material things that *may* make us happy, and then return to our lives of perceived misery and frustration. We are generally impatient when it comes to receiving satisfaction. We want what we want, and we want it now. More importantly, we want to exert very little effort to get it. How did we arrive at this place? Can we reverse this trend? Or is this the "new normal" we need to adjust to?

Our willingness to take risks, our tolerance for failure, our determination to rise every time that we fall, our motivation, and our persistence are all in peril if we cannot get back on a track toward appreciation, gratefulness, empathy, and engagement. Energy and excitement in the workplace and the classroom are contagious—but apathy and disengagement spread like a virus.

STOP WHINING AND START WORKING

As a father of two recent college graduates and a professor at the University of Maryland and the Georgetown University Law Center, I admit that I did have a bit of compassion for the "Occupy" movement that began on Wall Street in 2011 and spread throughout our nation. These are frustrating economic times with a highly competitive job market—certainly the prospect of student-loan debt coupled with no income and all the wrong skills upon graduation might motivate someone to carry signs, sleep in a public park, and stand out all day in the rain. However, as I always have told my children, be careful what you wish for, because you might just get it. In the case of the Occupy movement, that could mean the disintegration of the capitalist incentive structure, economic stagnation, and an uncompetitive and undereducated nation.

Is the goal of this movement really to disrupt the capitalism, entrepreneurship, and innovation that has defined the American Dream and made this country so great for nearly 250 years? Is there not more than enough historical evidence to demonstrate that an opportunity-driven, capitalist society offers economic security and a quality life filled with passion and challenge?

I suspect that many of you reading this book right now are among the wealthiest 1 percent that everyone appears to be frustrated with, or are at least in the 5 percent that still lives pretty darn comfortably, or in the majority of our citizenry that aspire one day to achieve the American Dream of owning a home and a car, having a good job, and enjoying a quality lifestyle. This is not a game of numbers; it is about putting your priorities, your energy, and your convictions in the right place and then pursuing your dreams with all of your might, passion and persistence.

Ask the immigrant who came to this country with $500 in his pocket and now runs a highly successful technology company—a person who is now in the 1 percent—if he sympathizes with these protestors. Ask the African-American partner of a global professional-services firm who grew up in the Deep South in abject poverty—and is also now in the 1 percent—if she sympathizes with these protesters. Ask the software entrepreneur who has overcome three different business failures, but whose persistence propelled his fourth company to success—and, yes, is now in the 1 percent—whether he sympathizes with the protesters. The lion's share of people making up this "dreaded 1 percent" are not hedge-fund managers or fifth-generation silver-spooners but are citizens like you and me who have worked very hard to get to where they are and to accumulate what they have. They, too, had to navigate through frustrating and volatile economic and social conditions to achieve their success. Let's not penalize their efforts with an unfair tax system or a political attempt to create a social divide that could destroy the very fabric of this nation.

According to *New York Times* article "In an Age of Privilege, Not Everyone Is in the Same Boat":

> *From 2010 to 2014, the number of American households with at least $1 million in financial assets jumped by nearly one-third, to just under seven million, according to a study by the Boston Consulting Group. For the $1 million-plus cohort, estimated wealth grew by 7.2 percent annually from 2010 to 2014—eight times the pace of gains for families with less than $1 million.*[59]

---

59   Nelson D. Schwartz, "In an Age of Privilege, Not Everyone Is in the Same Boat," *The New York Times,* April 23, 2016, http://www.nytimes.com/2016/04/24/business/economy/velvet-rope-economy.html?_r=0.

In Prince and Schiff's book, *The Middle-Class Millionaire*, they found that,

> *Overwhelmingly these millionaire households are headed by people raised in ordinary middle-class homes. Through their lifestyle choices and spending decisions, they wield influence in the overall economy in support of the same middle-class values and concerns they were raised with: security, health, self-betterment, family, and community.*[60]

The class represents people more willing to persist in the face of failure, of which 90 percent hold the belief that anyone who works hard enough can become a millionaire.

You can debate numbers all day long and pontificate on how much wealth is enough wealth, but in my mind, our core values as a nation and the principles upon which this country was built are not up for discussion. Earned affluence is nothing to apologize for; rather it is an aspiration we all share. At its essence, governance is about creating the framework and the resources to foster opportunity. So far, we have done a remarkably good job relative to the wealth and median living standards of other nations.

True opportunity cannot be fabricated to appease those who feel hurt by the system because they choose career paths in college that are becoming obsolete—or already are. Henry Hartman said, "Success always comes when preparation meets opportunity." As a society, our goal should not be to create more success; rather we need to focus on generating as much opportunity as possible. As individuals, we need to focus on preparing ourselves to adequately meet those opportunities. It is when prepared individuals meet society's oppor-

---

60 Russ Alan Prince and Lewis Schiff, *The Middle-Class Millionaire: The Rise of the New Rich and How They Are Changing America* (New York: Crown Business, 2008).

tunities that success is realized. If market opportunities are drying up, then we need to focus on the causes and potential remedies of economic stagnation. However, if the problem stems from a lack of individual preparation, the discussion needs to be framed around incentives, education, and retraining—not around overhauling the economic system. We must refocus our efforts, energy, and passion on making sure that this country remains a thought leader, innovation pioneer, and exporter of entrepreneurship.

THE MEDICAL CONSEQUENCES OF DISENGAGEMENT

Leonardo da Vinci observed: "Iron rusts from disuse, water loses its purity from stagnation, and inaction saps the vigor of the mind." Study after study has tied longevity of life to levels of activity and engagement postretirement—keeping a strong sense of purpose firmly in place. Alfred, Lord Tennyson said, "I must lose myself in action, lest I wither in despair." In October of 2015, researchers at Harvard and Stanford released a study concluding that work-related stress, apathy, and frustration can actually reduce your expected lifespan by as much as three to five years or more. Insecurity or disdain over the career path you are on creates a level of stress that can literally cut your life short.

Despair and lack of purpose or meaning in our work and in our lives can lead to clinical depression, another crisis that is on the rise in the United States and around the world. The economic impact of clinical depression rose to $210.5 billion in 2010, according to a study recently published in the *Journal of Clinical Psychology*.[61]

---

61   Paul E. Greenberg et al., "The Economic Burden of Adults With Major Depressive Disorder in the United States (2005 and 2010)", *The Journal of Clinical Psychiatry*, (2015), 76 (2): 155-162. http://www.psychiatrist.com/jcp/article/Pages/2015/v76n02/v76n0204.aspx.

This direct impact on economic productivity and lost revenues to companies is significant, with depression serving as the leading cause of disability today for people aged fifteen to forty-four, resulting in almost four hundred million disability days per year, significantly *more* than any other physical or mental condition. The number of people in the United States diagnosed with depression rose from 13.8 million to 15.4 million, with the fastest rate of increase seen among people over the age of fifty. And remember, this is just the *formal* set of people with diagnosed depression; it does not include the impact of workers or students who suffer from severe anxiety, posttraumatic stress, ADD/ADHD, despair, or isolation. All of that also affects productivity and profitability per worker. If you factored that portion of the population into the mix, you are likely to see four to five times the impact, and the annual loss spills into the trillions—having a significant impact on our GDP and our ability to remain competitive in the global marketplace.

OUR "RIGHT" TO BE HAPPY

The United States Declaration of Independence states that the "*pursuit* of happiness is an unalienable right." There can be no "pursuit" if we are guided by apathy and inaction. It is the *pursuit* that is protected by our Constitution, not the *happiness* itself. Too many of us have lost sight of that important distinction. *Engagement is a manifestation of our ability to embrace this pursuit.* It requires entrepreneurial individuals who are motivated. It is narrow-minded to assume that happiness can only occur outside the workplace or the classroom. We must return to finding passion in our work and in our love for learning and growing. After well over thirty years, I still love my work. Every day I experience pleasure in the acts of both teaching and learning. I feel blessed to be able to be this happy in my office and in the classroom, but I fear that I am part of a shrinking minority of Americans who don't only feel happy doing something other than working or learning.

At the heart of my happiness is *gratitude*. I am grateful—a concept I defined and discussed earlier—for everything I have, both the tangible and the intangible, and take nothing for granted. I expect that nothing will come my way without hard work and sacrifice, and I am relieved when I can see some causal relationship between effort and reward. I refuse to define my happiness or overall gratefulness by my bank accounts. Wealth to me is a holistic concept. I would never consider doing what I love for a career that pays more if it meant sacrificing my enjoyment of my daily existence. I accept that my path in life will be rewarded appropriately, but not always proportionately, to the value I create. There is no 1:1 formula; no guarantee that by the time my life is over that there will be equality between what I gave and what I received. By focusing on giving more than I take, I am much more grateful for what I have. I embrace empathy and try to walk in the shoes of another in order to understand his or her challenges. The discipline to focus on what I have accomplished and be proud of it stands in the way of trying to count the shekels of my neighbor. When we shed ourselves of envy, we open the door to reconnect, reengage, and reinvigorate—which fuels genuine appreciation and gratitude.

> *When we shed ourselves of envy, we open the door to reconnect, reengage, and reinvigorate—which fuels genuine appreciation and gratitude.*

THESE BOOKS (PURPORT) TO MAKE YOU HAPPIER		
The Gratitude Diaries By Janice Kaplan (Dutton, 2015)	The Myths of Happiness By Sonja Lyubomirsky (Penguin, 2013)	Positivity By Barbara L. Fredrickson (Three Rivers, 2009)
The subtitle says it all: *How a Year Looking on the Bright Side Can Transform Your Life.* Kaplan interweaves anecdotes from her year of living gratefully with interviews with doctors, psychologists, philosophers, artists, and A-list actors, teaching you that working at being happy pays off.	Following on her 2008 best seller, *The How of Happiness,* the author looks at the possibilities of increasing your happiness. In *Myths,* she focuses on the things that should make you happy but don't and contrasts that with the things that shouldn't make you happy but do.	A leading researcher in positive psychology, Fredrickson offers research to help readers create "an upward spiral" that carries them to a happier life. She explains how "positivity" is distinct from "happiness" and looks at the forms positivity takes.

THE REALITY OF REALITY

Let me pause here for a reality check. Living a life of passion and engagement is neither a panacea nor a pipe dream. There will be plenty of sacrifice, pain, and compromise along the way. We live our work lives and build our careers in parallel with our family lives, our social lives, and our lives as members of one or more communities. The illusive work-life balance is a myth; life is not about "balancing" work and life—it's about *integrating* work and life. Life is work, and work is life. We "work" at our jobs, our

> *Life is not about "balancing" work and life—it's about integrating work and life.*

families, our communities, our churches, and at our friendships. In some cases we get paid, and in many cases we do not. A life devoted to meaning and excellence during all of our working hours means just that: integrating all that we do toward that higher purpose.

HAPPINESS IS A CLEAR WINDSHIELD

I was born with a congenital cataract, leaving me blind since birth in my left eye. I do not have the same peripheral vision or depth perception that people with vision in both eyes do. In my youth, doctors told me to focus on sports with bigger balls, such as basketball and football. Unwilling to accept this life sentence of limitations, I sought out the sport with the smallest ball that I could find—squash—and by age twelve had won a local tournament in Philadelphia.

Many years later, the irony of my life is that while I do not physically see as well as 99.5 percent of the population, I am paid as a legal and strategic advisor to see the things that others cannot see for themselves. In building companies and organizations, leaders and founders are typically too close to the forest to see the trees. Outside advisors are brought in to help them have clearer vision of their growth path, to bring clarity to their mission, to help them understand the big picture, and to help them realize what business they are really in.

I recently spent a day with a company that had been in business for twenty-three years but did not understand what business they were really in and what assets they had available to harvest. I saw their strengths within an hour. Perhaps they were blinded by the light of opportunity or by the darkness of frustration. My malfunctioning eyes have served as the guide for hundreds of companies, from early-stage to rapid-growth to middle-market, Fortune 500, and even Dow 30 companies. Clarity of vision does not require a set of eyes that perform on a twenty-twenty basis.

We all have our burdens, restrictions, and afflictions to overcome. This is not a "woe-is-me" message but rather a wake-up call to never allow *what* you are to define *who* you are. Never allow your past to dictate your future. Never allow your physical impediments to be a barrier to your levels of accomplishment. Never allow the false perceptions of others to cloud your vision, goals, and dreams. The more you learn to appreciate your ability to overcome these hurdles, the more engaged in your career and your life you will be.

THE BLIND SPOTS IN OUR LIVES

Every car has a blind spot, some more than others. Where are the blind spots in your life? Where are things happening that may affect your fate but you cannot see and therefore cannot anticipate their consequences? How many times do we feel like *Man, I did not see that one coming!* and are relieved when there is no collision? In our cars, blind spots can often be minimized with mirror extenders as well as training ourselves as drivers to know where the blind spots are for a given vehicle and adjusting our driving accordingly. What steps can you take to mitigate the blind spots in your life? How are these blind spots getting in the way of your ability to feel truly engaged?

Recognize that you will never have all of the clarity that you would like to have at any given moment. The Swiss philosopher Henri Amyl once wrote, "The man who insists upon seeing with perfect clearness before he decides will never decide anything."

Our ability to thrive, succeed, and enjoy life relies on our ability to make the right decisions and to have all of the information and perspectives available to us to make these decisions. If we have the power to remove the impediments to our vision, we should do so with gumption and without delay.

It is often said, "Do something that you love and you will never work another day in your life." Finding your true purpose is critical to an enlightened and enjoyable existence, as well as to maintain clear vision on the road of life. Strength and inner peace come from knowing that we are doing with our lives what we were intended to do and contributing to society in ways that fully harvest our strengths. Everyone should ask himself or herself, *Is the job that I am doing and the tasks that I am performing my "highest and best use" to the organization, to society, and to myself?* Most successful people I know do not separate the concepts of work and play. To them, all of their actions meld together as being part of their life's purpose.

One common mistake made by people in determining whether they are on the right career path is the selection of a job or profession because they are good at it rather than choosing the thing that makes them happy. It is human nature to assume that because we are good at something it must be what we should be doing. But *good* and *should* are not the same. Fulfillment in life will not come from material things or money, but is more likely to come from understanding what makes us happiest. The challenge is whether we can achieve Zen-master status by finding a way to align the "good" and the "should" so that there is ultimately no distinction between the two.

When was the last time you experienced true joy or a fiery passion while doing the things you call work? Do you have the faith to put yourself on a path where those emotions can be an everyday occurrence? What hurdles stand in your way? I would urge you to examine these perceived barriers more closely.

DEFINING YOUR LIFE'S PATH

We owe it to ourselves, our families, our friends, and our coworkers not to go to the grave with our song still in our hearts. We owe it to ourselves and to each other to walk the path that we are intended to travel. Our inner peace and commitment are all harvested from the comfort of knowing that we are doing with our lives what is intended for us and that there is alignment between our talents and chosen occupation. Only then can we experience the benefits of a clear windshield.

To foster engagement in your work and personal life, take a minute to write down some answers to the following questions:

- What activities make me the happiest?

- What are my inner strengths?

- What am I as good at as anyone I know?

- In what ways do my own opinions of my strengths compare to how others perceive them to be?

- Is there an alignment between perceptions and reality?

Consider your answers carefully. Then take just a few more minutes to answer these questions:

- What is my game plan for life and my personal mission statement?

- How will I define my personal brand, values, and core beliefs?

- How will my legacy be defined?

- What impact will I make on this world?

- What are the things most likely to be said about me at my funeral?

- How will what is said compare to the true feelings of people who remember me?

- What might my epitaph and/or obituary say?

- Do they read the way I want them to?

- What will I do to change them now while I still have the chance?

There is a great story about Alfred Nobel, who had devoted his professional life to the study of explosives and was the inventor of dynamite. When a French newspaper in 1888 prematurely published his obituary and condemned him for his contributions to the world, it occurred to him that his legacy would always be as a person who pioneered a means of mass destruction. Hoping to change his legacy before it was too late, he endowed a series of five Nobel prizes, which are now some of the world's most recognized honors.

Since about the early 1980s, I have realized that my true path in life is as an educator. Finding your true purpose in life is very liberating and provides amazing clarity, though things do not always manifest themselves in traditional ways. For example, my calling in life as the "blue-collar scholar" takes on many forms throughout a typical week—as a corporate lawyer, author, public speaker, board member, MBA professor, husband, father, and friend. Not all forms of teaching yield the same level of economic rewards, and not all students will learn the same way.

Living your life as an educator also means devoting yourself to lifelong engaged learning. You must always keep your mind open to absorb process, and then share the benefits of your experiences and insights. A true teacher has the power to inspire others. A true master teacher is not the one with the most students but the one who has created the most masters. Being a lifelong teacher also means understanding how to adjust your style, your message, and your methodology to reach someone who is resisting what you are teaching. We all learn things in different ways, and your job as the instructor is to adapt your delivery accordingly. It also means to stay calm and patient when your students are slow to learn or refuse to listen. It is difficult to teach those whose minds and hearts are not open to improvement, to help those who do not want to be helped, or to offer a solution to those who refuse to admit they have a problem.

DON'T FEAR THE REAPER

I do not fear death. I fear not being remembered. I fear living an incomplete or disengaged life. I fear the possibility of not helping all who need assistance or not teaching all those who want to learn. I fear not loving enough. And I fear not living enough. We are all on this earth to make a positive impact and contribution to the greater good—an impact on one another, our community, and our society. An impact. Not a collision.

The impact of the events of 9/11, the sniper shootings at Columbine, the Colorado movie theater, the Umpqua Community College in Oregon, the Charleston, South Carolina, church, and other public places—all within a single decade—have been a horrible reminder of a simple truth: any day could be our last. That does not mean that we should take the phrase "Live each day is if it were your last" to the extreme, or we would all quit our jobs and go pursue whatever the number-one thing is on our bucket list. I would recommend that we take a slightly modified approach on a daily basis to ensure that we have minimal regrets on our deathbeds. Give some thought to the things you have always wanted to accomplish and the places you have always wanted to go, and then "chip away" at the list on a more modest and incremental basis. Remember, this is more than putting check marks next to items on a lifelong to-do list. Ask yourself how you want to be remembered. How have you made people feel? In what ways have you improved the lives of others?

Harriet Beecher Stowe once wrote, "The bitterest tears shed over graves are for the words left unsaid and the deeds left undone." When we keep our best thoughts to ourselves and our best acts inside of us, it constipates our existence. In the film, *The Bucket List,* Morgan Freeman's character explains to Jack Nicholson's that in certain cultures, only two questions are asked as conditions to admission to the pearly gates of heaven: Did you find joy in your life? Did you bring joy to others?[62]

These are not just my views and life philosophies. Dr. Martin Seligman of the University of Pennsylvania conducted a study which assessed the impact of the many approaches to improving one's life and outlook on life—which can in turn lead to a stronger sense of commitment and engagement. The study focused on three key things that everyone should do in the workplace that can produce consistent and successful results:

1. Practice daily gratefulness.

2. Commit to a life of serving others.

3. Be more thoughtful.

---

62 *The Bucket List,* directed by Rob Reiner, performed by Jack Nicholson and Morgan Freeman, IMDb, January 11, 2008, http://www.imdb.com/title/tt0825232/.

How do these three things weave together to fuel further engagement? First, our gratefulness for what we have gives us perspective—perspective on how blessed we are to live the lives we lead. Second, the saying that the more we give, the more we get is really true, but often misunderstood. The more we give creates a joy in giving, not in the expectation of return. It is the *act* of helping another that fuels happiness if you have the right mind-set, not the anxiety created by waiting for the favor or gift to be returned. And since that mind-set of expectation is only likely to be met with disappointment, which leads to disengagement, it's probably best to avoid it completely. Finally, we all need to embrace a higher level of reflection and mindfulness. The speed and pace of our lives leaves little time to pause and reflect on whom we are, what we have, and why we are really here. With no counterbalancing time to reflect on the blessings of our lives, we only have time for stress, anxiety, and a numbness that can lead to disengagement and even depression. The importance of living in the moment is at the heart of the teachings and writings of the Vietnamese Buddhist monk Thich Nhat Hanh. In *Peace is Every Step*, Hanh reminds us that the past is gone and the future has not happened yet, so all we have is the present moment in time.[63] We have the power to determine whether each moment will be engaged or not engaged, passionate or numb, connected or distant, happy or not. As it has been often said, "pain in life is inevitable, but suffering is optional." We control our paths to engagement and satisfaction with every step we take.

Returning to the marketplace, the cure for the crisis of disengagement begins with communication and culture. Knowledge and understanding of roles and responsibilities begets trust. And trust

---

63   Thich Nhat Hanh, *Peace is Every Step: The Path of Mindfulness in Everyday Life* (Bantam, 1992).

begets appreciation. Appreciation begets respect and collaboration. And it is very hard to be disengaged when an environment of trust, respect, appreciation, and collaboration surrounds you.

One element of communication is destroying misperception. The common misperception between workers and leaders is that the leaders of the company have the "perfect life" just because they have arrived at the top. Nothing could be further from the truth, yet we continue to foster the "99 vs. 1" wealth divide with our political, social, and media sound bites. CEOs suffer from significant fears and anxieties, and ironically the biggest fear is of being found incompetent—also known as the "imposter syndrome." This fear diminishes their confidence and undermines their relationships with others.

The most successful companies build cultures of trust and transparency in a way that provides everyone a sense of self-worth. It is not really about hiring skilled workers and then figuring out how to motivate them. It is about finding motivated and engaged people and finding ways to inspire them. We all have the abilities within us to be engaged and grateful, but our leaders need to be committed to strengthening the level of engagement with the right culture, incentives, and rewards that demonstrate genuine appreciation. Appreciated workers, students, and peers are *engaged* and *inspired*.

MENTAL HEALTH AND ENGAGEMENT

Depression is taking a huge economic toll on the United States. Annual costs in terms of medical, missed days of work, lost productivity and related direct and indirect costs are expected to reach well over $350 billion by 2018 according to multiple mental-health organizations. That figure only includes "diagnosed and known" cases of the psychological affliction of depression and does not include unreported cases or people who are deeply unhappy or frustrated at home or at work but who are not necessarily clinically depressed. If you add in the lost economic output, lost innovation, and reduced productivity of those who are unhappy and unmotivated, the costs start edging up closer to a trillion dollars per annum. Depression, on a standalone basis, is challenging enough to combat, but many of the direct and indirect consequences of this mental illness on our economy are also caused by the by-products of depression, also known as "comorbidities," which include anxiety, a lack of self-worth, substance abuse, and posttraumatic stress disorder, as well as physical ailments such as sleep disorders, migraine headaches, and weight gain. Diagnosed depression is the leading cause of disability for people aged fifteen to forty-four (resulting in more than four hundred million disability days—missed days at work per annum), affecting almost sixteen million US workers. The fastest rate of increase in depression was in those in people over age fifty. It is unknown how strong the correlation is between depression and career burnout, but is logical to conclude that they are often strongly related.

Gallup Polls have been instrumental not only in providing a link between engagement and better work performance of employees, but also showing that better employee engagement means better health. When employees are engaged, they feel less stress and anxiety, while simultaneously experiencing more joy and happiness at their workplace. Gallup's chief scientist of workplace management has explicitly asserted the significance of the relationship between the trifecta elements of work, stress, and health levels: the more stressful the work environment an employee is in, the higher the likelihood that the individual experiences potential negative health consequences. These manifest in employees as clinical depression and chronic anxiety, which then affect job performance.[64]

DON'T FEAR FAILURE

Do not be afraid to lose. Do not fear failure. To foster greater levels of engagement, embrace the life lessons and practical knowledge of defeat. The baby boomers created a trophy generation of millennials where even the team that came in seventh place was recognized because we became lazy and unwilling to teach our children the joys and lessons of defeat. Only from the roots of failure can success come. Only from necessity comes the mother of invention. Only from defeat comes an even stronger will to win. Ask most successful entrepreneurs what drives their hunger for success and they will answer by talking about the stomachache that comes from failure. If we raise an entire generation to believe that everybody wins all the time no matter what, then how will they overcome challenge, criticism, or even constructive feedback? How will they develop the determination, patience, and focus needed to overcome hurdles to succeed in all aspects of their lives. How will they learn to accept "No" as an answer and say "No" as an answer without frustration and disappointment?

If we begin to fear the risk of failure, then we try nothing, experience little, and become a nation of people who merely exist, but do not thrive; participate, but do not cherish; show up, but are not engaged; accept, but do not appreciate; and work, but are not fulfilled.

---

64   Jennifer Robison, "Disengagement Can Be Really Depressing," *Gallup Business Journal*, April 2, 2010, http://www.gallup.com/businessjournal/127100/disengagement-really-depressing.aspx.

CHAPTER 9

REFLECTIONS ON HOW RELEVANCE DRIVES ENGAGEMENT

BY GUEST ESSAYIST PHILIP R. STYRLUND

During the past several years, I have been speaking and writing about the topic of relevance—mostly as a sales-empowerment tool but also as a corrective for disengagement. Simply put, being relevant means mattering more to others than we do to ourselves. By definition, "relevance" literally means proactively seeking engagement, and once you are engaged, staying engaged, which by definition keeps you more relevant. And the kind of engagement we are talking about here means much more than passing on information like the billions of text and e-mail messages sent every day. Relevance is not a matter of what we know as much as it is a matter of how we know what we know matters to someone else.

Being relevant clearly demands that we aim higher in our relationships and we seek more than just superficial levels of interaction. I would like to share four "dynamics of relevance" that provide an exciting alternative to the "world of disengagement."

THE FOUR DYNAMICS OF RELEVANCE

Authenticity

Relevance begins with a journey inward to understand the individual, authentic self. Only by digging deep down into our "true self" can we come to a place of inner certainty. Understanding our complex strengths and weaknesses with clarity is as vital to a meaningful life today as it was in the time of the Greek sages. Remember, a citizen of Athens demanded to be educated and fully understand the personal and political factors involved in all the decisions they were called upon to make.

Mastery

In my formula for relevance, I've found that the movement from authenticity to mastery to empathy to action is most successful when it happens sequentially. It's not possible to dedicate yourself to mastering your signature strengths until you know, by first exploring your authentic core, what those signature strengths are.

It is wonderful to have a natural aptitude for speed or persuasion or musical composition, but aptitude isn't enough. The natural runner who never conditions her body or builds her endurance won't win a marathon by just relying on raw talent. Gifts, once identified, must be developed; and that requires discipline and dedication.

How do you make the gifts you've developed become relevant to others? Look for common ground, and seek to comprehend others through empathy. Until we fully comprehend that life is not about just us, it is not fully lived.

Empathy

We can think of empathy as the docking station of relevance with a three-step path signified by "them," "you," and "do." The first step is to focus on "them." What does your friend, colleague, or client care about? The second step is about asking "you" (yourself) what you can bring to their concerns. Finally, "do" focuses on defining the actions you can take to be an additive force to positively affect the concerns of others within your circle of influence.

The ability to assume someone else's perspective enables us to matter more to others and for others.

Action

The decision to put authenticity, mastery, and empathy into action is the great differentiator between the dreams of potential and the reality of accomplishment. Relevance requires authentic skills executed with mastery and reflecting an empathetic understanding of others. But the decision to act is not always an easy one. We can be reluctant to commit to a single path when we know it means foregoing others.

The ability to assume someone else's perspective enables us to matter more to others and for others.

Why is it that so many people seem to be living "self-limiting" lives through the decisions they make? Grab ahold of your life and realize that your life has meaning and consequence. Become relevant! Become value driven!

Our values represent our highest priorities and deeply held driving forces. They are part of our species' survival tool kit. You continually model or act on your values through personal and work behaviors, decision making, and many other parts of your life. Your life's very purpose is grounded in your core values.

Dr. James Gambone wrote in his book *ReFire Your Life!* that it is important to distinguish between *core* and *accumulated* values. We all value our homes, our position in society, our wealth, and many of our material possessions. However when we face a major crisis in our lives and we search for more solid ground to stand on, our core values often emerge and provide us with the more solid foundation—and our accumulated values become much less important.

There is a simple test for determining and clarifying the differences between your core and accumulated values. Just pick something that you consider to be one of your most important values and ask yourself the following questions: Did you choose the value from clear alternatives? Is the value something you practice on a regular basis? If someone really challenged your core value, would you be willing to stand up in public and defend it? If you take any of your own values through this clarification exercise and you can give a resounding and unqualified "Yes" to each of these questions, it is probably a core value.

Feelings are fleeting; core values are foundational.

In a society that seems increasingly bent on making important decisions based on how you *feel*, we need to distinguish and clearly understand the fundamental difference between feelings and core values. Let's have the courage to be countercultural here and not be afraid to say that feelings are fleeting and core values are foundational.

People say they feel good when they are on social media or when playing electronic games or fantasy sports. There is immediate gratification in these electronic media. The designers know full well that three of the most powerful senses we have as humans are touch, sight, and hearing. They make us feel good whether we know it or not because we are engaging those three powerful senses.

We see so many people living a good part of their days in virtual worlds. These people are not so concerned about seeking balance but seem focused on the immediate gratification they can receive anytime they pick up and use a phone/camera/text/e-mail-communications device.

Some business leaders have even told me that the real problem of disengagement at work is not that employees and managers are necessarily bored or dissatisfied with their jobs, but rather, they are distracted and seem almost addicted to their electronic, virtual connections.

We need to find ways to break the monopoly of "electronic engagement." Life can be so much richer and fulfilling. Are there actions companies and individuals can take to promote new rules of engagement?

To make these new rules of engagement *relevant*, they first need to have a strong value-based foundation. Ask yourself if your company currently provides employees and managers with significant degrees of autonomy, opportunities for personal and professional growth, a sense that any employee can have an impact on the business, and an environment that fosters good interpersonal relationships and connections inside and outside the workplace. If you are not doing these things right now, here are six new rules of engagement that you and your company may want to consider.

THE SIX NEW RULES OF ENGAGEMENT

Rule 1: Create a culture of service in your company.

It is very hard to *truly* serve customers or your coworkers and not be engaged. This culture of service starts with the leaders of the company. Make sure that other people's highest-priority needs are being served. Do those served, *while being served*, become healthier, wiser, freer, more autonomous, more likely to become servants themselves? If a serving and service culture becomes an integral part of your corporate culture, it is very hard to imagine being disengaged in this kind of workplace environment.

Rule 2: Develop mentoring programs that are conducted mostly in person.

Cross-generational mentoring programs in companies can provide a successful transfer of company culture using the "oral tradition" as well as electronic tools. Mentoring also provides an opportunity for more personal connections and interactions within the company. The strengthening of these relationships for many companies has resulted in a better overall understanding of the company's goals and values and a more common understanding of a company's products and how they're developed.

Rule 3: Promote and incentivize volunteering in your community.

There are many not-for-profit organizations that desperately need volunteer help. Companies that offer this kind of assistance have employees that get empowered, feel like they are making a difference, and want to continue this experience. If employees are also involved in the selection of the volunteer opportunities, a fuller engagement can be achieved. These company-sponsored volunteer programs enhance respect for the company brand. It is a win-win situation.

Rule 4: Set up a permanent "leaving bonus."

A few companies have set up a leaving bonus that is available to anyone in the company. Every year, employees must make a decision on staying or leaving the company. The amount of the bonus is determined by the particular value of the employee that may want to use it.

An important part of the leaving bonus is that it needs to be significant enough to have a person who is unhappy and dissatisfied take advantage of it. You want an engaged and satisfied workforce.

Rule 5: Consider a yearly "Relevance Awards Program."

Throughout the year, employees and management can nominate individuals who they think represent the best dynamics of relevancy. Have a small committee made up from all areas of the company make the decisions on which people should be honored with the Relevance Award.

It would be nice to attach a cash amount or an interesting perk to the award. This is yet another way of more fully engaging the workforce.

Rule 6 : Establish an e-mail- and text-free day.

Digital eye strain is the physical discomfort felt after two or more hours in front of a digital screen and is associated with the close-range to midrange distance of digital screens, including desktop and laptop computers, tablets, e-readers, and cell phones. Digital eyestrain could cause age-related macular degeneration.

What better way to break the electronic monopoly than to declare one day a week an e-mail- and text-free day. On this day, employees need to communicate personally with each other, their customers, and anyone else they come in contact with. Personal contact is preferred, but phone contact is also very acceptable.

Many will argue that this may put a business at a competitive disadvantage. But if you truly believe that distraction caused by social-media and wireless communication is resulting in losses for your company, some of those losses may decline when an employee experiences a more personal way of being successful with his or her work.

What matters is not the meaning of life but rather the specific meaning of life at a *given moment*. We may be reaching a tipping point in understanding how important it is to change the paradigm of disengagement. If disengagement means taking time to think and reflect—away from all of the distractions in our lives—then even disengagement could be looked at in a much more positive manner.

As CEO of The Summit Group, Phil is a recognized thought leader on business-value transformation as part of the go-to-market strategies of some of the world's premier organizations, both in the public and private sectors. In addition to his keynote presentations and engaging programs, Phil serves as a coach, mentor, consultant, and advisor to top leaders across a range of industries and has delivered sessions in more than forty countries. Recently, Phil was elected to the board of directors for SAMA (Strategic Account Management Association). He also leads the CEO Forum as part of the annual National Prayer Breakfast in Washington, DC.

Phil has written for, or been cited in, articles in leading publications that include: *The Wall Street Journal*, the *Los Angeles Times*, and *Fast Company*, as well as in several best-selling books, including *Adversity Quotient* and *The Power of Purpose*. In mid-2014, the book *Relevance: Matter More* was released, cowritten by Phil.

His career includes key leadership positions with US West and ADC Telecommunications. Phil also teaches in various university and executive education programs and has master's degrees in business administration and telecommunications science. He currently is engaged in a doctorate program at Middlesex University in London.

Phil resides in Minneapolis and Santa Barbara.[65]

---

65   Phil Styrlund et al., *Relevance: Matter More* (Riley Hayes Advertising, 2014).

CHAPTER 10

THE IMPACT OF DISENGAGEMENT ON INNOVATION, CREATIVITY, PRODUCTIVITY, AND PROFITABILITY

"Today more than ever, we must cultivate the creative and innovative potential of every employee in the organization. Everyone in the organization must be capable of thinking creatively and be willing to try new approaches which transcend their own roles, departments, and processes."

—ANDREW PAPAGEORGE, CHIEF INNOVATION STRATEGIST, GOINNOVATE!

It is hard to imagine that a disengaged workforce that spends the bulk of its time being distracted and dissatisfied will ever be a catalyst for the creativity and productivity in an enterprise. It is equally hard to imagine an employee who feels disconnected and unappreciated spending time thinking about ways to improve his or her workplace, products, or service. And it is harder still to imagine a disengaged manager spending the necessary time to figure out how to better engage employees.

Innovation within the organization (also known as *intrepreneurship*) refers to the actions and initiatives that transform organizations through strategic-renewal processes. Firms that consistently demonstrate durable corporate innovation are typically viewed as dynamic entities prepared to take advantage of new business opportunities when they arise with a willingness to deviate from prior strategies and business models to embrace new resource combinations that hold promise for new innovations.

In general, corporate innovation/intrapreneurship flourishes in established firms such as Google, Facebook, Netflix, Starbucks, Nordstrom, and 3M, and it's seen when engaged and motivated individuals are free to pursue actions and initiatives that are novel to the firm. Innovation initiatives are not limited to private enterprise—the boards of nonprofits, universities, nongovernment organizations (NGOs), and even government leaders must embrace principles of intrapreneurship. As Steven Brandt of Stanford University once said, "Ideas come from people. Innovation is a capability of the many."[66] However, as pointed out by Michael H. Morris, Donald F. Kuratko, and Jeffrey G. Covin in their book, *Corporate Entrepreneur-*

---

66   Steven C. Brandt, *Entrepreneuring in Established Companies* (Homewood, IL: Dow-Jones-Irwin, 1986), 54.

ship & Innovation,[67] to be successful, entrepreneurial activity must be carefully integrated into the organization's overall strategies.

There have been numerous articles and books written over the years advocating the importance of "unleashing the entrepreneurial potential" of individuals by removing constraints on entrepreneurial behavior (see for example, Gary Hamel's *Leading the Revolution*, Gifford Pinchott's *Intrapreneuring*,[68] and my 2012 book *Harvesting Intangible Assets*). Employees engaging in entrepreneurial behavior are the foundation for organizational innovation. In order to develop a culture of "corporate innovation," organizations must establish a process through which individuals in an established firm pursue entrepreneurial opportunities to innovate without regard to the level and nature of currently available resources. However, keep in mind that in the absence of proper control mechanisms, firms that manifest corporate-innovation activity may "tend to generate an incoherent mass of interesting but unrelated opportunities that may have profit potential, but that don't move [those] firms toward a desirable future."[69] Therefore, those factors that drive corporate entrepreneurial activity to produce high levels of innovation performance are likely contingent upon a firm's ability to judiciously use control mechanisms for the proper selection and effective guidance on entrepreneurial actions and initiatives.[70]

---

67   Michael H. Morris, Donald F. Kuratko, and Jeffrey G. Covin, *Corporate Entrepreneurship & Innovation* 3rd edition (Cengage/South-Western, 2011).

68   Gary Hamel, *Leading the Revolution* (New York: Penguin Group, 2000); Gifford Pinchot and Ron Pellman, *Intrapreneuring in Action* (San Francisco: Berrett-Koehler, 1999).

69   G. Getz and E.G. Tuttle, "A Comprehensive Approach to Corporate Venturing," *Handbook of Business Strategy* 2, no. 1 (2001): 277–279.

70   J.C. Goodale, D.F. Kuratko, J.S. Hornsby, and J.G. Covin, "Operations Management and Corporate Entrepreneurship: The Moderating Effect of Operations Control on the Antecedents of Corporate Entrepreneurial Activity in Relation to Innovation Performance," *Journal of Operations Management* 29, no. 2 (2011): 116–127.

In spite of the potential for corporate innovation to create value by contributing to improved organizational performance, many established companies overlook the critical importance of engagement and thus do not encourage intrepreneurial behavior, because executives worry about the images of chaos that innovation can portray. In addition, there are often structural impediments in place that prevent it from occurring, most of these being the product of bureaucratic routines that have outlived their usefulness. Developing an engaged culture that is capable of cultivating employees' interest in and commitment to effective entrepreneurial behavior and the innovation that can result from it is the product of effective efforts by managers at all levels.

There are a multitude of studies that emphasize the connection between truly engaged workers and better customer service, higher levels of creativity and productivity, higher sales margins, higher quality products, increased attention to safety, and lower turnover rates.[71] What businesses have also recognized, and research has supported, is that innovation within a company is one of the primary drivers of company success, determined through growth. The more interesting element to this equation is *where* that innovation is coming from: engaged employees. A *Gallup Management Journal* study found employees who were "engaged" indicated they "strongly agreed with the statement that their current job 'brings out [their] most creative ideas.'" [72] The reverse was true for those who indicated they were actively disengaged employees—in other words,

---

71   Kevin Kruse, "Why Employee Engagement? (These 28 Research Studies Prove the Benefits)" *Forbes*, September 4, 2012, http://www.forbes.com/sites/kevinkruse/2012/09/04/why-employee-engagement/.

72   Jerry Krueger and Emily Killham, "Who's Driving Innovation at Your Company?" *Gallup Business Journal*, September 14, 2006, http://www.gallup.com/businessjournal/24472/whos-driving-innovation-your-company.aspx.

the very disengaged individuals in the survey were the least likely to find their current job brought out their creative ideas.

Research also shows that engaged workers are more likely to foster a collaborative and innovative atmosphere among fellow employees by reacting positively to creative ideas of others on their team. A good example of this is Google, which fosters a variety of channels to enhance employee engagement through connectivity and the sharing of ideas. Some of the avenues for expression that the company facilitates is having Google Cafes, which serve as venues for individuals to interact across their regular team, or Google Moderators, a management tool that was created to allow anyone within the company to posit questions they would like to have answered. Through the Moderator outlet, employees can view existing ideas, questions, and suggestions.[73] This generates a symbiotic relationship between innovation and employee engagement, creating an inertial atmosphere.

For decades, workers were expected to know their jobs, do their work, keep their heads down, and only "bother" management with questions to avert a crisis. If a problem arises, know how and when to solve it, and don't interfere with the supervisor's valuable time. That mantra needs to shift if we are going to improve engagement in a way to drive more innovation and shareholder value. Employees at all levels need to be liberated to ask the "whys" and the "what ifs." They need to be able to ask (without retribution or punishment), "Why am I doing my job the way I am doing it?" and "Is there a better way?" and "What would it take to change and why?" Empowering your teams to ask questions also demonstrates humility by the

---

73   Laura He, "Google's Secret of Innovation: Empowering Its Employees," *Forbes*, March 29, 2013, http://www.forbes.com/sites/laurahe/2013/03/29/googles-secrets-of-innovation-empowering-its-employees/.

leadership team by admitting that they don't know all the answers, and it gives permission to the workforce to begin to organize its thinking around the unknowns instead of the knowns, which will foster greater creativity, innovation, and productivity. People are likely to be more engaged when they are empowered to think for themselves and permitted to question the "status quo" within reason and without the fear of retribution. Fostering curiosity is an elixir and a cure for disengagement and complacency.

CREATING A PROPER ENVIRONMENT SUPPORTING CORPORATE INNOVATION

Today's leaders must take responsibility to direct their managers to inspire their top performers to create a work environment that is highly conducive to engagement as the clear path toward creativity and innovation. Within such an environment, employees have the opportunity to step up to the plate, which can be either the fuel of their engagement or the oil of their frustration. Conditions in the internal culture dictate the perceived costs, benefits, and incentives associated with taking personal risks, challenging current practices, and devoting time to unproven approaches. Credible innovation is more likely in companies where all individuals' entrepreneurial potential is sought and nurtured and where organizational knowledge is widely shared. The managerial challenge becomes that of using workplace-design elements to develop an "innovation-friendly" internal environment.

As research on corporate innovation has evolved, numerous researchers have acknowledged the importance of internal organizational dimensions to promoting and supporting an environment for creativity and engagement.

This research has identified five specific dimensions that are important determinants of an environment conducive to entrepreneurial behavior including *top management support, work discretion/autonomy; rewards/reinforcement; time availability;* and *organizational boundaries.* These underlying organizational dimensions are required for individuals to perceive an innovation-friendly environment.[74] Let's briefly examine each one from the perspective of the organization's employees and as it may affect engagement.

1. *Top management support:* the extent to which one perceives that top managers support, facilitate, and promote entrepreneurial behavior, including the championing of innovative ideas and providing the resources people require to take entrepreneurial actions. Top management support has been found to have a direct positive relationship with an organization's innovative outcomes.

2. *Work discretion:* the extent to which one perceives that the organization tolerates failure, provides decision-making latitude and freedom from excessive oversight, and delegates authority and responsibility to lower-level managers and workers. Research suggests that entrepreneurial opportunities are often best recognized by those with discretion over how to

---

74   J.S. Hornsby, D.F. Kuratko, D.A. Shepherd, and J.P. Bott, *Managers' Corporate Entrepreneurial Actions: Examining Perception and Position, Journal of Business Venturing* 24, no. 3 (2009): 236–247; J.S. Hornsby, D.F. Kuratko, S.A. Zahra, "Middle Managers' Perception of the Internal Environment for Corporate Entrepreneurship: Assessing a Measurement Scale," *Journal of Business Venturing* 17, no. 3 (2002): 253–273.

perform their work, as well as by those encouraged to engage in experimentation.

3. *Rewards and reinforcement*: the extent to which one perceives that the organization uses systems that reward based on entrepreneurial activity and success. Reward systems that encourage risk taking and innovation have been shown to have a strong effect on individuals' tendencies to behave in entrepreneurial ways. Numerous studies have identified "reward and resource availability" as a principal determinant of entrepreneurial behavior by middle- and first-level managers.

4. *Time availability*: a perception that the workloads ensure extra time for individuals and groups to pursue innovations, with jobs structured in ways to support such efforts and achieve short- and long-term organizational goals. Research suggests that time availability among managers is an important resource for generating entrepreneurial behaviors and best practices. For example, the availability of unstructured or free time can enable would-be corporate innovators to consider opportunities for innovation that may be precluded by their required work schedules.

5. *Organizational boundaries*: the extent to which one perceives that there are flexible organizational boundaries which could be useful in promoting entrepreneurial activity because they enhance the flow of information between the external environment and the organization as well as between departments

and divisions within the organization. However, innovative outcomes emerge most predictably when innovation is treated as a structured and purposeful (vs. chaotic) process. Consistent with this point, organization theorists have long recognized that productive outcomes are most readily accomplished in organizational systems when uncertainty is kept at manageable levels, and this can be achieved through setting boundaries that induce, direct, and encourage coordinated innovative behavior across the organization. In short, organizational boundaries can ensure the productive use of innovation-enabling resources.

MEASURING READINESS: DIAGNOSING THE INTERNAL ENVIRONMENT

A firm's internal entrepreneurial climate should be assessed to evaluate in what manner it is supportive for entrepreneurial behavior to exist and how it is perceived by the managers. When attempting to inventory the firm's current situation regarding the readiness for innovation, managers need to identify parts of the firm's structure, systems, and culture that both inhibit and facilitate entrepreneurial behavior.

One example of an assessment instrument that can be used is the Corporate Entrepreneurship Climate Instrument (CECI),[75] which was developed around the five dimensions mentioned earlier: (1)

---

75   R.D. Ireland, D.F. Kuratko, M.H. Morris, "A Health Audit for Corporate Entrepreneurship: Innovation at All.Levels," *Journal of Business Strategy* 27, no. 2 (2006): 21–30; Michael H. Morris, Donald F. Kuratko, and Jeffrey G.

management support, (2) *work discretion/autonomy*, (3) *reinforcement*, (4) *time availability*, and (5) *organizational boundaries*. In addition, the instrument measures the degree to which a firm's culture supports entrepreneurial activity. Low scores in one specific dimension of the CECI suggest the need to focus on that particular dimension for improvement in order to enhance the firm's readiness for entrepreneurial behavior and eventual successful corporate innovation. This provides an indication of a firm's likelihood of being able to successfully use a corporate-innovation process. It highlights the specific dimensions of the internal work environment that should be the focus of ongoing design and development efforts. Further, the CECI can be used as an assessment tool for evaluating corporate training needs with respect to entrepreneurship and innovation. Determining these training needs sets the stage for improving managers' skills and increasing their sensitivity to the challenges of eliciting and supporting entrepreneurial behavior.

MEASURING RESULTS: ASSESSING YOUR FIRM'S ENTREPRENEURIAL INTENSITY

Organizations differ with respect to the levels of entrepreneurial activity they are capable of achieving, and boards should monitor the enterprises' capability and access to resources in these areas. Extending this thought a bit, we can say that organizations have different levels of *entrepreneurial intensity* (EI), which focuses on two basic questions: (1) How many entrepreneurial initiatives is the company pursuing (*frequency* of entrepreneurship)? and (2) To what extent do those initiatives represent incremental or modest steps versus bold breakthroughs (*degree* of entrepreneurship)? The degree

Covin, *Corporate Entrepreneurship & Innovation* 3rd edition (Cengage/South-Western, 2011).

of entrepreneurship indicates the extent to which an organization's efforts are innovative, risky, and proactive. This helps assess the actual results from innovative efforts.

To assess an organization's EI, frequency and degree of entrepreneurship should be considered together with any number of variances between levels of frequency and degree. Thus, a firm may be engaging in numerous entrepreneurial initiatives (high on frequency), but none of them may be especially innovative, risky, or proactive (low on degree). Another company may pursue a path that emphasizes breakthrough developments (high degree), but they are initiated only every two or three years (low frequency). Yet another firm might achieve a balance in terms of moderately high levels of both degree and frequency.

To assess a firm's degree of entrepreneurship, definitions are needed for innovativeness, risk-taking, and proactivity. *Innovativeness* refers to the seeking of creative or novel solutions to problems. Commonly, these solutions take the form of new processes as well as new products (goods and/or services). *Risk-taking* involves the willingness to commit significant resources to opportunities having a reasonable chance of failure as well as success. However, these risks should be carefully calculated based on potential gains and potential losses that could be associated with the decisions. *Proactiveness* is concerned with anticipating and acting in light of a recognized entrepreneurial opportunity. Proactiveness demands that firms tolerate failure and that employees be encouraged to persevere in their efforts to exploit opportunities that can be the source of innovation.

When developing measures for EI scores, it is important to know that norms for entrepreneurial intensity differ across industries. For example, the computer and information-technology industries tend to be quite entrepreneurially intense, while the consumer-foods industry is much less so. This is not to suggest that ever-increasing amounts of EI will always result in superior firm performance. Firms should view the pursuit of EI in *relative* rather than *absolute* terms, in that there is no absolute standard of EI that organizations should seek to develop.

PREPARING THE ORGANIZATION

Executive leaders must create an understanding of the innovation process for their employees. Key decision makers must find ways to explain the purpose of using a corporate-innovation process to those from whom entrepreneurial behaviors are expected.

Understanding and supporting a corporate-innovation process should not be left to chance. My experience suggests that executives need to develop a program with the purpose of helping all parties who will be affected by corporate innovation to understand the value of the entrepreneurial behavior that the firm is requesting of them. Let me provide a sample outline of this type of program.

CORPORATE INNOVATION DEVELOPMENT PROGRAM FRAMEWORK

Introduction to corporate innovation and entrepreneurship: an examination of the concept of corporate entrepreneurship and a corporate innovation strategy; an examination of some of the better-known innovations in established companies; and a review of several corporate-innovation cases.

1. **Innovative Thinking:** This thinking challenges participants to think innovatively and emphasizes the need for innovative leadership in today's

organizations. The misconceptions about thinking innovatively are reviewed, and a discussion of the most common inhibitors ensues. After completing a personal-innovation inventory, managers engage in several exercises designed to facilitate their own innovative thinking.

2. **Innovation Acceleration Process:** Managers explore how specific ideas are developed within the corporation, including structural barriers and facilitators. The concepts behind "idea stoppers" are examined. Video clips are used to illustrate some examples of entrepreneurial thinking.

3. **Barriers and Facilitators to Innovative Thinking:** This discussion of the most common barriers to innovative behavior includes examining a number of aspects of the firm's culture. Participants complete exercises that help them deal with barriers in their internal work environment. In addition, video case histories are shown to describe the entrepreneurial behaviors of innovators in the participants' firms who have positively contributed to implementing an innovation.

4. **Assessing the Innovative Culture:** The major thrust of this session is to learn how to assess the innovative culture in the organization. It is critical for managers to understand the methods they can apply to understand the "readiness" of their organization for innovative strategies. Some unique methods are introduced in which managers participate in order to gain experience. A unique assessment instrument

is provided, which assesses the level of innovative culture within the organization. Participants complete the instrument and discuss the areas for improvement based on the "perceptual" results.

These types of programs should be ongoing. As new innovative opportunities surface in a firm's external environment, as the internal work environment changes, and as new employees join the organization, it is appropriate for those from whom entrepreneurial behavior is expected to work together to find the best ways to implement a corporate-innovation process. In this sense, efforts to successfully engage in corporate innovation must themselves be innovative—changing in response to ever-changing conditions in the firm's internal and external environments.

RELEVANT ISSUES TO CONSIDER

Corporate innovation provides the context within which innovation takes place in an established firm. Here are the six most relevant issues that boards of directors and corporate executives need to consider when designing a corporate-innovation process for their organization:

1. Where does the firm want to be in terms of its level of entrepreneurial intensity? Does the firm seek a condition of (1) high frequency and low degree, (2) high degree and low frequency, or (3) some other combination?

2. To what extent are the firm's entrepreneurial efforts oriented toward starting new ventures outside the current portfolio of businesses versus transforming the existing

businesses with the objective of developing new products and/or serving markets that are new to the firm?

3. In what areas does the firm want to be an innovation leader versus being an innovation follower? In what market spaces does the firm seek to be a first mover? In what market spaces does the firm want to be a fast second mover?

4. In what areas of the firm are managers seeking higher versus lower levels of entrepreneurial behaviors? Which business product areas are expected to be the most innovative?

5. What is the relative importance over the next three years of product innovation (introducing new goods or services in the marketplace) versus process innovation (developing more efficient and effective ways to produce the firm's goods and services)? What is the relative importance of new versus existing markets?

6. To what extent are innovation stimuli expected to come from top-, middle-, or first-level managers? Are all managers clear about what the firm expects from them in terms of stimulating entrepreneurial behavior on the path to create product, process, and/or administrative innovations?

Dealing with these decision issues is important, in that innovation experience shows that entrepreneurial behaviors are more likely to become the norm in firms using a corporate-innovation process that is a product of developing answers to the decision issues listed above. Without such a process, managers and employees can waste significant resources on initiatives that make little sense for the firm or that have little likelihood of long-term success. Another benefit of a carefully designed and executed corporate-innovation process is

THE CRISIS OF DISENGAGEMENT

that regularly using such a process allows organizational knowledge to be shared across the firm.

DEFINING AND UTILIZING INTELLECTUAL ASSET MANAGEMENT

Intellectual asset management (IAM) is a system for creating, prioritizing, and extracting value from a company's various sets of intellectual-property assets. The intellectual capital and technical know-how of a company are among its most valuable assets, provide its greatest competitive advantages, and are the principal drivers of shareholder value. Yet rarely do companies have adequate personnel, resources, and systems in place to properly manage and leverage these assets. The combination of truly engaged employees who can interact with established IAM systems is highly likely to yield measurable and monetizable innovation. IAM, as a matter of strategy and competitive intelligence gathering, also involves monitoring certain developments in the company's marketplace, such as

- gathering intelligence on direct, indirect, and potential competitors;

- monitoring developments abroad;

- keeping one step ahead of a constantly changing landscape; and

- maintaining license agreements and streams-of-royalty payments on both an inbound and outbound basis.

Intellectual capital consists of many different types of human capital, intellectual property, and relationship capital.

IAM also involves an understanding of how and where intellectual assets sit in the strategic parameters and food chain of the company. Three strategic views toward the use of intellectual capital have evolved in the boardroom over recent decades.

1. **Traditional view.** Intangible assets enhance the company's competitive advantage and strengthen its ability to defend its competitive position in the marketplace; our intellectual properties are seen as a barrier to entry and as a shield to protect market share. This approach may be too passive and archaic in today's rapidly moving and highly competitive marketplace.

2. **Current view.** Intangible assets should not be used merely for defensive purposes but should also be viewed as an important strategic asset and profit center that is capable of being monetized and generating value through licensing fees and other channels and strategies, *provided* that time and resources are devoted to uncovering these opportunities—especially dormant intangible assets that do not currently serve at the heart of the company's current core competencies or focus (*proactive/systemic approach*).

3. **Future view.** Intangible assets are *the* premiere drivers of business strategy within the company and encompass human capital, structural/organizational capital, and customer/relationship capital. IAM systems need to be built and continuously improved to ensure that intellectual property assets are used to protect and defend the company's strategic position in domestic and global markets and to create new markets, distribution channels, and revenue streams in a capital-efficient manner to maximize shareholder value (*core focus/strategic approach*).

Board members and executives of companies of all sizes and in all types of industries are often guilty of committing a serious strategic sin: failure to properly protect and harvest the company's intangible assets. This is especially true at many technology-driven and consumer-driven companies. During the dot-com and Web 1.0 Internet boom, from 1997 to 2001, billions of dollars went into the venture capital, and the primary use of these proceeds by entrepreneurs was the creation of intellectual property. Ten years later, however, emerging growth and middle-market companies failed in many cases to leverage this intellectual capital into new revenue streams and market opportunities because of the singular focus on their core business.

Entrepreneurs may also lack the proper tools to analyze the value of the company's intellectual assets. Professor Baruch Lev, a finance professor at the Stern School of Business at NYU, has observed that only 15 percent of the "true intrinsic value" of the Standard & Poor's (S&P) 500 was found to be captured in their financial statements. Given the resources of an S&P 500 company, it is likely that smaller companies have their intangible assets even more deeply embedded, and the number for privately held companies may be as low as 5 percent. Imagine the consequences if you were to prepare to sell your business and 95 percent of your inherent value got left on the table! This gap in capturing and reflecting this hidden value points out the critical need for a strategic analysis of an emerging company's intellectual-property portfolio.

Leaders and boards of directors must understand that the inversion of the ratio of tangible to intangible assets as a percentage of total company value has been dramatic. According to multiple studies by Ocean Tomo in Chicago, in 1978, tangible assets (e.g., property, plant, equipment, and inventory) made up approximately

80 percent of the value of a typical S&P's 500 stock index company. By 2002, this was reduced to 20 percent of the total value, and the numbers continue to drop, especially in a virtual world. Today, for many emerging small- to-midsize enterprises (SMEs), the ratio of intangible to tangible assets can be as high as eight or ten to one.

The harvesting of intellectual capital is a *strategic process* that must begin with the taking of an inventory by the company's management team in order to get a comprehensive handle on the breadth and depth of the company's intangible assets. Corporate leaders have an obligation toward their shareholders to uncover hidden value and make the most of the assets that have been developed with corporate resources. The leadership of the company will never know whether it has a "Picasso in the basement" unless it takes the time to inventory what is hiding in the basement and has a qualified intellectual-capital inventory team capable of distinguishing between a Picasso and your child's art project. Once these assets are properly identified, an IAM system should be developed to ensure open communication and strategic management of these assets. At that point, the company is ready to engage in the strategic-planning process to determine how to convert these assets into profitable revenue streams and new opportunities that will enhance and protect shareholder value.

IAM helps growing companies ensure that strategic-growth opportunities are recognized, captured, and harvested into new revenue streams and markets.

IAM helps growing companies ensure that strategic-growth opportunities are recognized, captured, and harvested into new revenue streams and markets.

Company leaders should conduct periodic reviews of their IAM practices asking the following questions:

- What IAM systems, procedures, and teams are currently in place?

- How and when were these systems developed?

- Who is responsible or accountable for managing these systems within the company?

- To what degree are adequate systems for internal and external communication and collaboration now in place?

- What ideas/technology-harvesting filters and procedures for innovation decisional analysis (e.g., whether to move forward, budget allocation, and timetable) are currently in place?

- Are the strategy and the process for harvesting and leveraging intellectual assets reactive or proactive?

- What are the real or perceived internal (politics, red tape, budgeting processes, organizational structure) and/or external (market conditions, rapid changes in the state of the art, competitor's strategies) hurdles that stand in the way of better IAM practices and procedures?

- What can be done to remove or reduce those barriers?

BUILDING INTELLECTUAL ASSET MANAGEMENT SYSTEMS TO DRIVE ENGAGEMENT

As the stewards of both the tangible and intangible assets of the company, boards of directors and leaders must put IAM systems in place. The failure to do so not only is a breach of the fiduciary duty but may even rise to the level of board liability for being too complacent in harvesting the company's intangible assets. IAM systems drive engagement, collaboration, efficiency, and monetization.

When I speak at business conferences around the world to companies of all sizes and in all industries and ask them whether they have an IAM system in place, I am typically greeted with blank stares. When a few feeble hands go up, I then ask whether their IAM systems have been effective and yielded profitable opportunities, and even fewer hands rise. When I ask whether their organizational chart has been retooled to reflect the transformational shift toward an intangible asset–driven economy, they look at me as if I just arrived from Mars. And, finally, when I ask them to name the person in the company who serves as the chief intellectual property protection and leveraging executive they look at me as if I were from Venus. *How can we as leaders of companies and as fiduciary guardians of the entity's assets on behalf of our stakeholders continue to completely ignore the management and leveraging of our most important strategic assets?*

The time for all companies around the globe to commit time and resources for the deployment of an effective multidisciplinary IAM system to properly manage and harvest intellectual assets *is now*. As stewards of the assets of the company managers have an obligation to maximize the value of these assets, especially in a post-Sarbanes-Oxley regulatory environment. For more on this topic, see my 2012 book published by AMACOM entitled *Harvesting Intellectual Assets: Uncover Hidden Revenue in Your Company's Intellectual Property*.

CHAPTER 11

REFLECTIONS ON CREATIVITY, CULTURE, AND DISENGAGEMENT

BY GUEST ESSAYIST KAIHAN KRIPPENDORFF

Over the years, employees with ambition but who grew frustrated by their organization's willingness to accept new ideas had three choices:

1. **Quit:** They could quit their job and start a business, free from the entanglements of bureaucracy. In the United States, about 12 percent of employees choose this route.[76]

2. **Climb the ladder:** They could accept the system for a while in order to climb to a more powerful position from which they could later change the system.

---

76   Slavica Singer, *The Global Entrepreneurship Monitor*, 2014.

3. **Quit on the job:** They could give up on the idea that they should advocate for their creativity, quit without leaving their job, and push on until retirement. They quit on the job. They grow disengaged.

The first choice is risky. The second choice leads to a ladder that rarely ends (even if you become CEO, you lack the power you thought you would have to change the system). The third, in my opinion, leads to a life wasted.

Nearly 90 percent of employees find themselves choosing the third option. This alarming fact not only robs such disengaged workers of the purpose and passion that characterizes a life well lived, but it costs our society in measurable ways. A battery of studies proves the link between a company's performance and that company's ability to unleash creativity and entrepreneurial behavior in its employees. Companies that can unlock entrepreneurial intensity enjoy superior profits, income-to-sales ratio, rate of growth of revenue, rate of growth of assets, rate of growth of employees, and a composite measure of twelve financial and nonfinancial criteria.[77]

Engaged, entrepreneurial workers help organizations grow faster and more profitably and produce a broad spectrum of positive outcomes. Engaged employees introduce innovations that benefit consumers, families, and communities. And yet, of the 88 percent of working adults who decide not to engage in entrepreneurial behavior, nearly all feel disengaged. We are switching off human potential by creating a work context that encourages people to disengage.

---

77   Andreas Rauch, Johan Wiklund, G.T. Lumpkin, and Michael Frese, "Entrepreneurial Orientation and Business Performance: An Assessment of Past Research and Suggestions for the Future," *Entrepreneurship Theory and Practice* 33, no. 3 (2009):761–787.

Contrary to commonly accepted truth, only eight of the thirty most transformative innovations were first conceived of by entrepreneurs; twenty-two were conceived by employees. Without the inventiveness of intrapreneurs, we might not have the Internet, personal computer, mobile phone, DNA sequencing, magnetic resonance imaging, or fiber optics. Most transformative innovations (nine out of thirty) come to life when a larger community forms around the idea to develop it.

Teams do often play a role in the innovation journey, but they are less often small entrepreneurial teams and more often formal teams assembled by large organizations. When transformative innovations have been developed by teams, those teams are usually formally rather than informally connected, and they are usually larger, often more than ten people. Teams do matter (about 27 percent of the time), but the teams that develop the idea are usually larger and more often formally related than our entrepreneurial-hero myth would suggest.

We have pretty well dismantled the commonly held story about how innovations grow. Entrepreneurs don't come up with ideas; engaged employees do. Entrepreneurs don't develop ideas on their own or in informal teams; instead either communities or large formal teams do that work. But let's follow the story through the final phase and see who commercializes.

> *Entrepreneurs don't come up with ideas; engaged employees do.*

Only two of the thirty most transformative innovations were scaled by their original creators. More than 50 percent of the time (sixteen out of thirty), the innovator loses control of the innovation and competitors take over. Then, through a battle of players seeking to commercialize the innovation, the innovation scales. New entrepreneurial ventures don't scale innovations, competitors do.

Follow this path of innovation to its source. The transformative innovation—e-mail, MRI, DNA sequencing, mobile phone—is commercialized by a group of competitors. Those competitors are attracted by the work of a community or formal team. That community or formal team works on an idea generated by . . . an *employee*.

If we cannot engage employees, we cut transformational innovation off at the bud. Large companies, if they are forward-looking, are coming to realize that scale and creativity can coexist if you are willing to rethink how people find and pursue ideas.

The transition from bureaucracies that kill off engagement into newer forms of organizations that ignite and benefit from the creative power of engaged employees will happen—but it will happen slowly. Three of the most important things that intrapreneurs and organizations must both address are

- ownership mind-set;

- knowing where to look; and

- operating agility within structure.

OWNERSHIP MIND-SET

It's been long established that your mind-set plays a powerful role in what you see as possible and the choices you make. Research shows that people with a "growth mind-set" tend to see failures as learning opportunities, while those with a "fixed mind-set" see them as evidence of an innate weakness. Those with "growth mind-sets" seek to learn and improve from failures, while those with "fixed mind-sets" are less likely to do so.

To unlock the creative potential of employees and to become more effective at influencing your organization to adopt your creative ideas, it is critical to begin developing a growth mind-set.

KNOWING WHERE TO LOOK

A common complaint I hear from senior managers is that they ask employees for ideas, but the ideas employees share are simply of poor quality. What is typically missing is not creativity or strategic ability but an understanding of where to look.

It is helpful to ensure you and your employees are able to answer four questions before you begin generating new strategic ideas:

1. What is our business's mission or core purpose?

2. What is our five-year vision or strategic intent?

3. What are the top five priorities we believe will enable us to achieve our vision?

4. Is our primary source of competitive advantage due to our (a) having a superior product, (b) knowing the customer better than the competition, (c) excelling at people and culture, or (d) operational efficiency?

Until you can answer these four questions, ideas are likely to miss the mark.

OPERATING WITH AGILITY WITHIN STRUCTURE

The movement sometimes called "agile" or "lean" or "design thinking" or "scrum" has begun working its way into a variety of domains, from computer programming to science to entrepreneurship. This approach is starting to find its way into corporate innovation.

While some believe the approach—characterized by cycles of small experiments rather than long planning cycles—applies only to small companies, ever more large companies are figuring out it can work for them as well.

If we break down the paths of successful efforts of engaged employees pushing for creative innovations, we see they follow a rather predictable sequence of steps called by the acronym PINPOINT. The idea is that if an innovator can pinpoint just the right kind of idea that your core customer will love and your internal stakeholders will embrace, you are nearly guaranteed success. Innovators who are able to find this pinpoint follow eight steps:

1. **P**innacle user: They focus on the "pinnacle user," the most demanding core customer.

2. **I**nsight: They study this user to find an insight, usually an unmet need.

3. **N**eed assessment: They assess that need to ensure that meeting it represents a big enough opportunity.

4. **P**rototype: They then cycle through prototypes, starting with an inexpensive concept image and escalating the investment as they learn how the pinnacle user responds to each cycle.

5. **O**wn it: They give the resulting solution a memorable name.

6. **I**nternal alignment: They assess whether they are likely to win internal alignment.

7. **N**etwork alignment: They assess whether they would be able to win the support of suppliers, distributors, and other partners.

8. **T**ransferability: They assess if their idea would have useful application across other areas of the company and other businesses in the corporation.

An entrepreneur must primarily concern himself or herself with customer needs, but an *internal entrepreneur* must play a more complicated game, picking from the ideas that customers will love and only those that internal stakeholders and network partners will support.

The lack of engagement in the United States saps people of meaning, organizations of good ideas, and the community of the benefits that would come from those ideas. Engaged employees are the source of nearly every transformative innovation. Their disengagement creates a significant cost to humankind.

Though it is tempting to buy into the belief that large organizations simply cannot engage workers to act creatively and entrepreneurially, the facts point clearly to the challenge being possible. Your organization will either embrace this movement now or wait for others to get ahead of you.

Dr. Kaihan Krippendorff is a business strategist, keynote speaker, consultant, and best-selling author of four books, including *Outthink the Competition* (John Wiley, 2012). A former consultant with McKinsey & Company, he now writes one of the most popular blogs on FastCompany. com, *Outthinkers*, and is a recognized expert on innovation, business strategy, and creativity, appearing in key business media outlets including Fox Business, National Public Radio, *Bloomberg Businessweek*, Bloomberg Radio, and more.

He has trained more than six thousand executives and entrepreneurs in his unique business-strategy approach, The Outthinker Process®, and works with the leadership teams of a growing number of leading corporations, including Microsoft, Johnson & Johnson, Citibank, L'Oreal, United Technologies, Kraft, and Experian, to design innovative business strategies that disrupt markets and unlock new growth.

A sought-after keynote speaker, he is also a regular lecturer for Wharton Executive Education and Harvard Business School Press, as well as a guest faculty member for select business schools through the US and Latin America.

Dr. Kaihan Krippendorff received his doctorate of science at Abo Akademie in Finland. He has earned an MBA from Columbia Business School and London Business School, a BSE in finance from the University of Pennsylvania's Wharton School, and a BSE in engineering from the University of Pennsylvania School of Engineering and Applied Science.

He lives in Greenwich, CT, (just outside of New York City) with his wife and three children. He is fluent in English and Spanish with conversational command of German.[78]

---

78   Kaihan Krippendorff, "Dr. Kaihan Krippendorff, Business Strategist, Best-Selling Author, And Consultant," 2016, http://kaihan.net/.

CHAPTER 12

REFLECTIONS ON INSPIRING THE ENGAGEMENT OF YOUR CUSTOMERS AND PARTNERS

BY GUEST ESSAYIST ROBERT GAPPA

Engagement = meaningful connections that make me want to come back.

Anyone who has been engaged to be married and was truly in love with the person, and then got divorced, knows what it means to be both "engaged" and "disengaged." The activities engaged and disengaged people

Engagement = Meaningful Connections that make me want to come back.

223

do together are similar in process but different in frequency and intent. For engaged people, the end result is to make the other person desire to repeat the experience—with them. For disengaged people, the end result is "to get it over with."

So it is for rock concerts and theater plays. When the curtain drops or the last song is played, the musicians and actors want their audiences to clap for an encore. And the audience is there, anticipating to receive an "encore experience." If we experience an "encore performance" we are likely to go to the play again and to the rock concert when the band returns.

Likewise, for every shopping experience, whether it is the grocery store, the doctor's office, a movie, a vacation, or an online purchase—when we spend money with a person or a business, we are anticipating to receive at the very least, a pleasant transaction. All each of us wants is for the person or persons to whom we are paying money to "make me want to come back and spend money here again!"

This chapter is about how that is done and how it is done on a larger scale.

Engagement begins with the belief and desire to find what behaviors make customers and team members (including all employees from C-level to part-time hourly individuals, franchisees, and channel partners) grateful and thankful for the relationship they have with us—and leads to an enthusiastic anticipation of continuing and deepening the relationship.

To accomplish this we need to determine *why* each of these persons and entities is in a relationship with us as team members or customers. In other words, "What are the personal and business goals that we contribute to being achieved, either partially or completely?" When we know the answer, we can determine which beliefs, behaviors, processes, and technologies can be utilized to select, orient, train, develop, lead, and manage people who will have a desire to create inspiring, encore experiences—which make people want to come back.

Some of these experiences are face-to-face, and some are digital. When our intent to inspire team members is successful, we realize we have created a great place to work. We could be one of the "100 Best Companies to Work For," and we discover that retention, satisfaction, referrals, and productivity metrics improve. When our intent to inspire our business-to-business and business-to-customer clients is successful, we realize we have created a "great place to shop and spend money." Our retention of new and existing customers, as well as frequency, satisfaction, loyalty, and lifetime-value metrics all improve.

INSPIRING ENGAGEMENT IS YOUR BRAND'S MOST SUSTAINABLE COMPETITIVE ADVANTAGE

Everyone knows that the perceptions people have about us affect their attitudes about being around us. And we also know that we have a lot of control over the formation of these perceptions. We also know there are no easy fixes when it comes to winning the minds and hearts of team members and customers.

Since about the mid 1980s, almost every possible source of competitive advantage has been maxed out. Where can value be found when price becomes less and less of a factor and customers are tired of hearing that every brand's product or service is the "best?"

Consumers know better. So what do we do to retain a solid customer base and at the same time retain our most productive team members? The answer is to create a "great place to shop and spend money." Emotionally connecting with customers creates feelings within customers which drive frequency.

A great place to shop and spend money is half of the competitive formula. Simultaneously, great organizations create a "great place to work" in which their best performers can use technology and their individual strengths to implement the processes that make up the customer experience to create magical, memorable moments for each customer.

The challenge of personalizing a set process, energizes team members and customers alike, creating team members who are happy, satisfied, grateful, and engaged. When engaged team members utilize their strengths to create both a "great place to work" and a "great place to shop and spend money," they are not only providing the brand with an instantaneous, constant, long-term, real-time, sustainable competitive advantage that drives profits and growth but also, retaining long-term customers.

The positive emotions both team members and customers have as a result of great experiences result in customers receiving more than a product or service. They experience feelings that hold real value to them. These feelings are like currency—"emotional currency." This is the moment where everything changes, and the paradigm of business shifts. We are no longer exchanging our goods and services for the financial currency of the customer. We are exchanging the way we feel about the customer (most have already decided to buy our goods and services)—our "emotional currency" for their "financial currency." This "currency exchange" is the essence and core of understanding the new "experience economy" we are living and working in at this very moment. Dan Hill, the author of *Emotionomics* has created a mantra to help us understand the impact of emotions on our financial success: "Emotionomics Drives Economics."

We are all faced with extreme competition. We cannot maintain our margins from what were "normal operations" in this environment.

What causes this situation and problem is a customer relationship based solely on price. Competing on price makes a business a commodity. The solution is having a relationship with the customer overriding price. This demands managers and leaders who are more adept at psychology than economics. These leaders and managers understand how each individual team member connects with your customers and with your company.

A "great place to work" is one that nurtures team members' strengths and uses them to create great experiences for customers. The profit, growth, and long-term success of a brand depends on this dynamic. Management 2000's assessment process helps our clients identify where changes need to be made to create a competitive advantage for their brands by creating a "great place to work" for team members and a "great place to shop and spend money" for their customers. We conduct the assessment by asking hundreds of questions and look at the organization's competency.

> *A "great place to work" is one that nurtures team members' strengths and uses them to create great experiences for customers.*

Customer engagement is created when a brand is designed to enhance what a company's target market truly values. This type of engagement results in trusting, positive, and individualized experiences.

Consider the possibilities resulting from customers who experience positive, engaging, and individualized experiences:

- The brand can always and everywhere be trusted to keep the promises it makes.

- Customers are happy, content, and comfortable before, during, and after doing business.

- Customers, having been treated fairly, will stand behind the company's products and services.

- Customers will have pride in being associated with the brand and its products and services.

- The brand is essential to its customers' lives and somewhat irreplaceable, creating "separation anxiety" if the brand went away because the brand fits with the customers' personal needs.

- The brand is trusted to provide its customers with knowledge, information, and resources, through various mediums, to enhance their lives and the lives of their families and the communities to which they belong.

Some companies are very good at making emotional connections with their team members and with their customers. Most, however, are not. Companies that are successful benefit from stronger results—not only in cash flow and profit but in market share and shareholder value.

Engagement goes back to our earliest ancestors. With engagement comes peace and prosperity, and without it comes conflict and anxiety. My hope is that this chapter will help create an evolved "you" and will help you evolve your team members and customers into a more engaged community.

A MOST REVEALING ENGAGEMENT QUESTION: WHAT ARE YOU PAID FOR?

One very simple way to determine if a person is engaged is to ask him or her, "What are you paid for?"

I have found most people either do not know the answer, or they answer with a functional description of their job, i.e., "to serve food," or "to give you great service." At one customer-centric hotel brand the answer was, "Three results: you are very satisfied, you will return here or to one of our other locations, and you recommend us to your colleagues."

If you are a manager and your team members know the answer to this question, you must ensure each person has mastered the skills, knowledge, and abilities (SKAs) needed to implement the processes, use the technology, and manifest the behaviors needed to create guest experiences that makes them return and recommend the hotel to their colleagues. And the results can be measured. Once measured, team members can be involved in improving their SKAs, processes, technology, and behaviors to increase retention and frequency of those newly referred guests. Once team members are engaged, they will immediately ask themselves, *What can I do for this guest to ensure he or she returns here, goes to one of our other locations, and recommends us to his or her colleagues?*

If you consider yourself a leader, in addition to being a manager, and your team members know the answer to "what they are paid for," you can lead and inspire them to achieve the aforementioned three results for the guest. Both you and your team members will be engaged in accomplishing common inspirational results, and guests will have very strong, positive emotions about your brand. They will be bonded to the brand. They will be engaged guests who are loyal to the brand because of their experiences with it—all created by team members who understand that getting them to return and recommend the brand to colleagues is *what they are paid to accomplish*. Your team members are a team precisely because they have unified beliefs, which enable them to work together for the desired guest experience.

However, if as a leader and a manager you and your team members *do not* know what you are paid for, it is impossible to manage and achieve the desired results of communicating and inspiring people. That's because not one of the team members will be sure why you want things done in certain ways, what your communications mean, or why you talk about what you talk about.

So begin to ask team members, "What are you paid for?" and you will be amazed at the answers you receive. It will help you understand what you need to stop, start, keep, change, and improve in your beliefs, thinking, and behaviors to become a more engaged, inspired, and inspiring manager and leader.

WALT DISNEY'S ANSWER TO "WHAT ARE YOU PAID FOR?"

Walt Disney, a master of engagement and inspiration, understood that the essence of engagement was accomplished by ensuring that team members and guests experienced memorable, magical moments that made them feel happiness, inspiration, and joy—and a sense that they truly belonged. From the beginning, he wanted to create "The happiest place in the world." Walt Disney also wanted his brand to be a "source of joy and inspiration to the world," and it continues to be both.

Around 1940, Walt Disney said that each of the cast members were paid to "do what you do so well that they [customers] will want to see it again and bring their friends." In other words, they were paid to create encore experiences for one another and for guests.

Walt was a master at engagement. Disney team members, individually and collectively, have unified believing, thinking, and behaving. They measure what they manage, and manage what they measure. They have focus and concentration. Disney is the quintessential example proving individuals and their brand can lead, manage, measure, and inspire the engagement of team members and guests. The results, since Sunday, July 17, 1955, are new guests, the retention and frequency of existing guests, and the profit and growth of the brand as "The Happiest Place on Earth." If the brand Walt Disney created can be successful for so long, there is hope for the rest of us.

Before reading further, ask and answer the following questions:

- What am I paid for?

- What percentage of our team members know what they are paid for?

- What percentage of our team members are fully engaged, right now?

- (If appropriate) What percentage of our channel partners and franchisees are fully engaged, right now?

- What percentage of our customers are fully engaged, right now?

- How many of our customers are true believers that we, and only we, can give them the kind of experience they expect, want, and need?

- What precisely do we need to do to double that number?

- Do the team and I know what results I am managing to achieve?

- Do we measure what we manage?

- Do the team members know where I am leading them?

- How many customers, *not* transactions, does it take to produce our past twelve months' sales?

- What would our sales be if each customer had purchased once more in the past twelve months?

- If I could only have two financial metrics to determine the health of my brand, what would they be?

ENGAGEMENT AND INSPIRATION ARE PART OF MANAGEMENT AND LEADERSHIP

Disney is both well managed and well led. They know who their customers are, what their customers value, and how to enhance what they value. Disney delivers to the customers through their processes and technologies and by their well-trained team members. Personalized experiences lead guests to value the emotional feelings they receive during their stay more so than the money they spent. They experience a valuable "emotional currency" in exchange for the "financial currency" they paid to Disney. Disney knows that as long as emotional currency has more value to the guest than their financial currency, emotionomics will drive economics.

Most of us have been taught, "What we measure, we can manage." We also know *management is a science*. The science of management, according to Peter Drucker, involves seven processes (research, planning, organizing, delegating, directing, communicating, and coordinating) applied to each of the five resources (people, money, materials, time, and space) toward the achievement of results.

Leadership, on the other hand, is an *art*. Leadership is about teaching people the ways they need to believe, think, act, and behave, for the enterprise to be successful.

- Management is head, and leadership is heart.

- Management is intellect, and leadership is emotion.

- Management is bones, and leadership is spirit.

- Management is understanding, and leadership is meaning.

- Management is commitment, and leadership is conviction.

- Management is six sigma, while leadership is human sigma.

So the questions are as follows:

- Can we measure the engagement of our customers and team members?

- Can we manage what we measure?

- Can we inspire, measure, manage, and lead the engagement of customers and team members?

A TRIBUTE TO HISTORY: A PERSONAL REFLECTION

In 1976, I had the privileged good fortune to join Joe Batten's management-consulting company, BBH&S. Joe had authored *Tough-Minded Management* in 1963, and it became a best seller, printed in forty languages. He wrote a number of other best-selling management books, including *Beyond Management by Objectives, Developing a Tough-Minded Climate for Results, Expectations and Possibilities*, and *Tough-Minded Leadership*. Joe did not know it at the time, but he was establishing a set of management and leadership beliefs, philosophies, behaviors, processes, and technology to engage team members in creating great places to work and great places for customers to shop and spend money. We had clients who were some of the leading and emerging brands of the day, like Marriott, IBM, EDS, etc.

Here is the system we used then with our clients to increase productivity. Keep in mind what Joe called productivity is today called engagement. He believed there is only one reason why each and every team member is working in a company—to achieve his or her personal goals, which for Joe, were directly related to growth for the team members and those they cared about.

I remember that when I interviewed with Joe Batten he asked me what my biggest concern was in joining BBH&S. I said, "I have never sold anything." His response was: "I don't want you to sell. I want you to help clients discover that we can help them solve problems and take advantage of the opportunities. In other words, I want you to be of service. The clients will not be surprised when we send them an invoice."

This advice is the essence of inspiration and engagement as it reinforces the need for being of service to one another and to customers, meeting one another's needs, meeting customers' needs, and enhancing what customers value.

I started Management 2000 in 1982, with the conviction that a company with a strong culture, focused on teams that provided products and services customers wanted and needed, would be successful. Here we are thirty-five years later as of this writing, with more than 1,450 clients on our client list. Our mission, then and now, is "To give people what they expect and more." Our purpose is to help individuals and brands achieve profitable growth. I hope this chapter will help *you* achieve profitable growth.

WHEN MEASURING AND INSPIRING ENGAGEMENT WITH TEAM MEMBERS AND CUSTOMERS GOT INTENSE

Peter Drucker, in 1964, showed that he had great insight into inspiring engagement with team members and customers through the product when he said: "The customer rarely buys what the business thinks it sells him. One reason for this is, of course, that nobody pays for a 'product'. What is paid for is satisfaction. But nobody can make or supply satisfaction as such—at best, only the means to attaining them can be sold and delivered."

The September-October 1991 issue of the *Harvard Business Review* had an article, "The Service-Driven Company," by Leonard Schlesinger and James Heskett. The article challenged business leaders and stirred a debate and discussion within many companies, down to the present day, about the reason, purpose, and result of a business. Peter Drucker, in his 1964 book, *Managing for Results*, defined the *reason* for a business as *economic performance*, achieved by fulfilling its *purpose*—to *create a customer* and its *result*—a *satisfied customer*. The thinking and concepts in this book influenced, and continue to influence, CEOs to ask questions and shift paradigms. The questions go something like this:

- Do we want more sales, revenue, and profits, or do we want to create and retain more and more very satisfied promoter-customers who consume more and more of our products and services?

- Do we sell stuff, or do we establish relationships?

- Do our customers buy our stuff, or do they buy a means to an end—a need and a desire to be satisfied—when that need is met?

- Do we want a brand that is well-known? Or a brand that is emotionally loved, respected, and admired for the ways it makes people happy, comfortable, and feeling as though they belong to the brand and what it represents (Starbucks, Apple, Nike)?[79]

The groundwork was further established for what today is known as team-member engagement and customer engagement with these publications:

- Earl Sasser's book, *Service Breakthroughs: Changing the Rules of the Game*, 1990

- James Haslet's article, "The Profitable Art of Service Recovery" (*Harvard Business Review*, July–August 1990)

- Fred Reichheld's and Earl Sasser's article, "Zero Defections: Quality Comes to Services" (*Harvard Business Review*, September–October 1990)

Although terming has evolved over the years, essentially, these published individuals embraced the philosophies, processes, behaviors, and technologies used to create engagement. Inspiring the engagement of team members and customers is not new, but rather, it is something most of us need to catch up to structuring, doing, and living in our personal and business lives.

> A.G. Lafley, the chairman of the board, president, and CEO of Procter & Gamble, in the November 2009 issue of the *Harvard Business Review*, said the following about the effect

---

79   Leonard A. Schlesinger, "The Service-Driven Company," *Harvard Business Review* 69, no. 5 (1991): 71–81.

Drucker's definitions for the reason, purpose, and result of a business had on Proctor & Gamble:

> I learned many things from Peter over the years, but far and away the most important were the simplest: "The purpose of a company is to create a customer" and "A business is defined by the want the customer satisfies when he or she buys a product or a service. To satisfy the customer is the mission and purpose of every business."
>
> At P&G we keep Peter's words in mind with every decision. We declared that the consumer—not the CEO—is boss, and we made it our purpose to touch more consumers and improve more of each consumer's life. When we look at the business from the perspective of the consumer, we can see the need to win at two moments of truth: first, when she buys a P&G brand or product in a store, and second, when she or another family member uses that product in the home. (She buys the product because she is anticipating a memorable moment, and when she or a member of the family has a memorable moment, she is satisfied emotionally and bonded to the brand.)
>
> We knew that P&G's business model was Sesame Street simple, but deceptively so—typical of the wisdom that was the hallmark of Peter's lifework. By putting customers first, we've nearly doubled the number served, from 2 billion to 3.8 billion; doubled sales; and

tripled P&G profits in the first nine years of the twenty-first century.[80]

WHAT IS ENGAGEMENT?

A simple definition of engagement is: "meaningful connections and memorable moments making me [team members, customers, spouses, children, etc.] want to come back and recommend you to friends."

Engagement is all about feelings. Most men were brought up to "get over feelings" because they get in the way of commitment, dedication, and achievement. Besides, feelings made you weak, vulnerable, and susceptible to corrupting your intellectual capacity to make judgments and decisions.

Engagement is about behaving in ways that show you genuinely care about others—their wants, needs, desires, goals, and visions, as well as their fears, uncertainties, and doubts. It means

- taking the time to say "good morning" before going to your office in the morning;

- writing thank-you notes to people for a job well-done;

- giving twelve to fifteen compliments each day to people when the occasion calls for it;

- knowing about and discussing personal tragedies and triumphs with team members; and

- going to lunch with everyone, not just those with whom you are comfortable.

Successfully creating experiences for team members and customers has to do with possessing not just IQ, knowledge, and

---

80   Alan Kantrow, "Why Read Peter Drucker?," *Harvard Business Review*, November 2009, https://hbr.org/2009/11/why-read-peter-drucker.

understanding, but also possessing and implementing EI—emotional intelligence. Emotional intelligence is being aware that emotions drive our behavior choices and can impact people (positively and negatively) and learning how to manage those emotions—both our own and others—especially when under pressure.

Emotional intelligence is a necessary skill for managers and leaders, since their emotional stability and maturity has a direct effect on the ways people feel and on the depth of team members' and customers' beliefs that the company is a great place to work and a great place to shop and spend money.

At a "great place to work":

- I have the resources and training to do my job with excellence. I am working with a team of qualified people, whom I trust and respect and who trust and respect me.

- We are working toward the achievement of common goals, which gives me pride, satisfaction, and a feeling of personal accomplishment.

AN EXAMPLE OF ENGAGEMENT, USING BOTH EQ AND EI

Every person who works is working to achieve his or her personal income, lifestyle, wealth, and equity goals; a job with a company is a means to this end and not the end in itself. The same is true for customers. Believing this makes managers want to know and care about what each of their team members' personal goals are and how working at the given company will contribute to their accomplishment. Armed with knowledge about their team members' motivations, managers can make sure they and the company do everything possible to provide resources and opportunities for team members to achieve their personal goals. When team members perceive this intent on the part of their manager and the company, it shows the team member that the manager and the company are engaged in their lives. This increases the possibility of the team members reciprocating by being highly engaged with other team members, creating a great place to work, and in creating personalized memorable-moment experiences for customers.

Since it is true that engaged team members create experiences resulting in increased profit and growth from retained, frequent-user customers, it is easy to see why global brands put more and more emphasis on selecting managers who have both a high IQ and EQ.

THE BENEFITS OF ENGAGED TEAM MEMBERS AND ENGAGED TEAMS

It is impossible to overstate the importance an engaged workforce has on the company's growth, profitability, and shareholder value.

When a company looks for its competitive advantages, it needs to look to its workforce, from the C-Level to the frontline and maximize the potential managers have to inspire them to lead and manage the greatest resource of untapped potential—the existing workforce.

The measurable results of a culture of engagement inspire those companies who want to deepen their commitment to continue evolving it. To those who do not have an engaged culture, it must inspire them to evolve whatever they now have until it becomes one.

Here are some of the benefits of an engaged culture:

- unified believing and thinking

- alignment with corporate strategy

- better-quality products

- better experiences for fellow team members
- better feelings among all constituents
- meeting and exceeding goal expectations
- fewer sick days
- lower health-care costs
- decreased training costs
- higher-quality results
- higher team-member retention
- promoting from within
- greater contributions to innovations
- higher receptivity to change
- higher new-customer acquisition
- greater customer retention
- increased customer frequency
- increased average spend per visit
- new customers from referrals of existing customers
- fewer customer complaints
- increased customer trust of the brand
- customers promoting the brand
- a more stable workforce
- greater admiration for the brand
- increases in the number of loyal customers
- higher profitability and shareholder value

We know that the accountability of evolving an existing culture to an engaged culture lies with the C-level of management, but the responsibility to make it happen resides with everyone. Below are statistics that might cause us to wonder what our company might do with these statements. Management 2000's research show the following:

- Seventy-two percent of senior business leaders say the customer experience is the new competitive battleground and is the source of competitive differentiation.

- One hundred percent of senior business leaders said leadership was important.

- However, only 25 percent could give examples of how leadership was reinforcing a customer-experience culture in their businesses.

- Fifteen percent of senior business leaders say their companies are capturing customers' emotional experiences.

- Eighty-eight percent of senior business leaders said they had emotional brand values.

- However, only 45 percent could name them.

- And only 15 percent said they were ensuring their brand values were embedded in their customers' experiences.

- Forty-six percent of management team members and 37 percent of nonmanagement team members know what their company stands for and what makes it different from its competitors.

- Fewer than 50 percent of hotel guests actually felt they were valued during their stay.

- Five percent of consumers say social media influences their buying decisions, and 62 percent say it has no influence—that friends' recommendations, commercials, in-store displays, and even direct mail have more influence than social media.

Engaged team members tend to stay with their current employer at a considerably higher level than those who are disengaged, minimizing the cost of replacing a person.

- Total shareholder return (TSR) increases with increasing team-member engagement. In companies where 60–70 percent are engaged, the average TSR is 24 percent; where 49–60 percent are engaged, the TSR drops to 9.1 percent, and where fewer than 25 percent are engaged, the TSR is negative (www.dofonline.co.uk).

Today the research indicates the "number-one thing driving engagement with team members is their view of what senior management says and does—whether or not management is truly concerned about their well-being. There is a misconception that money is the biggest motivator. In reality, team members are motivated by leaders who *inspire* and demonstrate true commitment to them and the company. The idea certainly contradicts conventional wisdom but proves that companies have a great opportunity to improve engagement levels, beginning with listening to their team members."[81]

---

81 Gary Rhodes and David Whitlark, *Engagement*, ebook.

HOW ENGAGEMENT GOT STARTED: CREATING ENGAGED BRANDS

Edgar Schein, the guru of culture research, defines culture as "a pattern of shared basic assumptions that the group learned as it solved its problems of external adaptation and internal integration, which has worked well enough to be considered valid and therefore, to be taught to new members as the correct way you perceive, think, and feel in relation to those problems." When the business paradigm changed beginning in the 1960s, it meant the traditional "pattern of shared basic assumptions" was being questioned and slowly being replaced by new shared assumptions, such as:

- The reason for the existence of a business is economic performance.

- The purpose of a business is to create a customer.

- The result of a business is a satisfied customer who is committed to returning and recommending the business.

- Everyone is not your customer, so you must know who *your* customers are (various kinds of segmentation), what they value (what are they buying vs. what you are selling), and how *you* can enhance what they value (processes, behaviors, technology).

- Team members need to be involved in decisions affecting them.

- Contribution is the new work ethic.

- People want to work in teams.

- Positive emotions at work are important to job satisfaction.

- Results are more important than activities.

- The difference between good and great is discipline, i.e., having the skills, knowledge, and ability to follow a well-designed process and use technology appropriately to achieve consistent outcomes.

- Personal goals drive business goals, i.e., when the success of a business means personal goals are met or exceeded, it creates a high-performance organization.

- People want to have their strengths developed and utilized.

Through the decades of the sixties, seventies, eighties, and nineties, the likes of Peter Drucker, Walt Disney, Bill Marriott, Thomas Watson, Sr., Tom Peters, Michael Porter, Robert Kaplan, David Norton, Peter Senge, Edgar Schein, Joseph Pine, James Gilmore, Leonard Schlesinger, James Heskett, Earl Sasser, Fred Reichheld, and Dan Hill were teaching a new paradigm for business success. This paradigm was: *Well-trained, well-developed, and well-equipped team members who love doing what they do with quality, executing processes and using technologies designed to enhance what customers value, will create and retain very satisfied, loyal, frequent user, promoter-customers who will drive the profit and growth of a brand.*

The new paradigm emulated the work done by Juran, Deming, ISO, TQM, and Six Sigma, and created Human Sigma. GE is an example of a brand that utilized this paradigm. The experience-profit chain paradigm is illustrated this way:

Overview of the Profit & Growth Process

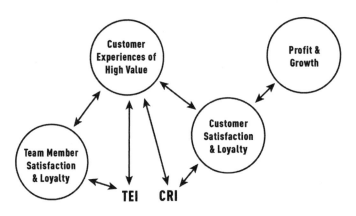

Empowerment, Involvement, Engagement, Collaboration, Communication, Cooperation, Personal Accountability for Results, Measure Team Member and Customer Satisfaction

When you ask a CFO operating under the new paradigm, "If you could only have one metric to tell you the health of the organization, what would it be?" he will more than likely respond along the lines of, "I need more than one, but if I could only have one, it would be *customer retention*. If I could have a second, it would be *frequency of purchase*. A third would be the *lifetime value of the customer*," and so on. This new paradigm took metrics that previously belonged to HR and made them the new predictive analytics of customer-centric brands. But the financial metrics of the past were not completely abandoned. The result was what Harvard called the balanced scorecard (BSC). Below is an illustration of a BSC. These kinds of metrics are the new normal of financial indicators.

THE BALANCED SCORECARD	
TRADITIONAL METRICS	PREDICTIVE ANALYTICS
revenue	new customers
cost of goods sold	customer retention %
labor	satisfaction %
material costs	frequency %
margin	loyalty %
marketing	employee turnover %
research & development	employee satisfaction %
fixed costs	average ticket price

Jan Carlzon, the CEO of Scandinavian Airlines, in his 1987 book, *Moments of Truth*, talked about the real assets of his company being his team members who engaged millions of customers every day in small fifteen-second "moments of truth," which would be "memorable moments" that determine the future success of the airline. He encouraged and trusted his team members to do the right thing and take care of the customers.[82]

Carl Sewel, a very successful Cadillac dealer in Dallas, in his book, *Customers for Life*, implemented one of Peter Drucker's business principles: "Ask customers what they want and give it to them again and again."[83] As more and braver business people implemented this paradigm, its success became well-known as not just isolated phenomena but a tried-and-true new way of doing business. One of the measurements of its success, when implemented over a period of years, is illustrated below for the years 2009–2012.

---

82   Jan Carlzon, *Moments of Truth* (Ballinger Publishing Company, 1987).

83   Carl Sewell and Paul B. Brown, *Customers for Life: How to Turn that One-Time Buyer Into a Lifetime Customer* (Doubleday, 2002).

COMPARISON OF PERFORMANCE						
average for four years	average growth in revenue		average growth in profits		average growth in market value	
	100 Best	S&P 500	100 Best	S&P 500	100 Best	S&P 500
	19.25%	9.25%	116.25%	11.25%	69.5%	22.25%

Christopher W. Hart in his March 2007 *Harvard Business Review* article, "Beating the Market with Customer Satisfaction," noted "the companies with high customer-satisfaction scores have blown the S&P 500 out of the water, especially over the last few years. Not only have they produced higher stock returns, but their stock values and cash flows have been less volatile."[84] These kinds of validations are still the case today. In addition, more and more private-equity funds are using, for their valuations, customer and team-member data as mentioned when discussing the BSC: new customers, new customers and existing customers retained, frequency of visits, satisfaction, loyalty, engagement, team-member engagement, and team-member retention. Management 2000's technology platform, XPERIEN-TRIX™, measures these metrics and delivers the results by location, manager, shift, type of purchase, franchisee, customer segment, etc.

After many years of implementing the new paradigm into Fortune 500 Companies, Heskett, Sasser, and Schlesinger, in their book *The Service Profit Chain*, lay out an integrated way of assessing and then following a detailed set of actions and corporate values designed to change the business paradigms. This change is from a manufacturing mentality that sells stuff to a marketing-and-relationship mentality that establishes inspiring relationships

---

84   Christopher W. Hart, "Beating the Market with Customer Satisfaction," *Harvard Business Review*, March 2007, https://hbr.org/2007/03/beating-the-market-with-customer-satisfaction.

between and among team members and with customers resulting in increased profit and growth. Among these detailed sets of actions is the mandate that *everyone in a company needs to be involved in helping to create positive customer experiences.*[85] Recently, Haskett was asked how difficult it has been for organizations to implement this approach of creating happy customers, who are comfortable and believe they belong to the brand. He replied, "Service-profit chain concepts are deceptively simple. They require an integrated set of management initiatives to achieve. The initiatives have to address team members first, then customers. And they take time."[86] He went on to say the hardest challenge is to change the assumptions that are the foundation of the existing culture and ask if these beliefs, values, behaviors, and processes reinforce service-profit chain relationships. Often they do not.

And it is hard to let existing paradigms go because we "don't really understand the new paradigms," or we know what is wrong with today's paradigms, but we do not know the devil in the new ones, and there is also the frustration of the time it takes to transition from the old to the new.

Heskett continues, "The difficult decisions include having to let go of people who, for whatever reason, are not managing by the new beliefs, values, behaviors, and processes. That is a difficult step for many organizations to take."[87] But it must be taken because for team members to be emotionally engaged and inspired, they must be supported by managers who lead by example and provide behaviors

---

85   James Heskett, Earl Sasser, and Leonard Schlesinger, *The Service Profit Chain* (New York: The Free Press, 1997).

86   Sean Silverthorne, *The New Math of Customer Relationships,* Harvard Business School, 2008.

87   James Heskett, Earl Sasser, and Leonard Schlesinger, *The Service Profit Chain* (New York: The Free Press, 1997).

consistent with the beliefs and value of a team member- and customer-centric culture. When this happens, team members become highly engaged, and a great place to work is created and sustained.

> • "84 percent of highly engaged team members believe they can impact the quality of their company's work product, compared with 31 percent of disengaged."
>
> • "72 percent of the highly engaged believe they can impact customer service, versus 27 percent of the disengaged."
>
> • "68 percent of the highly engaged believe they can impact costs in their job or unit, versus 19 percent of the disengaged."[88]

MANAGING YOURSELF TO ENGAGE TEAM MEMBERS

What would the impact on the climate of your organization be if each of your managers made the following pledge to their team members?

A MANAGER'S PLEDGE TO HIS OR HER TEAM MEMBERS

I pledge:

1. To set the right example for you by my own actions in all things.

2. To be consistent in my temperament so you know how to "read" me and what to expect from me.

---

88 "Towers Perrin Study Shows Less Than 1 In 5 Canadians Are Highly Engaged at Work," Insurance Canada, November 15, 2005, http://www.insurance-canada.ca/humanares/canada/Towers-Perrin-Workforce-511.php.

3. To learn what personal goals you each have that are motivating you to work here.

4. To involve you and get your opinions and recommendations on decisions affecting you.

5. To learn your personal and work-related strengths as well as the tragedies and triumphs of your lives—on an ongoing basis.

6. To be fair, impartial, and consistent in matters relating to work rules, discipline, and rewards.

7. To show a sincere, personal interest in each of you without becoming overly "familiar."

8. To seek your counsel on matters that affect your jobs and to be guided as much as possible by your judgment.

9. To allow you as much individuality as possible in the way your jobs are performed and in the ways you inject your unique personality into providing memorable moments for customers, as long as the quality of the end result is not comprised.

10. To make sure you always know in advance what I expect from you in the ways of conduct and performance on the job.

11. To be appreciative of your efforts, to demonstrate gratitude for your contributions, and to be generous in praise of your accomplishments.

12. To use every opportunity to teach you how to do your job better and help you advance in skill level, responsibility, and accountability.

13. To show you I can "do" as well as "manage," by pitching in to work beside you when my help is needed.

14. To help and support you in advancing your career.

Do you think having this pledge in place would change the ways managers currently behave? Do you believe these behaviors would result in higher levels of team-member engagement, profit, and growth?

HOW COMPANIES MEASURE TEAM-MEMBER ENGAGEMENT

Management 2000, with its technology platform called XPERIEN-TRIX™, measures the following engagement themes:

- pride in the company
- satisfaction with the company
- job, role, and function satisfaction
- feeling of fulfillment from having personal goals met
- opportunity to perform well in challenging circumstances
- recognition and positive feedback for results achieved
- personal support from management
- performance beyond expectation
- understanding of how one's job, role, and function is linked to the company's mission and brand promise
- opportunities for personal growth and increases in accountability and compensation
- depth of belief in staying related with the company for a long time

- ability to contribute to change and innovation

QUANTITATIVE CUSTOMER EXPERIENCE METRICS ARE NOT ENOUGH

Qualitative research can reveal how customers feel and what the company needs to stop, start, keep, change, and improve in its beliefs, behaviors, processes, and technology to create experiences for customers resulting in their becoming lifetime, promoter-customers.

This research can help companies determine which touch points have the most emotional significance. An example is the amount of time it takes to process your credit card for payment at a restaurant after the meal is over. This single touch point can turn a nine-out-of-ten experience into a five.

The touch points that carry the most emotional significance are called "moments of truth." Moments of truth are great opportunities for team members to create memorable moments and significant memories with customers. This will only happen if the team members realize the *why* of the way they are asked to behave and if they emotionally commit to making sure they create the why for the customer.

A client of Management 2000's in the quick-lube automotive aftermarket industry has some interesting data:

- Eighty-five percent of their oil-change customers were women, primarily single.

- Focus groups of women revealed they felt high negative emotions when they were approached by the male attendant, clip board in hand, to take information regarding their oil change.

- The women felt the man was taking the opportunity to look at their breasts and legs as he stood next to their open car window.

- This left them unhappy, uncomfortable, and angry, and no longer a customer for an oil change.

The results of this feedback were the following:

- A new process was implemented: this included the male attendant kneeling down next to the customer's open window to take the information regarding the servicing of her car.

- The focus groups also provided feedback regarding what the tangibles and ambiance of the waiting and reception areas should have in them to make women feel happy, comfortable, and like they belonged.

- The training-and-development program for corporate and franchisee managers and team members included sensitivity training, as well as do-and-don't behaviors regarding age, sex, diversity, etc.

Without the focus groups, we would not have been able to distinguish between feedback on the experience and feedback on what was *remembered* about the experience. Nobel Prize winner Daniel Kahneman, a leading pioneer in behavioral economics, explains the power of memory this way: Each person perceives reality from two different and sometimes competing perspectives—the *experiencing self* and the *remembering self*. The *experiencing self* is present at every touch point throughout the customer experience, but the *remembering self* takes inventory of the emotional significance of each touch point and ultimately decides which memories to keep. We want the "remembering selves" of our customers to be kept in the forefront of our frontline, engaging team members so our customers remember pleasant emotions.[89]

FINDING THE MOMENTS THAT MATTER

Management 2000's team-member, franchisee, and customer-quantitative experience platforms collect data at every touch point.

They cannot differentiate which moments are the most memorable and which matter most to team members, franchisees, and customers. Obviously, some moments will matter far more than others. By combining quantitative analytics with qualitative data collection and analysis, Management 2000 helps its clients explore which team member, franchisee, and customer touch points carry the most emotional significance—and which are the most likely to build team-member, franchisee, and customer engagement. Once these are identified, training and development can focus on how team members can inject their personalities into making those moments memorable for the customers.

One of the global brands in casual dining asked Management 2000 to analyze its restaurant guest behavior to determine the touch points that had the greatest impact on customer engagement. Management 2000 used qualitative and quantitative research methods to study guests and carefully observe their behavior across every customer touch point. This qualitative research determined that customers experienced seventy-seven touch points with the brand before, during, and after a typical dining occasion. After further analysis, Management 2000's predictive analytics boiled these down

---

89   John Timmerman and Ilana Ron Levey, "Quantitative Customer Experience Metrics Aren't Enough," Gallup, September 4, 2015, http://www.gallup.com/businessjournal/185345/quantitative-customer-experience-metrics-aren-enough.aspx.

to the eleven "moments-of-truth" touch points, which contributed to guests' most vivid memories—the key drivers that had the strongest influence on customers' emotional engagement with the company.

Identifying the key drivers didn't mean the company and its team members could ignore the other sixty-six touch points just because failure to deliver at one or more of these touch points would not likely disengage a guest. However, focusing on the "moments of truth" would yield a marginal return on investment compared with focusing on the key engagement drivers.

So team members were selected, oriented, trained, and developed in how to behave while implementing the processes designed to enhance these "moments of truth" for the guests. Quantitative measures tracked their success with guests, and this success was correlated to guest retention, frequency, and average ticket. We also tracked the team members' satisfaction, loyalty, retention, etc. With this system of both qualitative and quantitative measurement and validation in place, together with root-cause analysis to determine what needed to be improved in the beliefs and behaviors of team members—as well as what changes needed to be made to the processes and technology—managers improved their abilities to engage their team members, and team members improved their abilities to turn "moments of truth" into memorable moments for the guests. The restaurants increased their economic performance.

TEAM-MEMBER AND CUSTOMER WELL-BEING AFFECTS ENGAGEMENT

Much research has been written regarding the positive effect that team member well-being has on creating the real perception that the company is being loyal to them first. Some examples include

- providing health-care programs to part-time and full-time lower-wage team members;

- having a zero-tolerance workplace-violence policy;

- flexible work hours;

- telecommuting;

- workout facilities; and

- child care.

THE KEY DRIVERS OF INSPIRING THE ENGAGEMENT OF YOUR TEAM MEMBERS

- The brand has a mission and purpose that each person believes in and can directly contribute to being accomplished.

- Each person has at least one personal goal that is dependent on his or her job success for its being achieved.

- All people understand their duties and responsibilities and what is expected of them at work.

- Each person has the opportunity to learn and grow.

- Each person can manage his or her time and duties.

- Everyone is held accountable for his or her behaviors.

- People treat one another with respect and dignity.

- People can rely on what they are told at work.

- Individuals can provide input and believe that their input counts.

- The work environment is friendly.

- Fellow team members complete each other's work.

- Individuals and teams have periodic performance reviews.

- Having friends at work is encouraged.

- People enjoy what they do.

- Career advancement is available for those who want it.

- There is no discrimination in the workplace.

- People trust their managers.

- The workplace is safe and free from any and all physical, emotional, or psychological intimidation or violence of any kind.

EMBEDDING MECHANISMS DRIVE INSPIRATION

Noted psychologist Edgar Schein identified five primary mechanisms and five secondary mechanisms by which leaders change cultures.

PRIMARY EMBEDDING MECHANISMS

These are the five main ways by which leaders effect cultural change through their visible actions.

1. **Attention**

   The values, beliefs, priorities, and so on of the leader appear in where they place their attention. Followers look at what the leader is looking at and pay close attention to his or her emotions. When a leader gets particularly passionate or annoyed, then followers assume that the subject being attended to is important.

2. **Reactions to crises**

In a crisis, people's deeper values are exposed, whether they go into self-preservation mode or gallantly seek to help others first. The higher level of emotion in crises also means that we will remember what happens then more than at other times.

The result is that in a crisis, the leader's actions will be both remembered and also taken to be a truer example of who he or she really is.

3. **Role modeling**

People listen to the leader, and they watch carefully what he or she does. When there is a conflict between these, they will believe the leader's actions before his or her words. People also assume the behavior of the leader is what is right and will hence emulate him or her. How a leader behaves is how his or her followers will tend to behave.

4. **Allocation of rewards**

Rewards, from praise to promotion, are assumed to reflect desired behavior *as well as* desired results. If a cultural change to more collaborative behavior is desired, and someone gets a bonus for achieving an outstanding result through using selfish behavior, then it will be assumed that selfish behavior is okay. To change the culture, it would be necessary for that person to be censured, not rewarded, for his or her selfish behavior.

5. **Criteria for selection and dismissal**

Recruitment, promotion, and dismissal are all critical for choosing who does what and also the forms of reward and punishment. The criteria used should consider the style and personality as well as the technical competence of the person involved. In this way, the cultural aspects of the organization may be included in the selection-and-dismissal processes.

SECONDARY EMBEDDING MECHANISMS

These are the five secondary methods by which a leader may indirectly change the culture:

1. **Design of Organizational Structure**

"Function follows form" is a common saying and applies here. It has also been said, "First we create our organizations, and then they create us." The hierarchical shape of any organization will have a subtle effect on how it operates. Thus, to change the organization, changing its structure can be highly effective.

2. **Design of Systems and Procedures**

The systems by which an organization is run have a wide effect on how people think. These include budgeting, information systems, performance reviews, and management-development activities. Deliberate design of these can ensure alignment with desired cultural directions.

3. **Design of Facilities**

    The layout of offices often subconsciously reflects the values of an organization, both in terms of who sits near whom and also in the differentiation in benefits that individuals are given. More space, thicker carpets, window seats, bigger desks, and so on are all symbols of superiority. In some traditional organizations, these are chosen very carefully, according to management grade. In other companies, everyone has the same size cubicle with very little differentiation between management levels.

4. **Stories, Legends, and Myths**

    The stories that people tell and retell in organizations typically reflect the values and beliefs of the culture. Hence, changing the stories will tend to change the culture. This is particularly powerful as it is spread at the individual level, and hence has grassroots support and credibility.

5. **Formal Statements**

    Formal statements by the organization, although not always as credible as grassroots whisperings, are the public face of the organization, and hence demand attention. They also may later form the basis of formal arguments and actions, from decisions around allocation of resource to discipline and dismissal.

EXAMPLES OF EMBEDDING MECHANISMS THAT MANAGEMENT 2000'S CLIENTS HAVE USED TO REINFORCE MISSION, VISION, PURPOSE, AND CORE VALUES

First Example: Each payday, the manager of a team meets individually with each team member and goes through the following process:

- Manager says: Good morning Mary. As you know, today is payday and I would like you to tell me what our mission is, please.

- Mary responds: I'd love to. Our mission is "To create a friendly, inspiring shopping experience for our customers, resulting in their saying, 'I'll be back.'"

- Manager says: Thanks Mary. Will you share with me one or two times during the last pay period when you faced challenges to comply with, but you found a way?

- Mary says: I'd be glad to. (She tells the one or two examples and why it made her proud.)

- Manager says: Mary, I want to ask you, of your many strengths, which ones make those situations successful?

- Mary responds: Well I believe the strengths I used were _____ (Mary names her strengths.)

- Manager says: I agree those are definitely some of your strengths. In addition, I believe you used your _____ (manager inserts additional strengths and continues), all of which make you a very valuable team member.

- Manager continues: Today you are receiving your share of the customers' money, which we have because you and the rest of our team members create such great, inspiring shopping experiences that make customers come back again and again. Thank you very much.

Second Example: Begin *every* meeting of two or more people with the recitation of the mission statement or purpose. E.g., "To create a friendly, inspiring, shopping experience for our customers resulting in their saying, 'I'll be back.'" Then discuss recommendations and decisions, made with the mission, purpose, vision, and core values as guidelines. This primary embedding mechanism is repeated every payday, and it motivates team members to live the mission more intensely, so they will have incidents to share on payday for which they are proud. This embedding mechanism creates memorable moments and makes for more engaged team members who will inspire customers.

Third Example: Each team member, or the team as a whole, decides at the beginning of each month which core value each will work on individually and as a team to live more mindfully. Agreement is reached for each member to compliment others when they notice examples of the core value being lived—and for when the core value is not being lived, to have a discussion as a team. At the end-of-the-month meeting, the team provides progress on living the core value, and a new core value is chosen. This embedding mechanism creates memorable moments and makes for more engaged team members who will inspire one another and customers.

Fourth Example: When prospective team members are being interviewed, make the first question: "As a member of our team, what do you think you will be paid for?" (The answer is the mission and purpose) If the interviewee misses the answer, provide a card with the mission and purpose on it, and ask him or her to spend a few minutes memorizing them. Then resume the interview with the same question: "As a member of our team, what do you think you will be paid for?" This embeds the mission and purpose within the emotional psyche of the person, and he or she will not forget either—thereby creating a memorable moment.

Fifth Example: New team members wear either a T-shirt or a button that says: "Ask me what I am paid for." When a customer asks the inevitable question, the new team member says: "To create a friendly, inspiring, shopping experience for *you* today—resulting in you saying, 'I'll be back!' Now, how can I do that for you today?" This embedding mechanism creates memorable moments for both the team member and the customer. It also communicates that more than the purchase is the reason for being a customer, and it reinforces the importance of living the mission with every customer within the emotional psyche of each team member.

Sixth Example: The new team-member training is called "creating inspiring experiences," and the CEO always "drops in unexpectedly" and asks team members in training to recite the mission and purpose statements and tell why they are important. The CEO is provided with something personal to say about each person in the training class. This embedding mechanism will definitely create a memorable moment for the new team members, and it will make them more engaged.

Seventh Example: During the initial interview process, potential team members are asked which personal goals are linked to being employed with your company. This embedding mechanism is linked to something said earlier in this chapter: every person who works is working to achieve his or her personal income, lifestyle, wealth, and equity goals, and a job with a company is a means to this end and the end in itself.

Eighth Example: Have each manager commit to giving twenty genuinely deserved compliments every day when they observe achievements reflecting the use of a person's strengths or the living of the mission and purpose. This embedding mechanism provides team members with something they value and that creates engagement: recognition.

Ninth Example: Have all new and existing team members make their strengths more productive by listing a minimum of ten of their personal strengths, then having them categorize each according to how they are used. (For instance, those strengths that make me a better (1) team member, (2) spouse/significant other, (3) parent, (4) citizen, (5) person, etc. . . .)

Also, have each person lists the work-related strengths that, if developed, would make him or her more valuable to the company and to the customers. The manager can be collaborative in this process and give feedback. It will let the team members know the manager cares. And, it will build the self-esteem and confidence within the team members that will in turn create engagement.

Tenth Example: The manager asks his or her team members for feedback on what the manager needs to stop, start, keep, improve, and change in order to become more effective at creating a great place to work for each team member. This embedding mechanism will demonstrate vulnerability, listening, and a willingness and readiness to change. It will create memorable moments for each person, and it will create the same vulnerability within each team member.

Eleventh Example: Managers *must* know each individual, i.e., married, single, living with others, have children, parents dead or alive, tragedies he or she may have they lived through (or are living through), greatest accomplishments (and disappointments), and what sad and glad personal events are going on. Managers *must* celebrate the glad and have empathy for the sad.

USING PREDICTIVE ANALYTICS TO DRIVE LIFETIME VALUE OF TEAM MEMBERS AND CUSTOMERS

Management 2000's technology platform, XPERIENTRIX™, can measure

- if team members see opportunities;

- if they have their personal goals met by working for a company;

- if they have confidence in the future of the company;

- if they are as productive as they could be; and

- if they intend to stay with the company.

We can measure

- if franchisees are proud to be associated with your brand;

- if being associated with us helps achieve their goals; and

- if they believe they would recommend you to other potential franchisees.

When we know these metrics, it is like stepping on a bathroom scale and looking down to see a number. That number is the result of measurable key performance indicators, reflecting if people are living the brand's beliefs, behaving correctly, following processes, and using technologies correctly.

DO REWARDS AND LOYALTY PROGRAMS
TRANSLATE INTO CUSTOMER ENGAGEMENT?

The answer is a qualified yes—and a qualified no. Loyalty programs can be correlated to frequency of purchase, but not to the depth of commitment the customers who are using the loyalty program have to the brand.

The loyalty created by customer-engagement measurements needs to be correlated with those customers using the loyalty program to determine if the most engaged and emotionally committed customers are also the most frequent users of the loyalty program. If they are not, other strategies can be put in place to show recognition, appreciation, and gratitude to them for their commitment to the brand.

But these two do not often come together. What bonds us to a brand are the memorable moments and emotional experiences we have with team members (Nordstrom), with the products (Apple), and with the websites (Amazon). When a customer is bonded to the brand because of the reward points they receive, it is most likely because they have had an emotionally satisfying and personally enjoyable experience for which they are accruing points which they will eventually redeem. Their personal goals drive their business decision to go with a particular brand. The broader and more varied the use of points, the more consumers will be attracted to that loyalty program. Loyalty is really the emotional satisfaction customers get when they redeem their points and have their experience.

Consumers are aware of the fact that if companies did not *have* to offer a rewards program, they probably would not. The true key to winning the minds and hearts of customers is to ensure that each and every customer's experience includes at least one memorable moment and that the other parts of the experience are delivered flawlessly.

Customers remember memorable moments, not how many points they earned. Loyalty programs designed to create new customers, retain existing customers, and build frequency with customers will be successful at building real loyalty. On the other hand, when customers are loyal to the loyalty program and not the brand, the company will benefit from their loyalty program until a better competitive alternative comes along.

For more on this topic, study the *2015 Bond Brand Loyalty Report.*[90]

STEPS TO IMPROVE TEAM MEMBER AND CUSTOMER ENGAGEMENT

1. **Assess the current culture** to establish baseline data for measuring to what extent your company is a great place to work and a great place to shop and spend money. Segment team members and customers into engaged, passive, and disengaged categories.

2. **Analyze the current key influencers.**

   □ **The philosophy of the company:** What do various people and departments believe regarding people, promotions, compensation, diversity, opportunity, customers, suppliers, the brand, departments, senior management, etc.? How is the company philosophy conveyed and embedded?

   □ **The processes:** Are they documented, and are people who implement them trained enough to have mastered their delivery? Are processes designed to enhance what customers value? Are team members selected and

---

90 *2015 Bond Brand Loyalty Report,* Bond Brand Loyalty, http://info.bondbrandloyalty.com/the-loyalty-report-2015.

onboarded with an awareness and commitment to knowing "what they are paid for"?

▫ **The behaviors:** Are "behavior dos" and "behavior don'ts" clearly defined for situations between and among team members and with customers to create optimal experiences and memorable moments for all?

3. **Establish a plan and ROI for the project.** A multiunit retail chain with five hundred locations developed a forecast which demonstrated that if both team member and customer experiences were improved by 10 percent, 2015 vs. 2016, in six key result areas (new customers, new and existing customers retained, total number of customers, average number of visits, and average spent per visit) the return on investment (ROI) would be significant and definitely worth the effort.

4. **Involve a representative number of team members** who are high influencers / early adopters, and high influencers / high resisters, to work on a task force to beta test the changes and measure the results to validate the value of changing the culture.

5. **Design an algorithm to produce predictive analytics.** I.e., if the team-member and customer-engagement metrics changed by 10 percent and customer retention improved by 10 percent, and customer frequency improved by 10 percent, and the average spend improved by 10 percent, and team-member retention and satisfaction both improved by 10 percent, what would be the impact on the company?

6. **Implement the beta test.**

7. **Implement system wide:** measure, analyze, evaluate, improve, implement, repeat.

8. **Involve everyone in decisions that affect them.** Involvement leads to intellectual understanding, intellectual understanding leads to emotional buy-in, emotional buy-in leads to implementation, and implementation of changes leads to improved results.

GALLUP RESEARCH FROM 2008–2014: "STATE OF THE AMERICAN CONSUMER" (COMPRISING TWENTY-FIVE MILLION COMPLETED TEAM-MEMBER SURVEYS)

The single biggest decision that companies make that is validated by Gallup's research and not taught in business school is whom you select as mangers. Nothing fixes the bad decision of selecting the wrong manager—not compensation, not benefits, nothing. The toxicity it creates lasts longer than one can ever imagine. From Gallup Research:

- **Great Managers** produce engaged, inspired team members who create great experiences and magic, memorable moments for customers.

  □ Of the approximately one hundred million people in America who hold full-time jobs, thirty million (30 percent) are engaged and inspired at work, so we can assume they have a great boss.

- **Poor Managers** produce disengaged team members who create horrible experiences and hellish moments for customers.

  □ Twenty million (20 percent) team members are actively disengaged. These team members, who have bosses from hell that make them miserable, roam the halls spreading discontent.

- **Mediocre Managers** produce unenthusiastic, mediocre team members who create bland commodity experiences for customers.[91]

THE VARIABLES MANAGEMENT CONTROLS THAT CREATE A "GREAT PLACE TO WORK" AND HAVE A DIRECT IMPACT ON THE CUSTOMERS' EXPERIENCES

- who are appointed managers

- the processes

- the technology

- the embedding mechanisms

- the reward for performance

- behaviors that are highly valued and highly rewarded

- team-member mastery of the skills, knowledge, and abilities required for excellent performance

- how people are lead

---

91 "State of the American Consumer Report," Gallup, http://products.gallup.com/171722/state-american-consumer.aspx.

- the internalization of the brand's mission, core values, vision, positioning, and promise

- team-member recognition

- the identification and utilization of individual team members' strengths

- knowing who your customers are, what they value, and how you can enhance what they value

- an understanding of human behavior and the emotional connections that create full team-member and customer engagement and drive motivation, performance, and business outcomes

WHY DO TEAM-MEMBER AND CUSTOMER ENGAGEMENT MATTER?

Engaged customers tend to be loyal customers for life. If you have one hundred thousand loyal, engaged customers who are your customers for a lifetime and recommend you to others, they are of more economic value to you than one hundred thousand customers who do business with you for one year and then stop.

We have a client company with forty-five million customers in its database, with an average of two and a half transactions per year, and each transaction is worth $9.00. Retention and frequency are their most important metrics. Increasing the average two and a half transactions to three, with no change in the $9.00, would yield additional revenue of $202,500,000. Since this client is a franchisee with a 5.5 percent royalty, the additional royalty to the franchisor would be $10,125,000. With all of this information, you can calculate the lifetime value of these customers.

WHAT CAN BE DONE TO DRIVE TEAM-MEMBER ENGAGEMENT?

Develop a selection and onboarding process focused on the following areas:

1. Everyone knows what outcome they are paid to produce—knowledge that should be embedded in their behaviors, i.e., maintaining loyal, frequent users, and promoter-customers. (The mission: "To do what I do so well that they will want to return and bring their friends.")

2. Each team member has a personal goal that is dependent on his or her work goals being accomplished.

3. Each team member knows and understands the why of his or her job and how to convey the why in his or her behaviors. (The brand's purpose: to create "The Happiest Place on Earth.")

4. Each team member knows how he or she needs to behave in order to contribute to the why. (They use the uniqueness of their personalities to create magic moments for customers.)

5. Ensure that each team member has mastered the skills, knowledge, and abilities required to implement the processes and use the technology to create the magic moments.

6. Encourage and expect team members to see themselves as actors in a play delivering encore experiences for each customer.

7. Have team members consciously create memorable moments for their fellow team members as well as for each customer.

WHAT CAN BE DONE TO DRIVE CUSTOMER ENGAGEMENT?

1. Develop a strong brand mission and promise, expecting each team member to live it between and among one another and with customers in everything said and done.

2. Deliver great individualized customer experiences by consistently implementing the processes and using the technology correctly, thereby increasing customer engagement.

3. Increase customer engagement by designing processes and behaviors for each touch point within the customer's journey to enhance what you know your customers value, and convey consistent messaging and perceptions about the brand's promise.

4. Choose to measure the metrics that matter in the twenty-first century. And, once again, the two financial metrics that matter the most are (1) customer retention and (2) customer frequency.

5. Measure emotion. Historically, if someone had negative feelings, especially if you were a male, those feelings were easily dismissed with a statement along the lines of, "He will get over it." Today, we know customers do repeat business with a brand believing they will get a great experience the next time.

WHAT MANAGEMENT 2000 MEASURES FOR OUR CLIENTS:

-   Management 2000's customer recommendation index (CRI) tracks how the customers feel at the moment of a particular experience. This is very important for analyzing changes or improvements needing to be made to team-member behaviors or to the processes and technology used when creating customer experiences.

- Management 2000's customer belief index (CBI) tracks the "depth of belief" customers have regarding whether or not future experiences will be excellent and emotionally gratifying. These beliefs reflect the depth of the customer engagement reflected in their behaviors.

- Management 2000 has a franchisee engagement index (FEI) and a franchisee belief index (FBI) to help validate, for prospective new franchisees, the worth, value, and depth of validation existing franchisees will demonstrate to candidates deciding to join a company.

- Management 2000 also has a team-member engagement index (TEI) and a team-member belief index (TBI) to measure employee perception of the company as a great place to work and the degree to which they believe the company will continue to improve as such.

The CBI score is one of the most reliable predictive analytics providing the most valid correlation to future growth, revenue, profits, and shareholder value.

CUSTOMER AND TEAM-MEMBER ENGAGEMENT DRIVE FINANCIAL PERFORMANCE

Gallup and Management 2000 have found that fully engaged team members do a better job at creating fully engaged customers. Well-trained and committed team members who live the brand's beliefs in their behaviors with one another and with customers—while at the same time implementing the processes and using the technology comprising the customer experiences—will engage customers in the creation of magic moments. This makes the customers feel happy, comfortable, like they belong to the brand, and committed to returning and recommending the brand to their sphere of influence.

The measurement of these emotional and psychological attachments to the brand and its products—the CBI—are definite, reliable, and predicative analytics.

It needs to be noted that both the CEI and CBI scores can measure different shifts, different managers, different franchisees, area supervisors, field consultants, stores of different configurations, various segmentations of customers, etc.

Correlations can be made showing that the highly engaged managers and team members have higher customer retention and frequency of purchase rates than highly disengaged team members.

- Highly engaged customers of casual dining chains make 56 percent more visits per month than actively disengaged customers.

- Fully engaged hotel guests spend 46 percent more per year than actively disengaged customers.

- Fully engaged bank customers bring 37 percent more revenue to their bank than the actively disengaged customers.

Brand alignment and brand engagement is accomplished by:

- making *everything* people believe, think, do, and achieve related to the enhancement of the brand;

- embedding the belief with each team member that they are the brand;

- having team members know and understand the brand promise and the brand positioning;

- involving and engaging each team member in discussions regarding how they can influence enhancing the brand;

- ensuring the brand creates feelings of pride and respect within team members because of what the brand does for customers, team members, and society;

- empowering team members with the resources and permission to make decisions regarding protecting and delivering the brand promise in difficult and unusual circumstances;

- including an understanding of the brand promise in the selection and orientation and onboarding process of new team members;

- ensuring team members can see and believe they have an impact on customers' perception of and commitment to the brand;

- recognizing the team members who have the customer-facing roles when measurements show they are achieving the goal of creating and retaining engaged customers;

- regularly involving all team members in coming up with new and better ways to live the brand promise and the brand positioning between and among one another and with the customers; and

- internally publishing the measurement numbers when they reflect either an increase or a decrease in fully engaged customers, and involving the team members in the root-cause analysis of what changes need to be made to team-member behaviors, processes, or technology to stop negative trends or to increase the number and frequency of fully engaged customers.

CONCLUSION

Management 2000's clients are not those of McKinsey, Accenture, The Boston Consulting Group, and Bain—but we have great admiration for and spend lots of time studying their philosophies, theories, processes, programs, and practices. Management 2000 made a commitment when we began to help apply state-of-the-art business practices and the most traditional, solid, avant-garde, cutting edge, business-thinking practices and behaviors to the small- and medium-sized companies that make up the 1,450 brands on our client list. If you have questions or would like to discuss anything in this chapter, please contact us and let's discuss how we might help you become a "great place to work" for your team members and a "great place for your customers to shop and spend money."

Bob's background and experience has been in organizational development and design with a focus on building customer-centric brands and on strategic and organizational planning.

Bob graduated from Saint John's University in Collegeville, MN, with graduate work in German existential systematic theology. His career began as a college professor at Saint Leo College in Dade City, FL, where he served as president of the faculty and on the tenure and curriculum committees.

After years in education, Bob joined Batten, Batten, Hudson & Swab, a management-consulting company whose clients were primarily Fortune 1000 companies. He led a team of consultants who conducted hundreds of seminars all over the United States and was responsible for all marketing.

In 1981, Bob founded Management 2000 and has been its CEO since. His dedication to the franchise-business strategy has been very strong over the years. Bob has served as the director of education for the International Franchise Association (IFA) and served on the committee that created the certification program for franchise executives, called "The Certified Franchise Executive" (CFE). He's also worked closely with the Canadian Franchise Association over the years.

Bob has written several articles on franchising that are included in publications by Andrew Sherman; The IFA's *ICFE Study Guide for Franchise Executives*; and many more.

Bob has been involved in several franchise concepts, bringing to Management 2000 clients a perspective of the franchisee in addition to his other franchise expertise.[92]

---

92 "Robert Gappa, CFE," https://www.linkedin.com/in/robert-gappa-cfe-62aa6310.

CHAPTER 13

THIRTY THINGS YOU CAN IMPLEMENT NOW TO FOSTER, INSPIRE, AND SUSTAIN ENGAGEMENT

"The basic philosophy, spirit, and drive of an organization have far more to do with its relative achievements than do technological or economic resources, organizational structure, innovation, and timing. All of these variables weigh heavily in success. But they are, I think, transcended by how strongly the people in the organization believe in the basic precepts and how faithfully they carry them out."

—THOMAS WATSON JR., FORMER CEO, IBM

"Train people well enough so they can leave, treat them well enough so they don't want to."

—RICHARD BRANSON, FOUNDER AND CHAIRMAN, VIRGIN ATLANTIC

All of the ping-pong tables and free-bagel Fridays in the world will not inspire or engage an already disengaged, burnt-out, rudderless culture. People want and need to be led—to be part of something larger than themselves, and to be aligned with the core values and goals that are articulated by the leaders of the enterprise.[93] You can build a great team on paper, but until it performs, it means nothing. Just look at the preseason predictions for the Washington Nationals and Washington Capitals in 2015. People are hungry for transparency and candor, even if they disagree with what you say. Study after study proves that most of society wants to work for "something more" than a paycheck—but what exactly is that intangible known as "something more?" Is it so complex that it cannot be defined or achieved? Or is it so elusive that we spend our lives looking for it, thereby explaining the lack of loyalty and extensive turnover that so many companies face? Or are these turnover rates the "new normal," as we have become a more mobile, faster-moving, "me-driven" society? Clearly, to recruit, retain, and reward great people for the sustainable long term, company leaders *must* foster and sustain a culture of engagement. Companies must commit to having an engaged culture—as Southwest Airlines has committed to an enjoyable employee-centered atmosphere, or as Facebook and Google have emphasized an innovative culture.

---

93   Anthonia Akitunde, "Open-Office Backlash: Seeking Productivity in a Noisy World," March 28, 2014, https://www.americanexpress.com/us/small-business/openforum/articles/open-office-backlash-seeking-productivity-in-a-noisy-world/.

Best practices may vary from region to region, from industry to industry, and even from company to company, but here are thirty things you can do now to foster engagement and inspire your team:

1. TEAR DOWN THE WALLS BETWEEN PEOPLE, IDEAS, AND COLLABORATION

The Mars family never believed in corner offices standing in the way of a collaborative culture. On the reverse side, at New York City-based branding firm Collins, founder Brian Collins advocated against having an open-office plan. The thought of open-office plans without walls, cubicles, and other physical barriers has been dubbed a "polarizing phenomenon" with advocates arguing that the lack of isolation fosters community and collectivity—while opponents assert it is nothing more than a way for companies to save immense amounts of money under the veneer of creative development. Thought needs to be given to the way office space is laid out. Even though the theory of open-plan offices is easy to understand, the mechanics of how the space is designed and identification of teams that work together are critical.[94]

2. TEAR DOWN THE BARRIERS FOR AIRING GRIPES/GIVING AND RECEIVING FEEDBACK

If you work in a big company, chances are you are getting more feedback lately—whether you know it or not.

Recent revelations about Amazon's competitive work culture described a company-feedback system in which employees sent gripes to coworkers' bosses about their performance, sometimes without

---

94   Rebecca Greenfield, "Here Is an Open Office Any Employee Would Love," Fast Company, March 17, 2015, http://www.fastcompany.com/3043545/most-creative-people/here-is-an-open-office-any-employee-would-love.

the coworkers' knowledge. Invoking a workplace version of *Lord of the Flies*, workers said that some people used the tool, called *Anytime Feedback*, to gang up on rivals or oust low performers. The retailer's system may strike some as harsh, but peer reviewing has been in offices for a while, allowing coworkers and managers to weigh in on one another's performance.

Some companies have found innovative ways to allow employees to *anonymously* give feedback on the workplace environment. A Canadian restaurant chain, Earls, has modernized employee satisfaction and engagement surveys, moving from a more traditional annual employee survey to utilizing an anonymous app with a short survey to employee's mobile devices every three months.[95] This has actually led the management to focus more critically on employees' engagement. Hard talk is necessary talk in this situation, and if fueled by candor and transparency, you'll be able to clearly identify the problem, which puts you halfway to the solution.

Troubles can arise when employers lack a plan of action after employees learn more about their performance reviews, said Mr. Stewart, a former HR director at Ticketmaster and a vice president at Cornerstone. "Employees are receptive to the feedback, but when they go to look for training, resources, or mentoring, they are not there," he said. "That tends to defeat the purpose and create a negative sort of environment."[96] Unsolicited positive reviews motivate employees, but negative comments by workers rarely improve performance, since managers perceive it as "noise" and "whining," said Jason Averbook, a

---

95   "Apps Tell Boss What Workers Really Think," *Wall Street Journal Asia*, June 23, 2015, http://www.pressreader.com/china/ the-wall-street-journal-asia/20150623/281994671132194.

96   Lauren Webber and Rachel Emma Silverman, "Workers Get New Tools for Airing Their Gripes," *The Wall Street Journal*, August 25, 2015, http://www.wsj.com/articles/ workers-get-new-tools-for-airing-their-gripes-1440545279.

former workforce-technology consultant and now chief executive of TMBC, a firm that advises companies on managing performance.[97]

Other challenges arise when employees can covertly sound off to a colleague's boss, as noted in a *New York Times* story about Amazon in September 2015. Workers may rightly fear that their colleagues are stabbing them in the back or bringing up petty complaints, said Mr. Averbook. When that happens regularly, it indicates "a culture that's kind of childish and competitive," said Patty McCord, the former chief talent officer at Netflix Inc., a company that experimented with many types of feedback processes during her tenure.[98]

She helped craft a set of values for the company; one behavior aligned to those values was "You only say things about fellow employees you will say to their face."

> *Even when managers put such guidelines in place, criticisms are often leveled without any evidence, said Bruce Elliott, manager of compensation and benefits at the Society for Human Resource Management. As an HR executive in previous jobs, he found himself "going down rabbit holes to try to figure out the motivation behind" workers' critiques, to determine if the feedback was legitimate. That happened often enough to create frustration and a lot of wasted time. An Amazon spokesman said Anytime Feedback "is just another way for people to give feedback throughout the year—like walking into a manager's office, calling, or sending an e-mail." He added, "Most Anytime Feedback is positive, and it's up to each manager to decide how to use the feedback."*

---

97   Ibid.

98   Ibid.

Indeed, Employers worry they'll get too much positive rein-forcement and not enough honesty in peer review systems, said Jason Corsello, Cornerstone's vice president of corporate strategy and development. Managers are in an awkward spot when employees praise a member of a team, "but the manager thinks they're a low performer," he added. Human-resources executives struggle with encouraging managers and workers to offer candid comments, or "constructive criticism," in cubicle-speak.[99]

3. FOSTER A CULTURE OF NATURAL (AND ENCOURAGED) INQUISITIVENESS AND CURIOSITY

People who are inquisitive are usually engaged and vice-versa. We rarely wonder to ourselves or out loud how to make things better or how to do our jobs more effectively when we fail to care.

Every day, employees have the opportunity to learn new information that could improve their performance, yet many fail to take advantage of it. People are often hesitant to ask critical questions because they fear it will make them appear incompetent, said Alison Wood Brooks, an assistant professor at Harvard Business School. In fact, those who seek advice are perceived as more competent than those who do not, according to a recent paper that she wrote along with Francesca Gino, a professor at Harvard Business

---

99   Lauren Weber and Rachel Silverman, "Workers Get New Tools for Airing Their Gripes," *The Wall Street Journal*, August 25, 2015, http://www.wsj.com/articles/workers-get-new-tools-for-airing-their-gripes-1440545279.

School, and Maurice E. Schweitzer, a professor at the Wharton School at the University of Pennsylvania.

"Information sharing is very important in organizations," Professor Brooks said. "If everyone sat in their separate silos and never interacted with each other, they wouldn't learn anything from each other. By not seeking advice, you are missing out on a huge opportunity to learn from your co-workers."[100]

On the other hand, those in a neutral emotional state tend to take the advice they receive with a grain of salt according to separate research by Professor Gino. This stems from what psychologists call "egocentric bias," in which people think they know better than others.

Although a fair amount of research about how people respond to advice has been published, much less has been done on advice seeking—so that is the area that Professor Brooks, Professor Gino, and Professor Schweitzer decided to explore in their most recent study. Their findings suggest that unless you are feeling anxious, there is very little to lose if you seek advice.[101]

---

100 Phyllis Korki, "Smart Workers Seek Out Advice, Study Suggests," *The New York Times,* September 5, 2015, http://www.nytimes.com/2015/09/06/business/smart-workers-seek-out-advice-study-suggests.html?_r=0.

101 Ibid.

TEN EXAMPLES OF COMPANIES WITH ENGAGED CULTURES

While the culture that works for one company might not work for another, you can learn a lot from companies who are doing it right:

1. Zappos

Zappos has become almost as well-known for its culture as it is for the shoes that it sells online. What does that culture look like?

It starts with a cultural-fit interview, which carries half the weight of whether the candidate is hired. New employees are offered $2,000 to quit after the first week of training if they decide the job isn't for them. Ten core values are instilled in every team member. Employee raises come from workers who pass skills tests and exhibit increased capability, not from office politics. Portions of the budget are dedicated to employee team building and culture promotion.

Great benefits and a workplace that is fun and dedicated to making customers happy all fit in with the Zappos approach to company culture—when you get the company culture right, great customer service and a great brand will happen on its own.

Takeaway: Zappos hires according to cultural fit, first and foremost. It has established what the company culture is, and fitting into that culture is the most important thing managers look for when hiring. This promotes the culture and happy employees, which ultimately leads to happy customers.

2. Warby Parker

Warby Parker has been making and selling prescription glasses online since 2010. It designs its own glasses and sells directly to customers, cutting out the middleman and keeping prices low.

Company culture at Warby Parker instigates "culture crushes," and one reason for that level of success is a team dedicated to culture. That team ensures that a positive culture is on the forefront, setting up fun lunches, events, and programs. The company makes sure that there is always an upcoming event so the entire team has something to look forward to, and it uses methods to make sure the entire team works well together by insisting everyone helps to keep break areas clean or sending random employees out to lunch together.

Takeaway: Warby Parker has made company culture deliberate by creating a dedicated team tasked with coming up with events and programs to promote community. Great company culture doesn't happen on its own.

3. Southwest Airlines

The airline industry is often mocked for grumpy employees and poor customer service, but Southwest Airlines bucks those trends. Customers loyal to Southwest often point to happy and friendly employees who try hard to help.

Southwest isn't new to the game. It's been in operation since the early 1970s. Yet somehow, during all that time, the company has managed to communicate its goals and vision to employees in a way that makes them a part of a unified team. Southwest also gives employees "permission" to go that extra mile to make customers happy, empowering them to do what they need to do to meet that vision.

Takeaway: Employees who are convinced of a larger common goal are people who are excited to be part of a larger purpose.

4. Twitter

Employees of Twitter can't stop raving about the company's culture. Rooftop meetings, friendly coworkers, and a team-oriented environment in which each person is motivated by the company's goals have inspired that praise.

Employees of Twitter can also expect free meals at the San Francisco headquarters, along with yoga classes and unlimited vacations for some. These and many other perks are not unheard of in the startup world. But what sets Twitter apart?

Employees can't stop talking about how they love working with other smart people. Workers rave about being part of a company that is doing something that matters in the world, and there is a sense that no one leaves until the work gets done.

Takeaway: You can't beat having team members who are pleasant and friendly to each other and are both good at and love what they are doing. No program, activity, or set of rules tops having happy and fulfilled employees who feel that what they are doing matters.

5. Chevron

While oil and gas companies are prime targets for a lot of negative PR and public ire, Chevron employees responded favorably toward the company's culture. Employees compared Chevron with other similar companies and pointed out "the Chevron way" as being one dedicated to safety, supporting employees, and team members looking out for each other.

Chevron shows it cares about employees by providing health and fitness centers on-site or through health-club memberships. It also offers other health-oriented programs, such as massages and personal training. Chevron insists employees take regular breaks. In other words, the company shows it cares about the well-being of employees, and employees know that they are valued.

Takeaway: Your company culture doesn't have to be ping-pong tables and free beer. Simply providing employees with a sense of safety and well-being and creating a policy where everyone looks out for each other can easily suffice.

6. Squarespace

This successful dot-com startup is regularly voted as one of the best places to work in New York City. Its company culture is one that is "flat, open, and creative." A flat organization is one where there are no (or very few) levels of management in between staff and executives. This approach is more common among startups and can be tricky to maintain as a company grows larger, which generally requires groups to form.

Squarespace also offers robust benefits and perks, including 100 percent coverage of health-insurance premiums, flexible vacations, attractive office space, catered meals, stocked kitchens, monthly celebrations, relaxation spaces, and periodic guest lecturers. Solid benefits such as these help a culture but are not the sole instigator of a successful culture. Down-to-earth leaders and direct access to management have a great deal of impact.

Takeaway: Employees feel their voices can be heard when they aren't muffled under layers of management. This level of freedom and empowerment creates confident employees and improves morale.

7. Google

It would almost seem wrong not to mention Google on a list of companies with great culture. Google has been synonymous with culture for years, and it sets the tone for many of the perks and benefits that startups are now known for (free meals, employee trips and parties, financial bonuses, open presentations by high-level executives, gyms, a dog-friendly environment, and so on). Googlers are known to be driven, talented, and among the best of the best.

As Google has grown and the organization has expanded and spread out, keeping a uniform culture has proven difficult between headquarters and satellite offices, as well as among the different departments within the company. The larger a company becomes, the more that culture has to reinvent itself to accommodate more employees and the need for management.

While Google still gets stellar reviews for pay, perks, and advancement, there are also some employees who note growing pains that you'd expect from such a huge company, including the stress associated with a competitive environment. Hiring and expecting the best from employees can easily become a stressor if your culture doesn't allow for good work-life balance.

Takeaway: Even the best culture needs to revisit itself to meet a growing company's team. The most successful company culture leads to successful business, and that requires an evolving culture that can grow with it.

8. REI

For outdoor enthusiasts, REI has long been the company to turn to for great gear. Employees of REI, a cooperative where profits benefit its member-owners, also agree that this is a place where greatness happens, even beyond the beloved camping and outdoor products. REI's mission is to equip both customers and employees for the outdoors, not just to have fun but also in promoting stewardship of the environment.

REI says that its employees give "life to their purpose," firmly attributing company success to workers. The CEO of REI has acknowledged that employees can get benefits anywhere, but allowing outdoors-oriented employees to immerse themselves in REI culture is what makes it unique. Employees can win equipment through "challenge grants," where they submit a proposal for an outdoor adventure that would be challenging. Regular town-hall-style meetings are held, where employees can submit questions anonymously to help management understand what's happening in the company.

Takeaway: When your employees are completely immersed in the same interests as your company, the culture propels itself forward almost on its own. Culture that is owned and propelled by the same people puts value in their voices.

9. Facebook

Just like Google, Facebook is a company that has exploded in growth as well as being synonymous with unique company culture.

Facebook offers, as do many similar companies, lots of food, stock options, open office space, on-site laundry, a focus on teamwork and open communication, a competitive atmosphere that fosters personal growth and learning, and great benefits.

Yet Facebook has the same struggles as similar companies: a highly competitive industry that leads to a sometimes stressful and competitive workplace. Additionally, a free and organic organizational structure that worked for the smaller organization is less successful for the larger one.

To meet these challenges, Facebook has created conference rooms, has separate buildings, lots of outdoor roaming space for breaks, and has management (even CEO Mark Zuckerberg) working in the open office space alongside other employees. It's an attempt at a flat organizational culture, using the buildings and space itself to promote a sense of equality among the competition.

Takeaway: When your company depends on new hires that excel in a competitive field, your company culture and any associated perks will likely be the tipping point for applicants. You must stand out from other companies vying for attention.

10. Adobe

Adobe is a company that goes out of its way to give employees challenging projects and then provides the trust and support to help them meet those challenges successfully. While it offers benefits and perks like any modern creative company, Adobe's is a culture that avoids micromanaging in favor of trusting employees to do their best.

Adobe products are synonymous with creativity, and only through the avoidance of micromanaging are the people who create those products truly free to create. For example, Adobe doesn't use ratings to establish employee capabilities, feeling that that inhibits creativity and harms how teams work. Managers take on the role of coaches, more than anything, letting employees set goals and determine how they should be assessed.

Employees are also given stock options so that they know they have both a stake and reward in the company's success. Continual training and culture that promotes risk taking without fear of penalty are part of Adobe's open company culture.

Takeaway: Putting trust in your employees goes a long way toward positive company culture because trust leads to independent employees who help your company grow.

Remember that a truly engaged culture makes all employees feel safe and welcome, never excluded or uncomfortable. Focusing on "culture fit" alone makes it difficult to hire and welcome employees who are different from the prevailing culture, even if it would be an asset and great counterbalance at your company. Your company's level of

engagement may need adjustment if it causes you to end
up with a homogenized team who think and act the same.

---

4. COMMUNICATE EARLY, COMMUNICATE OFTEN

It can take many moons to build a culture of trust and only one
incident to dilute or destroy it. Logjams in communication create
logjams of trust. Logjams of trust quickly erode a culture. People
become disconnected, directionless, and distrustful when leaders are
playing their cards too close to the vest or becoming opaque in the
face of or crisis. We are living in a culture of transparency, and nearly
half of our workforce was raised in a society of transparency—so
it makes sense that our expectations have evolved. Perhaps in the
1940s or 1950s, the average worker just did his or her job and trusted
in management, but today's workforce wants to stay connected and
participate in the decision making that affects the future of the enterprise. Where there is a disconnect between leadership and perception of direction, people will let their minds wander to the worst
of scenarios—or worse, fill in the missing blanks of the corporate
mission or strategy with thoughts of their own, that are at best,
inconsistent and chaotic, or at worst, negative and destructive.

5. BREAK DOWN SILOS, CLIQUES, FACTIONS, CASTE SYSTEMS, REAL AND PERCEIVED GLASS CEILINGS, TURFMANSHIP, INTERNAL POLITICS, NEPOTISM, AND FAVORITISM

To foster engagement, build a true meritocracy. Foster selflessness
not selfishness. Reward what you know and how you apply it to
drive stakeholder value instead of whom you know and how you
manipulate it to drive favored behaviors. When a "cool-kids" clique

is encouraged and rewarded, too many of us feel uncool, left out, passed over, on the outside looking in, limited in our expectations of advancement, never understanding company culture fully, and thereby *disengaged.*

If you see a clique forming, kill it before it grows. Either we are all in it together or we are all in it apart—you choose!

6. YOU GET WHAT YOU GIVE

Invest in your people, or they'll vote with their feet. But do not assume that you know what they really want; the investments you make should yield short-, medium-, and long-term results and returns for both the company *and* the employees. Of course, cash is always nice, but it's a commodity with typically short-term impact. If you give an employee a $100 bonus for a week of hard work, it will likely be used to pay a bill or even for a nice dinner and then it's gone, with no greater impact than the famous "if you give a man a fish, he eats for a day, but if you teach a man to fish, he eats for a lifetime" saying. I would add, that if you teach a man to be a fishing guide, he teaches hundreds of others to eat for a lifetime—the multiples-and-catalyst effect.

The medium and longer mutually beneficial investments are focused on what is really important, such as training and education, peer recognition, and reward. Find the meaningful perquisites and benefits that will make a measurable difference in people's lives, and they will understand that you care about them, which will have a direct and sustainable impact on engagement.

7. ONBOARDING AND ORIENTATION (AND REPEAT)

We all know how exciting those first few days at a new job can be (or not) and how exciting those first few dates can be (or not). We are optimistic that things will work out and that we made the right choice. We are praying that there will be alignment between everything we were told when we were recruited vs. how things really are. And then it hits and it hits hard—either the company suffers from poor or mechanized orientation systems and/or we feel "bait and switched" or misled, finding that the culture we just joined is worse than the one we just left. And thus begins the slow-but-steady path to disenchantment and disengagement. Take a hard look at your current intake processes for new recruits—does your onboarding process foster accretion or dilution of culture right from day one? Does it create an affirmation that the employee made the right choice, or does it begin to cast doubt, thereby diminishing the potential productivity and success of the new hire right out of the gate?

Successful firms run focused boot camps, support new-hire training academies, foster the involvement of families in orientation, assign mandatory internal coaches and mentors, and run small-group integration brainstorming to ensure a seamless and successful transition into the company and its culture. Too many companies are spending too many resources on recruitment and too few resources on integration, leading to disconnects in prioritization and shared values. It is likely to only get worse, not better, from there. The old adage that "you never get a second chance to make a first impression" clearly applies here.

8. HEALTHY PEOPLE ARE MORE ENGAGED IN THEIR CAREERS, FAMILIES, AND COMMUNITY

Healthy bodies, healthy minds. Fostering wellness is not a three-hundred-square-foot gym in the building offered as an amenity by the landlord, only able to hold three people at the same time. Wellness is an attitude, manifested in dozens of different ways—from free flu shots to access to meaningful counseling, reimbursement for training and/or entry in fitness events, diet and weight-loss contests, flexible work hours, and "mental-recharge" time.

9. PAYING IT FORWARD: CORPORATE SOCIAL RESPONSIBILITY

At the leader level, executives are themselves highly engaged and demonstrate their commitment through their actions, decisions, and words on a daily basis. People feel like they are part of something larger than themselves and that the organization's commitment to their well-being and development fosters a sense of pride, loyalty, and trust. Employees are emotionally invested in the success of the enterprise in the same way that their leaders are, regardless of their status or compensation, as long as they feel that they are being fairly treated relative to their level of productivity and the productivity of the company overall. The organization demonstrates its responsibility to the careers of its people through training, education, advancement opportunities, and a commitment to the community overall.

They feel a sense of purpose, especially when everyone, including the C-suite, articulates and follows a set of nonnegotiable core values. Employees at all levels clearly understand their roles and contributions to the organization's overall success and how their own rewards and recognitions are aligned with the organization's goals and objectives. The actions of leaders and managers are *always* guided by principles of mutual respect, transparency, and integrity. Corrective action is taken when someone or a group strays from these core values, without exception. There is accountability and a lack of finger pointing; leaders take responsibility for the problems as crises occur within their organizations.

10. CAREER PATHS AND CAREER TRACKING

Most of us like to know what tomorrow will bring and that we are on a career path that is aligned with our personal goals, interests, and desires. And we want to know that the path we think we are on is in sync with the path that the company thinks we are on—and will support if milestones and growth goals are met. Engagement is often the collective manifestation of everyone in the company having a clear sense of where they are going and how they are going to get there. When that happens, the company glides across the water as seamlessly and as beautifully as a well-oiled rowing crew, guided by a veteran coxswain.

11. THE WAR FOR TALENT

Multiple headlines over the course of late 2015 and early 2016 reminded business leaders that they were the generals in a war of talent. Employee mobility, aggressive recruitment, and active poaching have run rampant. As an example, Tesla's success has created wars between all competing automakers in recruiting engineers and software experts in the driverless-car and electric power-sources/battery-life arenas. To drive engagement, develop detailed strategies to get and keep your most talented workers. Their enthusiasm and genuine dedication and engagement will be contagious and will only enhance existing recruiting programs. Companies with clear skill gaps in sales, technology development, finance, and strategy will be left behind as their companies become increasingly irrelevant to the marketplace and its targeted customers. Commit to developing dynamic career tracks that are less linear and more matrixed so that top talent can develop skills in a wide variety of areas from strategic thinking to financial acumen, operational excellence, and growth-strategy execution. Think of career mapping as driven less by an organizational chart and more like the old computer game "Doom," where players work their way through a maze and pick up new useful tools and weapons for each smart decision that they make or battle that they win. Expose your top talent to a more diverse set of skills and aspects of your company, and give them a seat at the planning-and-strategy table when it is warranted and earned. CEOs must allocate resources to ensure that talent acquisition, learning and development, career mapping, and leadership mentoring are all tools positioned for victory in the war of talent.

12. CREATE CLARITY

To drive engagement, the leadership team of the company must commit to the development of a clear vision as to what each team member needs to do each day and why. Engaged employees want to understand how what they do relates to others and to overall company goals. They hunger for a defined path and access to resources for a career path, mapping, direction, and development. (They want to know what are the five to ten things they need to do really well to advance to the next level within this company.) People are generally happier, more focused, and more engaged when they are clear as to what is expected of them and how they contribute to the overall value of the enterprise and how it relates to a clearly defined and communicated incentive-and-rewards program. Management must clearly define core expectations. For example, create the baseline of behaviors expected as part of the job vs. behaviors that are truly above and beyond that get rewarded.

13. MAKING A COMMITMENT TO COMMITMENT

What is it about our inability to commit to commitment? Our impatience and inability to focus and to build long-term meaningful relationships as a nation is chipping away at our ability to make genuine commitments.

Let's take a minute to deconstruct the word "commitment." A commitment is a promise—which people depend on—to undertake a duty or obligation; to promise to do or not do something, the breach of which can have significant consequences to those depending on the promise. When a candidate commits to serve on a board of directors or an executive commits to a leadership position, it is expected that he or she will commit to undertake the legal and moral obligations that go with these fiduciary positions—with vigor, passion, and enthusiasm.

In the context of leadership and governance, we need board members and executives to be accountable to the success of the company and fully committed to the best interests of the stakeholders—not just check-ins that periodically contribute and are merely kept informed of the company's progress.

At every level of the organization, commitment is crucial for breeding innovation, solutions to problems, and internal improvements. Organizational leaders can influence proactive behavior by developing a greater sense of commitment to the organization by creating programs that form stronger bonds and establish employee identities within the organization so that individual employees feel they can contribute to the whole in a valuable manner. Commitment is the accountability that separates activity from results, the manifestation of your actions speaking louder than your words. Commitment is all about character and integrity. It has been said that the primary difference between an interest and a commitment is that if you are merely interested in doing something, then you'll only do it when circumstances permit—but when you are committed to do something, you'll accept no excuses, only results. To combat a persistent global recession, we cannot depend on the mere promises of leaders to dig us out of our holes; we need a concrete and implementable game plan.

Vince Lombardi once said, "Most people fail not because of a lack of desire [or talent], but due to a lack of commitment." Commit. Inspire. Engage.

14. EMULATE WHO YOU ADMIRE

Which cultures of other companies do you admire? Which culture(s) would your employees want to emulate? Take a page from the playbooks of the companies that you and your team admire most. For example, if your culture of engagement will be driven by customer service, you may want to start talking to your team about being the "Nordstrom" or "Four Seasons" of your industry. What would that mean? What would need to change to accomplish it? Will your current and targeted customers value and appreciate this shift in your focus? There is no need to reinvent the wheel as long as you customize the initiatives to meet your company.

15. YOUR EMPLOYEE'S ENGAGEMENT WILL BE A MIRROR IMAGE OF YOUR OWN

Founders of companies are motivated by a wide variety of things when they start and build their businesses. And those things may evolve over time. Companies driven by founders' strong desire to feed their ego or pocketbooks tend to have lower levels of engagement. The reasons are obvious—employees respond to the founder's motivations, and if it is only all about *you*, then there is little reason for others to feel a part of that vision. When the objectives are expanded to include excellence in customer service, building enterprise value, or peer recognition, the overall vision is more inclusive and thereby more engaging. Founders and leaders committed to genuine value creation can empower teams of value creators. Couple this vision with a stock-option pool, performance warrants, profit-sharing plans, phantom stock, sale-of-company bonuses, or other mechanisms that allow your team to participate in the growth of the company—having a stake in the outcome will increase levels of engagement. Often missing in what is supposed to be a two-way street and two-way communication are core principles of *empathy* as a genuine two-way approach to understanding one another. Leaders must walk in the shoes of each employee in order to lead with engagement; workers must understand the pressures and challenges of leadership to see that the job is not as easy as it may be imagined.

16. STREAMLINE WORK PROCESSES AND SYSTEMS

Protocol and processes are an important component of any business, but when the "systems pendulum" swings too far, it creates red tape and bureaucracy that dampen engagement and innovation. If employees need to fill out five different forms and seek three different approvals to step outside the box and develop innovative approaches, many will not bother. This leads to a dilution in creativity, an increase in apathy, and eventually the more innovative employees will move on to other companies. Take a hard look at your processes and look for opportunities to streamline. Adopt project-management principles, processes, and the overall mind-set to deliver value and eliminate waste and drive efficiency and client satisfaction. Be a problem solver. If winning is about 10 percent planning and 90 percent execution, do not make it too hard for your teams to execute without insurmountable hurdles.

17. CUT OUT FAT, BUT BE CAREFUL NOT TO PIERCE CRITICAL MUSCLE AND BONE

The business media seems to be announcing workforce reductions for companies of all sizes almost daily. Downsizing and rightsizing are effective tools to cut the fat and the deadwood out of your overhead and organizational structure, but if you go too far by slicing the muscle and the bone, you will cripple your remaining people with too much to do and too little time or resources to do it. Workers who are legitimately overworked and underpaid are rarely engaged and are much more likely to be frustrated and disenchanted. Create dynamic systems and programs to match workload to head count and human-capital resources—use temporary workers and outsourcing solutions to fill short-term demand until it matures into sustainable medium-term to long-term demand.

18. INSIST ON CAMARADERIE, COLLEGIALITY, AND COOPERATION

Incivility in the workplace is toxic and contagious. Leaders must be civil, treat others as they seek to be treated, and create both rewards for teamwork and penalties for behaviors that lead to disrespect. Mid to lower-level workers will not buy in to a commitment to camaraderie when they witness back-stabbing, politics, and infighting among leaders of their organizations. Give your people chances to work together and discourage maverick projects. Repeated studies have demonstrated that employees' relationships with their coworkers were the second-highest factor related to their engagement and their overall commitment to the organization.

And it does not always need to be in the workplace—other ways to foster collegiality include organizing teams to participate in such things as sports leagues; community support and charitable projects; team-building retreats and educational events; evening classes on cooking and wine tasting; happy hours; and trips to the movies, museums, theatre, or other cultural activities that can be done in small groups and generate cohesion and understanding.

19. BE A MONOTONY-BUSTER

Most of us are creatures of habit. We feel more comfortable when practices and expectations are predictable. But that can also lead to low productivity and boredom, which lead to disengagement. Find a few ways to mix things up a bit, whether by changing work teams, lighting and furniture, meeting flows, impromptu lunches, or staff-meeting agendas. Change things enough to keep things interesting and foster greater levels of engagement—but not too far to destroy the benefits that are the security of predictable routines, especially if they are working. Consider allowing employees to spend a few days working in other departments to foster trust in how other functions of the organization affect their day-to-day work.

20. REIN IN LEVELS OF TECHNOSTRESS

Automation has had a profound effect on our workplace, and robotics is still in the earliest stages of development. There are already too many of us suffering daily from e-mail overload and drowning in an ocean of technology updates. Every time I learn a system, it gets updated and I need to learn it again. Every time I am about to get up from my desk to go to a face-to-face interaction, ten more e-mails arrive in my inbox. Our smartphones are with us 24/7, which enhances responsiveness and client service but rarely allows any time to think quietly or ever really be "offline." Many of us fear the future impact of automation and robotics on our jobs. As leaders, do what you can to alleviate the anxiety of technostress.

21. THE MODERN FAMILY IS HERE TO STAY

The popularity of the television series *Modern Family* is not an aberration or a fad—modern families are here to stay. To foster engagement in a changing world, employee-benefit programs must be reflective of the "new normal," inclusive of same-sex partner benefits, daycare, elder care, maternity and paternity leaves, infertility and adoption-services support, on-site basic health care, substance-abuse and stress counseling, or other related "new-normal" benefits. Some companies are shifting away from traditional "long-term" financial benefits such as a 401(K) match and turning to more short-term and immediately accessible benefits, such as monthly allowances for house-cleaning services, meal-delivery services, home-health visits, on-site auto care, and flex days. Give people what they really want, not what you think they want. An October 2015 article in CNBC.com reported that the workers most in demand did not actually want more money; they wanted more flexibility and more creative benefits that met their needs and their evolving family commitments. In the published survey, flexible worker hours trumped higher pay, free food, unlimited vacation time, retirement plans, and even child care. People were happiest when they could take care of "life stuff" as it arose and were empowered by technology to work remotely. Quality of life beat out the quantity of a fatter paycheck, even when coupled with a brand-new foosball table in the coffee room.

22. ENGAGE THE MIDDLE TO INFLUENCE THE WHOLE

The Gallup data referred to throughout this book (citing that more than 70 percent of workers are disengaged) is not limited to the masses. Even more concerning is that middle-level managers and even higher-level executives have an engagement level of only 35 percent, only a few points better than lower-level employees.

Middle-level managers need to take a lesson from the Disney Institute. At Disney Institute, they believe that every leader is telling a story about what he or she values. That story is being told based on each middle-level manager's behaviors; so it's critical to role model the right behaviors. To foster a highly engaged work environment, you must be a highly engaged team member yourself. Here are six characteristics of an engaging team environment. Ask yourself how you can personally role model these characteristics with your team:

1. **Clear goals and commitment to team goals:** How will I demonstrate enthusiasm and commitment to solving challenges as a team?

2. **Accountability to the team:** How will I demonstrate that I am personally invested and responsible to the team?

3. **Supportive climate and behaviors:** How will I praise and recognize others for their hard work and achievements?

4. **Mutual trust and respect:** How will I openly share my own strengths and opportunities?

5. **Results focus:** How will I reward and celebrate the achievement of specific goals?

6. **Good communication and constructive conflict:** How will I engage in open and passionate debate of ideas and opinions?

23. DEVELOP AND COMMUNICATE KPI'S

To foster engagement, develop a set of clear and transparent metrics, key performance indicators (KPIs), key industry ratios, and other key numbers on a dashboard that everyone understands and embraces. Develop training programs that give employees the tools they need to meet these metrics, and reward employees who drive increases in KPIs. Be transparent in explaining how certain behaviors will help metrics be met and how they drive the goals and objectives of the organization overall. Employees who better understand *what* is expected of them and *how* they will be measured will be more engaged and empowered.

24. LEADERS MUST BE VISIBLE AND ACCESSIBLE

Employees are more engaged when their leaders are visible, accessible, acknowledge people, show genuine gratitude, listen to ideas, and transparently make decisions. Being humble makes you more human and will be mimicked by your leaders and everyone else throughout the organization. Simple manners, common courtesy, and periodic feedback will directly impact employee retention, peer-to-peer respect, and, ultimately, levels of engagement.

25. REDEFINE THE PARAMETERS OF EMPOWERMENT

Do the people in your organization say they value empowerment but then seem to do the opposite in their actions? Actions speak louder than words. Empowerment leads to trust, and trust fosters engagement. Here are a few concrete ways to actually empower your people:

- Allow people to really speak their minds. Give them a forum to voice their concerns, and foster and reward candor. Then listen and actually act.

- Allow your people to focus on what they truly enjoy and truly do best.

- Involve more people in the hiring process based on criteria that they help develop.

- Seek and develop talent from the inside first; create and foster real opportunities for upward mobility in multiple lanes that will directly increase levels of engagement. Keeping positions always filled from the outside usually makes people feel like opportunities for advancement are limited and that their skills are undervalued.

- Allow your employees to weigh in on a wide variety of work variables that mean something to them (within reason), such as dress code, holidays, peer recognition, flexible work hours, charitable giving, regularity of bonuses, and range of benefits.

- Be participative and collaborative with your work teams on customer-service standards, branding guidelines, quality-control standards, ethics and codes of conduct, and other work processes or external communications strategies where a shared sense of pride and trust will drive engagement.

26. FIGHT "STALL-OUT" WITH A FOUNDER'S MENTALITY

Bain & Company recently surveyed eight thousand global companies and found that more than two-thirds have suffered from stalled growth periods or even steep declines over a ten-year period, in some cases multiple times. In a "stall-out," growth, innovation, productivity, and profitability begin to stutter and then halt, in part due to apathy, lack of leadership, and upticks in overall disengagement.

These energy-starved and rudderless companies fell into the trap of internal dysfunction, and it fueled a downward spiral in growth and opportunity. How did they break this dangerous cycle? Chris Zook and James Allen, both at Bain, found that companies that reversed the cycle and got back on a plan of sustainable growth adopted the following three core beliefs and made them critical components of their culture:

1. They viewed themselves as insurgents, fighting on behalf of the unserved or underserved target market(s) and customer(s).

2. They had an obsession with performance at the frontline, e.g., where the business meets the customer (and the rubber meets the road).

3. Most importantly, they fostered a "founder's mind-set" at all levels throughout the company. The founder's mentality looked at decision making and resource allocation with the same conviction, passion, deeply rooted core values, and

frugality that the original founder or cofounders brought to the table at the inception of the company. By turning back the hands of strategic time, the fire under the feet of the workforce was reignited, and core values were significantly reengaged.

27. LEARN MORE VS. PAY MORE

The "knee-jerk" reaction by many employers when culture and engagement reach intolerable low points is to retool the compensation system and pay more money. Money alone does not inspire motivation; rather a tangible increase in real wealth inspires commitment, loyalty, and a sense of security. But most of America's workforce is in ill financial health. More money just equates to more expenses if financial literacy programs are not put in place to inspire financial planning and budget disciplines.

Give your employees the gift of financial literacy to better manage the money that they already have as a precursor to just paying more. Not only will they appreciate the commitment to education, but they also might learn to do more with less—both personally and in establishing budgeting disciplines and accountability within the company. It is hard for workers to focus on productivity, creativity, and innovation when their minds (and wallets) are burdened with monetary debt pressures and broken retirement aspirations. Not only is debt distracting, but it may be the root of many baby boomers fighting to hold on to jobs well past the peak of their productivity because they are well short of their retirement goals.

28. WE MANAGE WHAT WE MEASURE

How are you measuring engagement? What key metrics or performance indicators can you develop and regularly monitor on your engagement dashboard? What key questions would you ask—either in general or tailored to your company's current challenges and speed bumps? Consider the staff survey results from a midsized tech company, and use this set of responses to develop your own measurement tools:

overall staff satisfaction:	6.12 percent
employees who have a close understanding of their career and progression path:	28 percent
employees who feel "fairly" compensated relative to their roles and responsibilities:	48 percent
employees who feel that they can reach their full human potential if they spend all of their career here:	17 percent
employees who believe that we as a company authentically live and operate aligned with our values:	37 percent
employees who would reapply for their current role:	31 percent
employees who see themselves working here one year from now:	48 percent

Your survey question to measure engagement may look very different, but there is clearly room for much improvement for the company above. Employees in the company above also cited a lack of a succession plan, a lack of individualized career maps, a lack of accountability and consistence, muddied core values, lack of standard operating protocols (SOPs), and a lack of an investment in training and development as the core sources of their levels of disengagement and dissatisfaction.

29. PEOPLE WANT TO BE LED BY LEADERS

Notwithstanding all of the emphasis and demand for empowerment, individuality and personal expression, social media, and embracement of diversity, people for the most part still want to be *led* by *leaders*. They crave a sense of direction and guidance as to what constitutes excellence and what is unacceptable. They want to know which swim lanes they should stay in and what criteria will be used to evaluate their performance on a fair and consistent basis. They want and need to know how the company is doing overall, what they are doing to drive shareholder value, and what role they can play to solve problems as to mitigate risk or drive opportunity. Silence breeds fear, resentment, rumor mills, and disengagement. People want to trust their leaders and count on them to create the appropriate levels of transparency. Sunlight may be the best form of disinfectant, but nobody wants to get sunburned, either! Leadership is not necessarily about educating every employee as to "how the sausage gets made," *but* it is about explaining how and why we are in the sausage business and how and why we sell *this* type of sausage to *this* type of customer, and what metrics we use to determine our success. To drive higher levels of engagement, be sure people learn *what* they can do to contribute to the success of the enterprise and how their performance will be judged in alignment with the company's overall goals and objectives. Constantly reinforce communication about how the company is doing overall and what each employee can do to accelerate or enhance the company's progress. If you want people to be truly engaged, you must educate and lead them as to how they can maximize their contribution to the enterprise and then reward them fairly and consistently when they actually perform.

30. STOP PROMISING A WORK-LIFE BALANCE ONCE AND FOR ALL

Let's face it, the notion of a work-life balance is illusive and misleading. I have yet to meet anyone who truly feels that his or her life is in perfect balance. And instead, most of us feel frustration, resentment, guilt, and anger when our lives are out of balance in either direction.

Well, get used to it. Your life is likely to be out of balance in some way for the rest of your life. Leaders and managers who promise their teams a work-life balance are misleading their people and only setting them up for failure and rebellion. Employees who stress themselves out looking for the balance will wind up disengaged and disillusioned and generally resentful of their workplace, which will surely get in the way of any desire or motivators to go the extra mile. Just embrace the chaos, anticipate the change, and deal with the fact that balance is a pipe dream getting in the way of the reality of imbalance, which can still be very fulfilling on the work and personal front.

> "The master in the art of living makes little distinction between his work and his play, his labor and his leisure, his mind and his body, his education and his recreation, his love and his religion. He hardly knows which is which. He simply pursues his vision of excellence at whatever he does, leaving others to decide whether he is working or playing. To him he is always doing both."
>
> —Zen Buddhist text